Decolonizing Africa and African Development

T0326532

Africa in Development

Volume 15

Series Editor: Jeggan C. Senghor
Institute of Commonwealth Studies
University of London

Anthony Victor Obeng

Decolonizing Africa and African Development

The Twenty-First-Century Pan-Africanist Challenge

PETER LANG

Oxford · Bern · Berlin · Bruxelles · Frankfurt am Main · New York · Wien

Bibliographic information published by Die Deutsche Nationalbibliothek.
Die Deutsche Nationalbibliothek lists this publication in the Deutsche
Nationalbibliografie; detailed bibliographic data is available on the
Internet at http://dnb.d-nb.de.

A catalogue record for this book is available from the British Library.

Library of Congress Control Number: 2016949839

ISSN 1662-1212
ISBN 978-3-0343-0758-1 (print) • ISBN 978-1-78707-107-0 (ePDF)
ISBN 978-1-78707-108-7 (Epub) • ISBN 978-1-78707-109-4 (mobi)

© Peter Lang AG, International Academic Publishers, Bern 2017
Hochfeldstrasse 32, CH-3012 Bern, Switzerland
info@peterlang.com, www.peterlang.com, www.peterlang.net

This publication has been peer reviewed.

Printed in Germany

To all who fought, fight now and will fight in future for the reconquest of the freedom and dignity of Africans and people of African descent everywhere

Contents

viii

Preface

Many are those, and not only in Africa, who do not regard the world order which has framed 'African development' for centuries positively. This book takes a dim view of the present world order, 'African development' and the African development industry spawned by the first two. The devastating effects on the African people of the development of Africa's underdevelopment described by Walter Rodney and others should speak for themselves. But facts, unfortunately, do not always speak for themselves. To add insult to injury, every turn of the underdevelopment screw and scream of its victims is met by its architects and principal beneficiaries with more programmes and language designed to supplement or replace existing 'opiums of the people'. And their consistent and predictable long-term effects are to worsen the dependency complexes of the 'beneficiary-victims', strengthen the power of the development industry over them – with spill-over job opportunities in the allied humanitarian-aid industry – and lock them further into the under-development cycle. Tony Blair's use of the African people's relentless misery as a pretext for more of the politics of crocodile tears, 'politics of pity' and 'white-saviour-complex'-loaded meddling in African affairs (after his conde-scending 'scar-on-the-conscience-of-the-world' declaration) is a case in point.

Exposing the chicanery and its fallouts is a conscientized African's duty. But it cannot be done as truthfully and pointedly as needed without disturbing the squeamish or offending those whose comforts and tranquil-lity demand the least possible unearthing or repetition of inconvenient truths – or their presentation in language so opaque that the inconvenient truths are effectively buried. Like Michelle Alexander's *The New Jim Crow: Mass Incarceration in the Age of Colorblindness*, this book is not and cannot be for everyone. Writing a book that will not disturb the many myths, half-truths and outright lies about underdevelopment and poverty in Africa is, frankly, not among my limited supply of talents – or consistent with my sense of duty as an African, a Pan-Africanist and a human being. *I offer this explanation as a pre-emptive apology to any friends and intellectually honest readers who would have preferred to see some of the language of the text watered down or some inconvenient but relevant facts, ideas and materials excluded from it completely.* I hasten to assure my respected readers, however, that while the book does not bow to unreasonable tastes and sensibilities, they will find no gratuitous insults in it either. Nor will they find in it any of the licentious exploitations of the freshly minted 'right' to offend the *weak, unprotected and unpopular* – or 'give 'em hell' – which has come to be peddled by uncouth new-age norm setters as 'the right to insult religion' or extensions of the cynically defined and just as cynically practised 'freedoms' of speech, the press and expression!

The trickier challenge which this book had to manage from the planning to the execution stages was how to satisfy between two covers readers who are already familiar with the lives and works of the likes of Kwame Nkrumah, W. E. B. Du Bois, Frantz Fanon, Amilcar Cabral, Thomas Sankara, Archie Mafeje, Walter Rodney and Samir Amin from Africa and the African Diaspora, and of Noam Chomsky, Susan George, Naomi Klein, among others, from the non-African world, on one hand; and those who are not, and would rather their cosy worlds were not disturbed by inconvenient truths, on the other. To square this particular circle, if that is what it is, the book relies on the hope that established and aspiring intellectual freedom fighters who are not averse to learning from or revisiting the leading lights in intellectual activism, dead and alive, and *the comfortable of the earth* who would rather see, hear or read no evil, will find common grounds, and interest, in the following quotable quotes which have driven and informed it in several ways:

1. 'You cannot fool all the people all the time.' (Abraham Lincoln)
2. 'Men [and women] do not only make history but also learn from it.' (Archie Mafeje)
3. 'The future will have no pity for those men [and women] who, possessing the exceptional privilege of being able to speak words of truth to their oppressors, have taken refuge in an attitude of passivity, of mute indifference, and sometimes of cold complicity.' (Frantz Fanon)

4. 'The highest purpose of man is the liberation of man from his bonds of fear, his bonds of poverty, the liberation of man from the physical, spiritual and intellectual bonds which have for long stunted the development of humanity's majority.' (Ahmad Sukarno)
5. 'Dare to invent [a better] future.' (Thomas Sankara)

For the further and specific reflections of those who are already persuaded that this is not the best of all possible worlds – and a better world needs to be invented in its place – it is additionally submitted that:

- An aide-memoire is not necessarily a bad thing;
- New generations often need to have their old wines in new bottles;
- In view of the fact that imperialism has lost none of its appetite for global hegemony, effective annexation of other people's countries and the expropriation of African resources whenever and wherever it deems it in its strategic or 'national security' interest to do so, it is irresponsible to withhold any information, insights and other intellectual tools available to freedom fighters that may be useful in the struggles for African liberation and development and a better world; and
- The myth that the enslavement of Africans in Africa and of their kith and kin in the New World was abolished by devices like black empowerment (aka 'independence') on the mother continent and in parts of the Caribbean, 'affirmative action' and 'civil rights' in the United States, and 'democracy' or 'racial democracy' elsewhere, demands debunking without mercy and by all means necessary, including books such as this – in the interest of justice in general and racial justice in particular.

This retelling of the African liberation and development saga promises, moreover, to do 'more than add to the catalogue of what we already know', to quote Howard Zinn's characterization of people's histories.

I would, finally, urge those (African and non-African) who are bound to find the book hurtful, to resist their natural instinct to want to smash the mirror. They may well find it more rewarding to accept, instead, that the 'You' in Lincoln's observation that 'You cannot fool all the people all the time' applies to them as well – and Africans are among the people who cannot be fooled all the time. No apologies can be offered, on the other hand, for knocking down a few masks for a good cause.

Acknowledgements

For good personal reasons I have taken a special interest in African and world developments since 1943. A combination of the accident of birth, life and work experiences has long given me an urge to share with peers and my younger family and friends my reading of the events and pseudo-events of my lifetime which I deem important to them. The formative experiences include a childhood happily spent under the influence of senior extended family members and their peers who militated alongside Kwame Nkrumah for the independence of the Gold Coast and Africa, and served in his governments in various capacities – and some thirty-five years of a relationship with the African development industry as a student, observer, participant and reviewer.

The urge I got to write this book thus derives partly from a desire to do for others that which my own family elders, mentors and peers have done for me through a lifetime of formal and informal political and development education. Acknowledgement is thus due to them for helping to make me who I am. But by the same token they cannot escape blame entirely for my principles and foolhardiness in recklessly dishing out in the following pages the sacred facts and educated opinions about the politics of Africa's development and underdevelopment which more cautious individuals would rather leave unsaid.

But, as I researched and wrote the book, the conviction that keeping to myself the knowledge, opinions and alternative African development ideas I had acquired or independently developed was not a morally defensible option was only strengthened by persistent affronts to the African people which mainstream academic and public commentators tend to ignore and which too many of their African victims accept with the same fatalism with which they accept taxes and death! For, as I continued to watch the rebranding of the unreconstructed 'civilizing missionaries' as 'development partners' it became increasingly obvious to me that it was cowardly and irresponsible not to contribute the power of the proverbial pen at one's command to the cause of Africa's liberation from informal but real 'post-colonial'-colonial subjugation and to the development of the continent for the benefit of its peoples at home and abroad.

Much of the credit or blame for my choice of engagement over the peace of comfortable retirement belongs, as hinted above, to my beloved offspring, nephews, nieces and their friends whose love, friendship, respect and thirst over the years for my 'take' on a wide range of issues left me without the freedom to shirk my parental, *mzee*, and African liberation and development responsibilities in the form which many of them insisted upon; that is, a book. It is a further mark of their faith and kindness, which I also salute, that they have accepted this modest response as the most important legacy they can expect from me.

While thanking my multiracial and cosmopolitan group of young relatives and friends for their contributions in their own special ways to the idea and execution of the book – and hoping that it will benefit them and their own descendants and friends – I hasten to absolve them from responsibility for its contents. I do not expect them, in particular, to agree with everything I write in the following pages any more than they have agreed with everything I have told them verbally over the years.

But I hope that the book will add clarity and more force to their already formidable moral compasses and cognitive maps and help them navigate their ways through a world which is often bewildering and treacherous; help them, in particular, to demystify 'poverty' in Africa and 'African development'; and further help them avoid the low self-esteem which has condemned too many of their elders and some, I fear, of their own peers, to the wretched life of agents of the underdevelopment of their mother continent and impoverishment of their own people. For rewarding me with the cathartic benefits I have derived from researching and writing the book I cannot thank my children, family and young friends enough for their own courage in persuading me to write anyway, knowing as they did the risks even they could face on account of their association with one who tells truth to power.

Pressure of a related kind came from other irresistible sources I can easily identify. Dr Jeggan C. Senghor, a fellow Pan-Africanist; former UN colleague; friend and soul brother of some forty years standing;

Senior Research Fellow at the School of Advanced Study, Institute of Commonwealth Studies, University of London; and General Editor of Peter Lang's *Africa in Development* series, is a leader among those who bear special responsibility for the book. Having earlier succeeded in getting me to write the chapter on 'Vassal States, Development Options and African Development' for *Towards Africa's Renewal* (2007), which he co-edited, Jeggan pushed his luck and provoked me into writing this follow-up book by persuading me that the alternative to writing what turned out to be the book before you was to join the ranks, eventually, of the African ancestors and contemporaries we had both privately condemned on numerous occasions for taking valuable knowledge and skills with them to their graves, rather than share or leave them behind in accessible forms for possible future use.

To the above pressures was added another irresistible one from Dr Hashim Gibrill, professor, former chair of the political science department and a brain behind the international development programme of Clark Atlanta University, USA, the iconic W. E. B. Du Bois' old university. Hashim's kind offer to me, in March 2007, of the forum of his department's graduate students' seminars, open to the faculties and students of other Atlanta-based universities was, indeed, a multiple blessing. Above all, it gave me precious post-retirement exposure to the thinking, concerns and determination of some of the brightest, cosmopolitan and conscientized youth I have been privileged to interact with. It was also particularly energizing in confirming to me that the quest for a new and better world order and the Pan-Africanist ideals articulated and defended by the founding fathers are not dead, despite the worst efforts of the neoliberal globalizers and their continental and Diaspora-African collaborators and front men and women. In addition to providing me with another opportunity to recharge my intellectual batteries, the forum was thus encouraging in confirming to me that a book such as this would have waiting audiences worth investing in. I am profoundly grateful to Hashim and the staff and students of Clark Atlanta University and the other Atlanta-based universities who attended my seminar for these precious gifts.

It will be evident to all who read this book that I am indebted to many more people and sources for orientation and content than I can name here. The references to books and articles that helped to shape my thoughts in diverse ways constitute a partial acknowledgement of this debt. But I take this opportunity to salute the many uncited thinkers, scholars, intellectual freedom fighters, other activists and 'ordinary folks' who have shaped my understanding of the politics of Africa's underdevelopment over the years, and enabled me to contribute this book to the intellectual and political struggles for the liberation of Africa and its development from their external and internal hijackers.

I must also, at this juncture, acknowledge, without thanking or saluting them, the Africa and African development hijackers, external and internal, who, taking advantage of the collapse of African nationalism since the independences and civil rights achievements of the 1960s and the end of the 'Cold War' in the West's favour, have returned to vintage imperial arrogance and practices – and the 'useful idiots' who have facilitated the rollback of many of the nationalist and Cold-War-era concessions to African interests and pride – for making it impossible for me to turn a blind eye to their sins of commission and omission, and compelling me to exhale as vigorously as I hope I have done in this book.

To those who are familiar with their immense contributions to the development of social and economic research and analysis in and about Africa, my indebtedness to two great African intellectuals and freedom fighters, the South African-born Professor Archie Mafeje and the Egyptian-born Professor Samir Amin, for their guidance and insights will be obvious. Nonetheless, I must take this opportunity to acknowledge upfront their contributions to my intellectual and political development in ways which may not stand out as clearly as they should in the following pages.

Besides acknowledging and thanking Archie Mafeje for the privilege of his company as my professor and academic adviser in The Hague from 1968 to 1969 – and my mentor, role model, elder brother and very close friend thereafter until his death in March 2007 – I am also happy to celebrate him as one of the Pan-Africanists to whom this book is dedicated. But, like others whom I acknowledge in these pages, I cannot presume that Archie would have agreed with everything I have had to say. What I do know, on the other hand, is that he would have applauded my saying it anyway. For, while he was always a robust scholar and debater who did not suffer fools gladly, he abhorred sycophancy and never attempted to make disciples of his students, ex-students and younger friends. I thank him especially for challenging me to always strive to make a difference and not to waste my life and mind while I still have them.

Samir Amin, one of Africa and the world's most profound thinkers and political economists, distinguished and probably proud non-recipient of the Nobel Prize in Economics and – among other past and current responsibilities – former Director of the United Nations African Institute for Economic Development and Planning (IDEP), Director of the Third World Forum and Chair of the World Forum for Alternatives, is another major contributor to my political and intellectual development. I am also happy to single him out for special acknowledgement as a godfather of this book. It all began with his 1974 invitation for me to join his research and teaching team at IDEP. The honour and good fortune gave me the best and most satisfying job I have ever had, exposing me as it did to some of the best development thinking, networks, thinkers and sources of intellectual energy in the world from which I still benefit.

I can only hope that in this book I have proved worthy of the trust, investments and friendship of Archie and Samir.

My 'ideologically bankrupt' friends are not of the offensive and reactionary kind: theirs is the sin of extreme moderation. Most of them are, in fact, no less outraged by the 'sincere ignorance', injustices, cynicism, frauds, imperialist meddling, collaborationism and other banes of the African people than the rest of conscientized humanity. It is no accident, for instance, that it was one of their number who, in a routine political discussion, first drew my attention to Kobina Sekyi's classic, *The Blinkard and the Anglo Fanti*, a book-length denunciation of the phenomenon more widely known as 'black skin, white masks' some forty years before Frantz Fanon's justly celebrated book of that title was first published in 1952. More generally, however, another of their qualities is that they pack considerable intellectual power, and routine interactions with them invariably turn into intellectual feasts which help nourish the brain – in spite of their ideological bankruptcy. But I am, above all, grateful to them for their friendship, for keeping me in touch with some of the thinking on 'the other side', for their infectious intellectual dexterity and personal integrity, and for aiding and abetting the book's production with positive energies.

My dear mother, Madam Mary Obeng (better known by her matriarchal name, Maame Dufie) of blessed memory, easily bears the greatest responsibility for the moral tone of the book. It was she who inculcated in me the fearlessness, love of truth, justice, decency and respect for those, and only those, who deserve it that, I hope, permeate its pages. It is my fervent hope that in this book I come close to being worthy of her life, example and teachings.

My indebtedness would not come close to being wholly discharged without acknowledgement of the valued editorial support I received on an early draft from my nephew and friend, Professor Augustine Nuamah Mensah, and another close friend whom I cannot name publicly. Kofi Mensah cleaned up the zero draft of the manuscript for presentation to the publishers and subsequently provided much-appreciated final editorial touches. The editorial advisor I cannot name because I was unable to use his recommendations is a retired senior officer of ECOWAS, the pioneer African regional economic integration body. While I was unable to use his suggestions in the end because they were overloaded with a religious faith and neoliberalisms I do not share, the commitment to Africa's development and eagerness to help a friend succeed in an enterprise he judged worthy which he demonstrated through the support he offered are more deeply appreciated than he has known until now. I take this opportunity to salute him for both.

Gratitude, goes, finally, to Lucy Melville, Publishing Director of Peter Lang Ltd, and her team for their professionalism and support; to Jeggan, in his general editor capacity, for proving to be the 'user-friendly' editor I expected him to be; and to the obviously resourceful anonymous reviewer who, early in my seventieth year, gave me the best New Year's present I could have hoped for, in the form of his encouragement and support, generous comments on the book and precious editorial suggestions.

Abbreviations

ACP	African, Caribbean and Pacific Group of States
AFRICOM	United States Africa Command
AGOA	African Growth and Opportunity Act
AMISOM	African Union Mission in Somalia
ANGOP	Angolan News Agency
AU	African Union
BRICS	Brazil, Russia, India, China, South Africa
CAAT	Campaign Against the Arms Trade
CAR	Central African Republic
CARICOM	Caribbean Community
CIA	Central Intelligence Agency
CIS	Commonwealth of Independent States
DRC	Democratic Republic of Congo
E/TCDC	Economic and Technical Cooperation among Developing Countries
ECDC	Economic Cooperation among Developing Countries
ECOWAS	Economic Community of West African States
EU	European Union
FAO	Food and Agriculture Organization of the United Nations
GDP	Gross Domestic Product
HERF	Haiti Emergency Relief Fund
ICC	International Criminal Court
ICJ	International Court of Justice
IGAD	Intergovernmental Authority on Development
IMF	International Monetary Fund
INGOs	International Non-governmental Organizations
LPA	Lagos Plan of Action for the Economic Development of Africa, 1980–2000
LRA	Lord's Resistance Army

MINUSTAH	Mission des Nations Unies pour la stabilisation en Haïti (United Nations Stabilization Mission in Haiti)
MPLA	People's Movement for the Liberation of Angola
NAACP	National Association for the Advancement of Coloured People
NAM	Non-Aligned Movement
NATO	North Atlantic Treaty Organization
NEPAD	New Partnership for Africa's Development
NGO	Non-governmental Organization
NIEO	New International Economic Order
NWIO	New World Information Order
NWO	New World Order
OAS	Organization of American States
OAU	Organization of African Unity
OPEC	Organization of Petroleum Exporting Countries
PAIGC	Partido Africano da Independencia da Guiné e Cabo Verde
PANA	Pan-African News Agency
SADC	Southern African Development Community
SAP	Structural Adjustment Programme
SIPRI	Stockholm International Peace Research Institute
TCDC	Technical Cooperation among Developing Countries
UN	United Nations
UN-ECA	United Nations Economic Commission for Africa
UNESCO	United Nations Educational, Scientific and Cultural Organization
UNIA-ACL	United Negro Improvement Association and African Communities League
UNITA	National Union for the Total Independence of Angola
UNSC	United Nations Security Council
URTNA	Union of National Radio and Television Organizations of Africa
USAID	United States Agency for International Development
WAGP	West African Gas Pipeline
WTO	World Trade Organization

Introduction

> Those who do not learn from history are doomed to repeat it.
> — GEORGE SANTAYANA

> A people's history does more than add to the catalogue of what we already know.
> — HOWARD ZINN[1]

As it celebrated the fifty-fifth anniversary of its 'independence' a think piece in the online publication, *Ghana Nsem* (or 'Ghana Palaver', in loose translation), mocked one of the many colonial constructs in Africa pretending to be states as follows:

Those who for 500 years nationalized and refined armed robbery and rape are now our 'development partners'. Those merchants and industrialists of slavery who globalized pillage and serial genocide are now born again and immaculate. They are the defenders of human rights, guardians of morality, arbiters of virtue and enforcers of justice, for the world. They dominate the web of international organizations and impose rules which they flout at will, with eloquent brute force. These ravenous creditors masquerade as generous 'donors', guiding us with compassion ever nearer the horizon of 'development'.

Instead of criticizing their lucid pursuit of their own interests for half a millennium, we must recognize our tendency to grovel. We have forgotten what independence means. Deeply hooked, we allow foreign 'aid' to dictate our priorities. Most of our poorest people are food farmers, so we import more food. Local manufacturing is dying, so we import more manufactured goods. Someone said, 'We will sit down for somebody to come from Iceland to tell us how to keep warm'. Another said, 'Rudderless and without imagination, we are being driven by outside forces'. We

---

1   Howard Zinn, Preface to The New Press People's History Series (Boston, MA: 2000).

have no vision of ourselves, of Africa, as proud and strong at global level. We have no plan for how to become strong. Worse still, we don't even think we need a Plan.[2]

The author's beef is widely shared in progressive African circles. The immediate targets of his ire are just as familiar: they include the 'states' and 'governments' in Africa that appear to have been custom-designed to serve foreign powers and interests at the expense of the people they call their own and the 'intellectual enablers' who service the 'mendicant rulers' and their foreign patrons.[3] The violence of the language in which these banes of the African people are denounced – and not only by the likes of Bentsi-Enchill and Olufemi Taiwo – is, indeed, a measure of the contempt held by a growing number of Africans for the collaborator 'post-colonial' 'states' and 'governments' concerned. But many more in-depth studies of the relevance and quality of Walter Rodney's opus on how Europe underdeveloped Africa before and during the trans-Atlantic slave trade[4] – and as 'white race authority' thereafter[5] – are needed if the critiques of the entire underdevelopment history of the continent are to go beyond nationalistic

2   Nii K. Bentsi-Enchill, 'Silence means consent – A note on 55 years of in-dependence', <http://ghanansem.org/index.php?option=com_content&task=view&id=251&it emid=345> (accessed 12 June 2013).

3   Olufemi Taiwo 'Africa's Mendicant Rulers and their Intellectual Enablers', *Pambazuka News*, 5 February 2014, <http://pambazuka.org/en/category/comment/90438> (accessed 5 February 2014).

4   Walter Rodney, How Europe Underdeveloped Africa. London: Bogle L'Ouverture Publications, 1972.

5   Robert Anthony Eden (or Anthony Eden, for short), who gave the colour-coded description of imperialism quoted above, was British Prime Minister from 1955 to 1957. The description was attributed to him by Vijay Prashad, on page 47 of *The Darker Nations: A People's History of the Third World* (New York: The New Press, 2007). It is, undoubtedly, such associations of power with 'whiteness' which give rise to 'reminders' by the likes of Ta-Nehisi Coates (*Between the World and Me* (New York: Spiegel & Grau, 2015), 8)) that 'the elevation of the belief in being white, was not achieved through wine tastings and ice cream socials, but rather through the pillaging of life, liberty, labour, and land; through the flaying of backs, the chaining of limbs; the strangling of dissidents; the destruction of families; the rape of mothers; the sale of children; and various other acts meant, first and foremost, to deny (the others) the right to secure and govern their own bodies.'

and pious indignation to yield lessons for present and future generations of African freedom fighters. Bentsi-Enchill's recognition, rare among post-Rodney commentators on Africa's underdevelopment history, that chattel slavery, colonial slavery, neo-colonial slavery and the slavery of the vast majority of African peoples who fall on the wrong side of globalization are part of the same rob-and-rape continuum deserves to be celebrated, accordingly, as yet another potentially productive response to the cynics and the brainwashed who continue to divide the African people between alleged beneficiaries and victims of chattel slavery and between descendants of 'free' Africans and the descendants of 'former slaves', for instance, ignoring the fact that most Africans who escaped chattel slavery ended up as colonial slaves and remained unfree 'to secure and govern their own bodies (and resources)'.

The challenges which Africans and peoples of African in the Diaspora can only hope to address effectively, with the right combination of thought and practice, informed by correct appreciations of the African condition in Africa and abroad, include:

- 'the new Jim Crow' 'in the age of colour blindness' in 'God's own country' described by Michelle Alexander;[6]
- the enduring sufferings of the Caribbean people of African descent outlined by the CARICOM Reparations Commission (CRC) and recalled below;
- the return to Africa of unbridled imperial arrogance decades after the continent's alleged decolonization;
- persistent anti-African and anti-black 'racism' in its traditional citadels, in the forms of 'racist' gestures by psychopaths, and subtle-and-crude insinuations by current representatives of white-race-authority and their propaganda organs that Africans have a duty to only 'trust and obey' their so-called development partners' leads and instructions on what to think, what to do, how to govern themselves, how to feel, which sexual orientations to allow and which ones to continue to disallow – because the West is yet to promote them from the monkeys,

6   Michelle Alexander (2011).

parrots and apes they were once openly said to be to fully-human status; and
- the conditions of peoples of African descent in, for instance, parts of Latinized America, the Arab and Arabized worlds and Asia.

In a book with the decolonization of Africa and African development as its lead title the starting point is, logically, the deleterious effects of the colonization of the continent and its development. The following chapters will hopefully demonstrate to all concerned and beyond all reasonable doubt that Pan-Africanism is the answer to all the challenges listed above – and more.[7]

That Pan-Africanism is, indeed, a weapon which the peoples of Africa and African descent elsewhere can ill afford to ignore in their struggles against racial bigotry and oppression and the defence of the gains of their struggles can also be inferred from the fact that while the insults and assaults on them may be personal and local the evidence from the Americas, the Caribbean, Arabia and Asian is conclusive enough that personal and local solutions without the backing of collective black and African power are doomed to suffer the fates of the thousand and one confrontations, rebellions and revolts in the five centuries of African and black history which Bentsi-Enchill alluded to in the above quotation. The repackaging of 'imperialism' (a 'dirty' or 'objectionable' word in the twenty-first century) as 'globalization', of 'empire' (once a source of bragging rights, as in 'the empire on which the sun never sets') as 'the global village', of colonies as 'Overseas Territories', indirect-rule chiefs as Presidents, etc., can also thus be seen for what it is: a ploy to deny that *plus ça change, plus c'est la même*

---

7   It is disappointing but not too surprising in this connection that in her otherwise excellent book Alexander acknowledges 'a shifting domestic and international political environment' (Alexander, ibid. 37) as a contributor to the civil rights gains in America in the 1950s but fails, unlike civil rights activists of an older generation, to acknowledge the role of Pan-Africanism in stimulating both the civil rights movement and that shifting international political environment.

chose and thereby deny victims of the enduring *status quo* the lessons of their own history.[8]

For proof that Africa remained, and remains, their 'possessions' in the minds of the 'former colonial masters' turned 'development partners' one needs look no further in this day and age than the West's intermittent frenzy over the spectre of 'global China', a new scramble for Africa or 'poaching' by China in its African game reserve 'despite the fact that the PRC (People's Republic of China) only (accounted) for a tiny fraction of direct foreign investment there – 4 per cent for 2000–10 compared to 84 per cent for the Atlantic powers'.[9] The many British-led Western moves

8   For concrete examples of the subterfuge note the reference by the British to Africa's Chagos Islands as British Indian Ocean Territory (BIOT) and by the French to La Réunion and Mayotte as 'overseas departments' of France. Unimpressed by such tricks 'globalization' is treated throughout this text as imperialism by another name except where the context dictates otherwise. Note also in this connection that the game of attaching fancy names to colonies is almost as old as imperialism itself: in practice the distinctions between colonies designated as such and those labelled as 'protectorates' or 'trust territories' were essentially cosmetic even before the Soviet and Chinese threats and Pan-Africanism forced the concessions to African nationalism which globalization has since all but nullified. The only issue for serious debate, it seems, is whether globalization evolved as imperialism's response to new opportunities and challenges – or a backlash against the restraints and concessions previously imposed on it by Pan-Africanism and the exigencies of the 'Cold War'. Note finally in this connection that the formalities of 'plausible deniability' have been dropped, presumably as unnecessary, in the execution of globalization's interventions in domestic affairs in Africa and worldwide (including by coups d'état or 'regime change' and assassinations) – and mercenaries have become 'private security contractors', for instance.

9   Ching Kwan Lee (2014). Conn Hallinan's 'The New Scramble for Africa', *African Agenda*, Vol. 14, No. 3, 2011 and Jason Hickel's 'Trading with the enemy' (in the same issue of *African Agenda*) in which Michael Battle, then US Ambassador to the African Union warned that 'if we (in the United States) don't invest on the African continent now, we will find that China and India have absorbed its resources without us, and we will wake up and wonder what happened to our golden opportunity of investment' (11) are further examples of both the mindset and the implied contempt for the African inhabitants of Africa. The fact that the said Michael Battle was himself an African-American also serves as additional warning against the use

to replace the Mugabe government in Zimbabwe with one more acceptable to the 'former' colonial master and more liable to maintain Britain's
preferred 'willing-buyer-willing-seller' land policy for that country are yet
more giveaway indications of the civilizing missionaries' congenital inability
to let their 'former' colonies go.[10]

But as Cabral and others have also pointed out the Western imperialist
machine in Africa has always worked on two engines: the weaponry of the
imperialist powers themselves and facilitation by collaborator elites and
others in the subjugation and exploitation of the continent and its peoples.[11]
The contributory mindsets and sins of commission and omission include:

- Fatalism, superstition, the fetish of power and power holders and
  other faith- and culture-moulded mindsets which incline subjects
  to be submissive towards 'constituted authority', no matter how vile
  or shamelessly and openly subservient to foreign governments and
  interests;[12]

---

of ancestry and skin colour as sufficient evidence of an individual's Pan-Africanist
orientation. Battle, himself, was, in fairness, US Ambassador to the African Union,
not the African-American Ambassador to the African Union. But few, and particularly few 'non-cynical' Africans, would have expected him to conduct himself as what
Jason Hickel called him in another think piece: 'US imperialism's Ambassador to the
African Union'. See Jason Hickel, 'Michael Battle, US Imperialism's Ambassador to
the African Union', <https://revolutionaryfrontlines.wordpress.com/2010/10/17/
michael-battle-us-imperialisms-ambassador-to-the-african-union/>.

10   For independent views of the Zimbabwe saga see Baffour Ankomah, 'Zimbabwe:
     The Land Has Come Back' (12–15); the interview on the same issues with David
     Hasluck, director of Zimbabwe's white Commercial Farmers Union, CFU (48–52);
     and the letter by Clare Short, then British 'international development' minister,
     which sparked the British-Zimbabwe land dispute (52–3) all in *New African*, 415,
     February 2003.

11   Cf: Cabral (1974).

12   One of the more primitive versions of the superstition – assertions of the divinity of
     kings and queens – is, obviously, not an African monopoly. But between the partici-
     pation of some African chiefs in the trans-Atlantic slave trade, the use by imperialism
     of others as tools of indirect rule and the ready supply of indirect-rule presidents
     in the neo-colonial and globalization eras continuing recognition of rulers in the

- The matching of the colonial masters' white-saviour complex by an equally palpable white-saviour-dependency complex, as a direct consequence of centuries of colonial indoctrination and the virtual imperialist monopoly of the means of mass propaganda;
- The unending flow of the African 'quisling' at the service of the predators denounced by Cabral;[13]
- Internalization of the perverse doctrine that development is about building on 'colonial development' to 'catch up' with 'the already developed' nations and states with the help of the 'international community' and on its terms – a recipe for colonial-style servitude – and, by the same token, general loss of the sense that development is about the growth of a people's capacity to sustain themselves and meet their physiological, social and psycho-spiritual needs with the resources and means at their disposal and under their control;
- The free reins given to the purveyors of Western ideologies of various sorts, advocacy non-governmental organizations in fact and in name only riding various hobby-horses, 'independent' 'Think Tanks' which serve in practice as voices of Western paymasters, psyops operators pretending to be independent journalists with mandates rooted in imperial psychology to 'inform, educate and entertain' their regional and global audiences and other special-interest bodies to do as they please with African minds, values and morals;
- The pretence – in spite of their lamentable failure to do more than serve as machines and mechanisms for looting the continent and dispossessing its peoples in some half a century of 'independence' – that the geopolitical constructs and dependent-development strategy inherited

---

service of foreign interests as divinely ordained deserves to be called and treated as an 'African disease' even if it also manifests elsewhere!

13 In 'Guinea and Cabo Verde against Portuguese Colonialism' (Cabral, 1974, 14) Cabral lists the 'quislings' and 'faithful lackeys' as 'traditional chiefs and bandits in the times of slavery and of the wars of colonial conquest, gendarmes, various agents and mercenary soldiers during the golden age of colonialism, self-styled heads of state and ministers in the ... time of neo-colonialism'. The past is, of course, history. Contemporary freedom fighters may wish, no doubt, to update Cabral's list for current and future purposes.

from colonialism are capable of transforming Africa from a collection
of 'idiotic neo-colonial states'[14] to instruments for the defence, development and welfare of the African people;

- The superstition – subsequently blown apart by US President Barack
  Obama, no less – that the United Nations Organization, the so-called
  UN Development System and the Bretton Woods institutions, among
  others, are common-wealth organizations serving all the world equally,
  honestly and impartially, not the instruments of US power and domination long denounced as such by discerning observers;[15] and

- The evidence in the following pages that by their various acts of commission and omission Africa's 'traditional' and 'modern' elites, peoples
  and institutions have lent and continue to lend their support and
  cooperation to the US-led forces of globalization as effectively as their
  forebears did to the colonial and neo-colonial powers.

This book will not be a game changer any more than more illustrious publications before and alongside it have been, or can be, game changers. It may
not even change many minds. Silence, on the other hand, is not an option
for those who both have an interest in the decolonization of Africa and
African development and wish to escape the ignominy of 'cold complicity'
which Fanon warned against.

This attempt to escape the sin of cold complicity combines a people's
history of the development and maintenance of Africa's underdevelopment

---

14   Ayi Kwei Armah (1995), 10.

15   For Obama's superstition-buster see 'Remarks by the President at the United States
      Military Academy Commencement', 28 May 2014, where he boasted that 'after World
      War II, America had the wisdom to shape institutions to keep the peace and sup-
      port human progress, from NATO and the United Nations, to the World Bank and
      I.M.F (thereby) … *reducing the need for unilateral American action*' [my emphasis].
      For related independent 'intelligence' see Akyaaba Addai-Sebo, 'Never again! Why
      Africa can no longer believe in UN neutrality', *New African*, 509, August 2011, 12–18;
      Anne-Cécile Robert, 'Interventions militaires en Libye et en Côte d'Ivoire: Origines
      et vicissitudes du "droit d'ingérence"', *Le monde diplomatique*, 686, May 2012; 'Otan,
      bras armé de l'Onu?, *Afrique Asie*, April 2011; and Tor Krever, 'Dispensing Global
      Justice, Judging the ICC' (January/February 2014).

for other people's benefit with an indicative list of issues for consideration and action by freedom- and development-loving Africans, peoples of
African descent and their allies.

As a curtain raiser Chapter 1 throws a Pan-Africanist's searchlight on
some of the wilder claims about the benefits to Africa and the so-called free
world (to which the continent belongs as property, not a member) of the
Allied victory in what the West calls the Second World War. In particular
it subjects to critical examination the myths, not to say lies, that:

- the West saved Africa and the rest of the non-Western world not only
  from Italian Fascism and German Nazism, as specific historical phenomena, but from the underlying ideologies as well, including racism
  itself; and
- enlightened by the 'Second World War' and the spirits of resistance to
  Fascism, Nazism and the Atlantic Charter the West graciously decolo-
  nized Africa, and has followed that process with an African 'development' agenda which is not a mere makeover of its earlier 'civilizing'
  or 'Westernizing' mission.

In lieu of the pretence in the opposing political and intellectual camp that
its version of the history of the period covered in Chapter 1 is, somehow,
'objective' and ideologically neutral we acknowledge here that ours is una-
voidably ideological and Pan-Africanist. But it is not a work of fiction: it is
based on knowledge and insights from existing and reliable previous works;
confidential information provided by trustworthy participant-observers,
some of which may or may not have seeped already into the public domain;
personal observations; and educated interpretations of noteworthy events,
non-events and processes that occurred in the period of interest.

Chapter 2 recalls how France and the United States have acted, individually or jointly, to underdevelop Haiti throughout its existence as an
'independent' nation, and draws attention to some of the already observable replications of the 'Haiti treatment' in 'independent' Africa. It further
warns the peoples of Africa and the Diaspora that they ignore the lessons
from two centuries of Haiti's imposed underdevelopment at the peril of

repeating that country's history as their own future. As grounds for this warning the chapter points out, inter alia, that:

- the 'aggressive North Atlantic alliance that could not imagine their world inhabited by a free regime of Africans' in Haiti, and '(continues) to have a primary interest in that country's current condition'[16] is as alive and active as ever;
- the 'Alliance' has no more reason to tolerate free regimes of Africans in Africa and the rest of the African world than it has demonstrated over Haiti;
- the 'Alliance' has given, and continues to give, ample proof of its determination to do to the rest of the African world what it has done to Haiti;
- Africa and the rest of the African world have not lacked Duvalier-regime lookalikes created or sustained by imperialism as tools of indirect rule *and* 'living examples' of the dangers of entrusting power to 'black people';[17] and
- many of the tools which were employed in the nineteenth century to recapture Haiti for France and turn it into a Franco-American condominium have since been successfully applied to other rebellious African and black states.[18]

16 Hilary Beckles, 'The Hate and the Quake', *The Barbados Advocate*, 19 January 2010, <http://www.barbadosadvocate.com/newsitem.asp?more=letters&NewsID=8490> (accessed 20 April 2014).

17 For two of the most conspicuous examples of the cynicism in living memory see Pat Hutton and Jonathan Bloch, 'How the West Established Idi Amin and Kept Him There' in *Dirty Work 2* and, among other sources, *The Dictator's Handbook* on the United States and Mobutu Sese Seko of the Congo-Zaire. It is no secret, either, that then Defence Minister of the Central African Republic, Jean-Bedel Bokassa, who was to make a laughing stock of himself, his country and Africa by crowning himself emperor, was first made president of his country by France. See <http://www.nytimes.com/1996/11/05/world/jean-bedel-bokassa-self-crowned-emperor-central-african-republic-dies-75.html#h[AcoMBl,1]> (accessed 22 November 2015).

18 Ama Ata Aidoo – the literary legend – has worried, privately, that the nightmare scenario described above is, for all practical purposes, already here. The effective bantustanization of African territories in Africa and abroad which once attempted,

Using what has come to be regarded by many, including many discerning black people, as *the* democratic ideal since his famous Gettysburg Address (despite well-grounded doubts that Abraham Lincoln himself considered 'black people' as 'people' for his definition or purposes),[19] Chapter 3 critically examines the West's 'democracy' template and latter-day democratization-of-Africa project which have replaced the West's traditional 'good governance' recipes for Africa.[20] It points out, in any case, that true democracy is impossible without the true and effective self-government and self-determination which the West continues to deny the African people by words, deeds (including covert and overt military means) and 'conditionalities', despite 'decolonization' – and democracy will remain a fraud for as long as Africa and its development remain effectively colonized.

On the basis of the not unreasonable proposition that Africa cannot solve its development and indeed existential problems with the thinking and other elements that have locked it in underdevelopment, chronic poverty and attendant humiliation for its people for centuries Chapter 4 proposes the development of Africa by Africans and for Africans as the only real alternative to the continuing development and maintenance of Africa's underdevelopment. A few foundation ideas in support of this vision are offered for consideration and possible follow-up.

Chapter 5 argues that failure to recognize the development industry's version of African development as no more than a reincarnation of

---

claimed or promised independence may be proof enough of the effectiveness so far of imperialism's Haitianization-of-black-states machine. This is not to imply that there is no escaping it, of course.

19 As Coates (op. cit., 6) put it, 'when Abraham Lincoln declared, in 1863 that the battle of Gettysburg must ensure "that government of the people, by the people, for the people, shall not perish from the earth" ... the question is not whether (he) truly meant "government of the people" but what (America) has, throughout its history, taken the political term "people" to actually mean. In 1863 it did not mean your mother or your grandmother, and it did not mean you and me' – i.e. the people who are labelled 'black'.

20 For irrefutable evidence that America, for one, did not always favour 'democracy' in the West's *de facto* colonies and that US interests, not 'good governance', dictate the forms of government it promotes overseas see Chapter 3.

'colonial development' in Africa can only be described as politically mis-
chievous, intellectually naive, uninformed, misinformed and – in view
of the glaring evidence – scandalous. The chapter is just as dismissive of
'African development' prescriptions designed to, *inter alia*, mislead the
uninformed about 'how rich countries got rich and why poor countries stay
poor', as Erik Reinert puts it,[21] and give the false impression to vulnerable
Africans that it is within their continent's power to follow the 'development path' of the 'early developers', knowing full well that even the most
'powerful' African states are in no position to impoverish other people for
their enrichment. The chapter accordingly rejects the italicized words in
Susan George's description of 'development' as 'the password for imposing *a new kind* of dependency, *for enriching the already rich world* and for
shaping other societies to meet its commercial and political needs'.[22] The
true story of the underdevelopment and impoverishment of Africa and
the cause and effect relationship between these processes and the wealth
of George's '*already rich world*', partly retold in this chapter, sets the stage
for the chapter that follows.

Chapter 6 makes the case for the revival of Pan-Africanism as an
African liberation and development tool. In doing so it cautions that Pan-
Africanism can be raised as a liberation and developmental force if and
only if it reincarnates as a mass or popular movement. For, regardless of
its glorious past, Pan-Africanism cannot expect to be able to count on the
popular support and sacrifices necessary for its revival and mission without
taking on board Cabral's wise counsel that:

> The people [do not fight] for ideas, for the things in anyone's head ... [but] to win
> material benefits [for themselves] ... live better and in peace ... see their lives go for-
> ward [and] ... guarantee the future of their children.[23]

On the basis, additionally, that the dignity of the peoples of Africa and
of African descent across the globe is indivisible and that an affront to

---

21   Reinert, *How Rich Countries Got Rich and Why Poor Countries Stay Poor*
      (London: Constable, 2008).
22   Susan George, *How the Other Half Dies*, 17.
23   'Tell no lies, Claim no easy victories', in Cabral, op. cit., 70.

Africans anywhere is an affront to Africans everywhere, the chapter calls for greater Pan-Africanist attention to the liberation, development and welfare needs of all the Diaspora poor. It reiterates, in this connection, the importance of incorporating in Pan-Africanism's twenty-first-century agenda the defence, freedom, development and welfare needs of previously 'lost', silent, silenced and otherwise neglected 'tribes of Africa', notably, the Afro-Latinos, Afro-Indians and the formally or informally enslaved African-descended minorities in some Arab-majority states.

Protecting the movement from trivialization by the innocent or naive on one hand and hijacking by fraudsters, other opportunists, quislings and infiltrators on the other is also highlighted in this chapter as a major housekeeping concern of our age. The chapter ends with some actionable ideas for tackling some of the twenty-first-century Pan-African and Pan-Africanist challenges flagged in previous chapters.

The epilogue is a mixture of more actionable Pan-Africanist ideas and parting thoughts.

Africa and the World from 1943 to the Present

Imperialism knows no law beyond its own interests.
— KWAME NKRUMAH

He who controls the past controls the future. He who controls the present controls the past.
— GEORGE ORWELL

Only those who know the past can draw lessons and build a good future.
— ANGELA MERKEL, *at the commemoration of the 100th anniversary of the 'World War One' battle of Verdun*

If you don't like someone's story, write your own.
— CHINUA ACHEBE

An independent African's perspective

The freely acknowledged purpose of this book – to contribute to stakeholder thinking on the recovery of Africa and the transformation of African development into an African project by Africans primarily for Africans – would strike many as a show of positive defiance. But therein lies its value for those with a stake in African development as a development project rather than an 'insider' industry for 'insiders'. For, with Steve Biko's very apt observation that 'the most potent weapon of the oppressor is the mind of the oppressed'[1]

---

[1]   <http://www.brainyquote.com/quotes/authors/s/steven_biko.html> (accessed 1 January 2015).

as a call to arms and the real story of Africa's underdevelopment, which remains only partially told, as sufficient provocation the book is designed to contribute to the following development objectives:

- Cleansing of polluted African minds of toxic myths about Africans and the darker peoples of Africa, in particular, as an inferior 'race', the better to secure their acceptance of the dictatorship of their former slave and colonial masters turned 'development partners';
- Empowerment of the African people to work for the development of their societies and continent with themselves as prime beneficiaries; and
- The liberation of the more redeemable of Africa's 'development partners' from the mindset, complexes, wants and desires which give some of their number their attachment to African resources and the suppression and exploitation of the African people as matters of their strategic interest and 'national security', make them compulsive meddlers in African affairs and condemn them to degrading reliance on the denigration of 'the African' for 'racial', national and individual self-esteem.[2]

Walter Rodney's *How Europe Underdeveloped Africa*[3] and works of similar genre, such as E. A. Brett's *Colonialism and Underdevelopment in East Africa: The Politics of Economic Change 1919–39* and Rhoda Howard's *Colonialism and Underdevelopment in Ghana*[4] make it unnecessary to trace the underdevelopment of Africa to its sources, fortunately.[5] The fact

---

2   This may not be a fool's errand if Kwame Anthony Appiah's thesis in *Honour Code* (Chapter 3, 'Suppressing Atlantic Slavery', 101–36) that 'honour' helped to convert morality into the political force which drove parts of the anti-slave trade and anti-slavery movements has any merit.

3   Rodney (1972).

4   E. A. Brett, *Colonialism and Underdevelopment in East Africa: The Politics of Economic Change 1919–39* (Ibadan and Nairobi: Heinemann, 1973) and Rhoda Howard, *Colonialism and Underdevelopment in Ghana* (London: Croom Helm, 1978).

5   General dependency theory has also offered valuable tools for understanding underdevelopment and impoverishment processes in Africa and elsewhere in the Third World. For some of the basic texts on the subject see, André Gunder Frank, 'The

that the 'treaties, aggression and fraud' blamed by Abraham, along with 'simple carelessness' on the part of some African leaders, for the continent's original loss of its independence[6] can resurface as 'force, pre-emptive attack, deception' in the advocacy by a latter-day Western-Establishment advocate of imperialism in the twenty-first century[7] – and be all too openly applied in the name of 'globalization' by the 'former' colonial masters, individually and collectively – makes the history and beneficiaries of Africa's underdevelopment hard to miss. The development of Africa's underdevelopment began centuries ago, of course. And the 1943–2015 period in that long process may or may not be more devastating than other identifiable periods before it.

But the period packs enough examples of toxic myths, dubious claims, subterfuges, plain falsehoods, imperial arrogance, brutality and general cynicism on one hand and native 'carelessness' (in the sense of Abraham) and other political or politically significant social, moral and mindset-derived weaknesses, among others, on the other hand, to make it a deserving period for focused attention by activists and students of the development and maintenance of Africa's underdevelopment. Notable among these are:

- The claim that the Allied victory over the Axis powers in the 'Second World War' was a victory for human decency, a just world order, the rights of peoples to self-determination and the primacy of right over might generally; and that the West is mandated to police observance

---

Development of Underdevelopment' and 'Economic Dependence, Class Structure and Development Policy', both in James D. Cockcroft, André Gunder Frank and Dale L. Johnson, eds, *Dependence and Underdevelopment: Latin America's Political Economy* (Garden City, NY: 1972); Samir Amin, 'Underdevelopment and Dependence in Black Africa'; and Samir Amin, *Le développement inégal: essai sur les formes sociales du capitalisme péripherique* (Paris: Les Éditions de Minuit, 1973). See also, Kwame Nkrumah, *Neo-Colonialism*; Patrick Bond, *Looting of Africa* (London and Pietermaritzburg: Zed Books, 2006) and 'How Africa Developed Europe and USA' (the cover story), *New African*, 444, October 2005, 10–13.

6 'Independence Lost and Regained' (Chapter 3) in W. E. Abraham, *The Mind of Africa* (1962), 116.

7 Robert Cooper, 'The new liberal imperialism'.

by others of this glorious 'post-war' moral order – for its good and the good of all of humankind;[8]

- The big lies, or variants of the above false claim, that the proclamation of the Atlantic Charter in 1941 by Franklin D. Roosevelt and Winston Churchill, President of the United States and Prime Minister of the United Kingdom, respectively, made respect for the rights of peoples to self-determination a cornerstone of the two imperial powers' so-called 'foreign policies' – and the Allies' victory in the Second World

[8] 'Second World War' is put in quotes to draw attention to the fact that the description of the 1939–1945 war as the Second World War is ideological and open to dispute. To W. E. B. Du Bois, for one, the 'First' of the 'World War' series was no more than a 'war for empire, of which the struggle between Germany and the Allies over Africa was both symbol and reality' (quoted in Howard Zinn, *A People's History of the United States: 1492 to the Present* (New York: Harper, 2005, 363 from W. E. B. Du Bois, 'The African Roots of War', *Atlantic Monthly*, Vol. 115, No. 5, May 1915, 707–14)). That has to make the integrity of the descriptions of the two wars as World Wars questionable. Note, also, that to Samir Amin, another free thinker, the first and second 'World Wars' were, in reality, no more than sequences in a 'thirty-year war between the United States and Germany to inherit Britain's defunct hegemony'. (See *Obsolescent Capitalism: Contemporary Capitalism and Global Disorder* (London: Zed Books, 2003, 9)). Independently, and reflecting much informed African opinion, Herbert Ekwe-Ekwe ('The concatenation of the African role in the war of 1914–1918 or World War', *Pambazuka News*, 693, 11 September 2011, <http://pambazuka.org/en/category/features/92864> (accessed 11 September 2014)) rejects the myth – repeated in 2014 by George Carey, a former Archbishop of Canterbury' (and 'Spiritual Head of the worldwide Anglican communion') in 'Why I, as a Christian, believe we have to banish evil British jihadists from these shores', *The Mail on Sunday*, 23 August 2014) – that the two 'World Wars' were fought against totalitarianism and for the survival of democratic virtues – as a self-glorifying untruth about wars in which European powers used Africans to fight their wars, and Africans were placed in 'the double-jeopardy of conquered and occupied peoples at once fighting wars for and against ruthless aggressors'. In view, moreover, of the fact that two of the principal heroes on the side Carey extols, British Prime Minister Winston Churchill and Charles de Gaulle, leader of the 'Free French Forces', were dead against the decolonization of Africa – and of other 'wartime' and 'post-war' facts which the West 'forgets' – the Western preference for describing the World Wars by numbers, rather than purpose, for instance, should, itself, be of more than academic interest!

War was not just over enemies who happened to be Nazis and Fascists but over Nazism and Fascism as well;

- The myth that the West and 'the free world' are other than new codes for Anthony Eden's 'white race authority' plus 'honorary white' Japan[9] and under US leadership;[10]

- The decolonization fraud which enabled former French President Charles de Gaulle, for his part, to mock African 'independence' as the transformation of colonization into cooperation[11] and trapped

9　'Honorary white' was, of course an accolade granted to Japan and the Japanese by apartheid South Africa (with the consent, no doubt, of the rest of white race authority) and never really repudiated by Japan or any quotable Japanese.

10　The description by Louis J. Freeh, a former director of the US Federal Bureau of Investigation of the president of the United States as 'the President of the free world' (Louis J. Freth with Howard Means, *My FBI: Bringing Down the Mafia, Investigating Bill Clinton, and Fighting the War on Terror*. New York: St Martin's Press, 2005, 53) is by no means unusual. Sycophantic reporting by Britain's BBC of the travels, activities and words of US presidents and other US political, defence, diplomatic and commercial, industrial, banking and entertainment 'heavyweights' and 'celebrities' also gives the impression that to that 'World's Radio' at least the United States is the 'free world's' (if not 'the world's') leader to be impressed upon the world at every opportunity as such. The sycophancy often extends to the obliteration of information that casts the US in an unfavourable light: BBC listeners who were reminded in May 2016 of Operation Condor (the notorious campaign of political repression and state terror involving intelligence operations and assassination of opponents of the corporate dictatorships of Latin America between 1968 and 1989) were 'spared' the fact that it was backed by the US, and its poor listeners were left in the dark by the BBC in the same month and after the conviction of the brutal African dictator Hissène Habré for war crimes that he had been a US ally, for instance. No one who has ever heard a BBC news bulletin can possibly doubt that the power which kept such vile company would have been named and shamed (as in 'Russian-backed Ukrainian rebels) if it had not been 'the leader' of the 'free world'.

11　De Gaulle's exact words, quoted by Edem Kodjo in *Et demain l'Afrique* (Paris: Editions Stock, 1985), 123, were, 'Nous avons changé la colonisation en coopération'. For some of the forensic evidence on the fraud see Kwame Nkrumah, *Neo-Colonialism: The Last Stage of Imperialism* (New York: International Publishers, 1965) and Ngugi wa Thiong'o, *Detained: A Writer's Prison Diary* (London: Heinemann, 1981). For quick and ready examples of how imperialism proceeded to mock Africa after the fraud see Ellen Ray et al., eds, *Dirty Work 2: The CIA in Africa* (London: Zed Press, its victims in the informal colonial state described by Nkrumah as 'neo-colonialism';[12]

- The myth that the 'Cold War' (which was anything but 'cold' outside the 'white lands') was a holy war between a holy (Western) empire and its evil (Soviet) enemy;

- The further myth that the 'Cold War' defeat of the Soviet Union and the globalization of both the Russia of the oligarchs and post-Maoist Communist China were triumphs of 'capitalism' over 'socialism' and 'communism', and proof of the superiority of 'capitalism' to any other socio-economic system and political economy imaginable by man;[13]

- The determination by the West that non-Western and non-capitalist societies and territories such as those of Africa have no choice but to accept incorporation by the West, willy-nilly;

1980). French President, Valéry Giscard d'Estaing's shameless appropriation of the African nationalist slogan – 'L'Afrique aux Africains' ('Africa for the Africans') – in the initial French attempts to 'ward off' the American 'intruders' in the early stages of the 'globalization' of Africa is also a measure of how the French continued to see themselves as 'African' (in the sense in which the British continue to see themselves as an Indian-ocean power by virtue of their continuing occupation of the Chagos Islands) even after their ostensible decolonization of their African empire. No one appears to have bothered, finally, to explain where 'the dual mandate' under the old colonial order ended and *le droit d'ingérence* under the 'new' 'co-operation' regime began!

12   'The essence of neo-colonialism', as Nkrumah pointed out, 'is that the State which is subject to it is, in theory, independent and has all the outward trappings of international sovereignty (but) in reality its economic system and thus its political policy is directed from outside' (*Neo-colonialism*, ix).

13   On the globalization of Russia and China see, for instance, 'Bonfire of a Young Democracy: Russia Chooses "The Pinochet Option"', in Naomi Klein, *The Shock Doctrine. The Rise of Disaster Capitalism* (New York: Picador, 2008), Chapter 11; 'The Capitalist Id: Russia and the New Era of the Boor Market', Chapter 12; 'Slamming the Door on History: A Crisis in Poland, a Massacre in China', Chapter 9; and 'The Shock of Tiananmen Square', 232–41.

- The frequent disguise of 'the West', 'the free world' and 'white race authority' as the 'international community', to confuse those who are wont to take words at face value;[14]
- The invention of 'globalization' as a deceptive alias for imperialism;
- Margaret Thatcher's decree that 'there is no such thing as society' and, following from it and the mindset which produced it, pressures on African countries by the world's Anglo-Saxon Establishment and its surrogates, in particular, to legitimize as a 'human right' an unusual sexual orientation which the generality of African societies find abhorrent;[15]
- The American doctrine, insidiously, routinely and sometimes crudely repeated by other propaganda organs, that what is good for America is good for the world and America has the right and duty to act unilaterally where necessary and multilaterally where possible to secure its 'uninhibited access to key markets, energy supplies, and strategic resources' – and it is a form of roguery to stand in America's way;[16]
- The Western masters' insistence that the Market-State system under which The Market or Market Forces rule – under the management and control of the 'force multipliers' named by Obama, bilateral and other

14 Reportedly letting this particular cat out of the bag was the prominent 'neocon' (for neoconservative) and former US Permanent Representative to the UN, John Bolton, no less, according to Noam Chomsky who quotes Bolton as bragging that 'There is no United Nations. There is an international community that occasionally can be led by the only real power left in the world – that's the United States – when it suits our interests and when we can get others to go along'. See Noam Chomsky, *Failed States: The Abuse of Power and the Assault on Democracy* (New York: Metropolitan Books, 2006), 86. As if on cue or by command the state-owned Western media, notably the BBC and France's RFI, generally conflate the United States, the West, the world, and 'the international community' in their reportage.

15 Then British Prime Minister Margaret Thatcher, talking to *Women's Own* magazine, 31 October 1987. For more on the 'sexual revolution' which the Anglo-Saxon Establishment has attempted to export to Africa, notably through US President Barack Obama and British Prime Minister David Cameron, see below.

16 For examples of the ventilation and analysis of this doctrine and associated doctrine of 'American exceptionalism' see President Obama's *Commencement Address at West Point on May 28*, 2014, Chomsky, *Failed States* and Chomsky, *Rogue States*.

multilateral 'development partners', the Credit Rating Agencies, etc.,
determine how Africa is 'democratically' governed, how its governments are funded and 'development projects' are financed and who
gets what, when and how generally – is the only 'development' system
available and permissible to the African people;[17]

- The fib that on the backs of successful 'wars of national liberation',
clever political manoeuvring or negotiations, the magnanimity or
acknowledgement by some colonial and apartheid bosses at the right
time of 'the winds of change', 'magical tea parties' or some combination of the above the African continent and peoples were freed from
imperialism and apartheid for ever;[18]

- The processes by which the African Union, African 'states' and 'responsible' African leaders have been manoeuvred into accepting as 'development partners', 'protectors', and more, the same NATO, NATO
members and NATO interests which are notorious for their past
support for apartheid in South Africa and its occupation of South-
West Africa (Namibia); collaboration with Portuguese colonialism in
Angola, Mozambique, Cape Verde and Guinea-Bissau; unspeakable
atrocities against the peoples of Kenya and Algeria, among others;
harbour in their establishment the likes of Robert Cooper (author of

17   On the concept of 'market state', as Philip Bobbit describes it in *The Shield of Achilles*,
see Chapter 3 below. On the havoc which 'market-state' thinking unleashes on development, democracy and development and democracy theory see Colin Leys, *The Rise
and Fall of Development Theory*, Thandika Mkandawire, 'Globalisation, Structural
Adjustment and "Choiceless Democracies"' and Samir Amin, *'Mondialisation et
démocratie, une contradiction majeure de notre époque', Recherches Internationales*,
No. 55 (1999).

18   It is a measure of the power of this deception that many African 'leaders' accepted
'independence' from France on the proverbial silver platter in 1960, after first rejecting independence in a 1958 referendum, paving the way for Charles De Gaulle's boast
quoted above. 'Lancaster House' agreements sealed similar donations of 'independence' in 'Commonwealth Africa' and the only constitutionally designated Prime
Minister in Ghana after Kwame Nkrumah, a certain Kofi Abrefa Busia, campaigned
for 'dialogue' with South Africa in 1970–1971 as a means of ending apartheid – on
the grounds that all problems with the 'white man' could be solved over tea!

'The new liberal imperialism', op. cit.) and the authors of the regime changes in Cote d'Ivoire and Libya noted above; and continued to treat Africa at the time of writing as their game reserve;

- The myth that the African Union is, and ever was, an authentic African liberation, integration and development tool;
- The myth that Rhodesia was fully liberated in 1980 with the birth of Zimbabwe, South West Africa with the birth in 1990 of Namibia, apartheid ended in 1994, and that with these developments Africa ceased to have a colonial problem;[19] and
- The addition of 'the war on terror' to the myriad excuses for continuing imperialist command and control of Africa.

If the following account by Jeremy Keenan of how the Sahel became a 'war on terror' theatre is even partly true, the African people today have every reason to worry about where their American, AFRICOM and NATO protectors – and the complicity of their leaders, as 'partners' or mercenaries in that war – will take them next, within or beyond the globalization phase of imperialism:

> In 1998, US dependency on foreign oil supplies surpassed the psychologically critical 50% level. The Cheney Report (2001) estimated Africa would provide 25% of US oil imports by 2015. That, because of the shale oil revolution, is now part of history.
>
> However, at that time, the US wanted to militarise Africa to secure its oil resources. To do so, it used the pretext of the Global War on Terror (GWOT). The only problem was that Africa did not have much, if any terrorism at that time. The attacks on US embassies in Nairobi and Dar es Salaam in 1998, and a Mombasa hotel in 2002, were in East Africa, far from its major oil resource regions and not enough to justify the launch of a new front in the GWOT.
>
> The US' need for more terrorism in Africa was provided through Washington's post 9/11 supposed 'counter-terrorism' alliance with Algeria. Instrumental in the development of this alliance was Rumsfeld's Proactive, Pre-emptive Operations Group, known as P2OG, which was put into operation in late 2002. Its primary objective was to create false flag incidents to justify military intervention.

---

19   The mischief in this particular myth lies not just in the concession of places like the Chagos Islands to their colonial occupiers but in the gratuitous acceptance of the myth that colonization has, indeed, been transformed into co-operation, as alleged by General De Gaulle.

In February 2003, 32 European tourists were kidnapped in the Algerian Sahara. It was the first act of terrorism in the region post-9/11. Like so many actions during the Dirty War of the 1990s, it was almost certainly a false-flag operation undertaken by the DRS (Département du Renseignement et de la Sécurité of Algeria at the time), probably on behalf of the US ...

The operation provided the Bush administration with the publicity and propaganda it needed to justify the launch of a 'Sahelian' or 'second front' in the GWOT. January 2004 saw the deployment of some 1,000 US forces across the Sahelian states of Mauritania, Mali, Niger and Chad. Bush called it the Pan Sahel Initiative (PSI). Locals called it the 'US invasion of Africa'.[20]

The development of Africa's underdevelopment, 1943 to the present: Another narrative

Africa and the 'development and freedom' problematic

Development and freedom have come to enjoy the quality of virtues everybody loves. Amartya Sen, the Nobel-Prize-winning development intellectual, raises development, presumably 'safely', to the level of 'a process of expanding the real freedoms that people enjoy'.[21] The late African intellectual giant of a more radical persuasion, Archie Mafeje, agreed and went further, in 'South Africa at Crossroads: Liberation or Betrayal?' to equate development with liberation, and both with 'emancipation from an undesirable social status to a more desirable one'.[22] It is hard to disagree.

Not surprisingly, therefore, and with typical cynicism, 'development' and 'freedom' have also been appropriated as their contribution to civilization by those who have historically made it impossible for others to enjoy

20   Jeremy Keenan, 'How terror came to the Sahel', *New African*, 560, April 2016.
21   Amartya Sen, *Development as Freedom* (Oxford: Oxford University Press, 1999), 3.
22   Archie Mafeje, 'South Africa at a Crossroads: Liberation of Betrayal?', *In Search of an Alternative: A Collection of Essays on Revolutionary Theory and Politics* (Harare: SAPES Books, 1992), 74.

one or the other or both blessings of civilization. Worse, still, the deniers of freedom and development to others were doing so in their names long before 1943 – and not only at the expense of the peoples of Africa. The poem in which the English poet, Rudyard Kipling, invented 'the white man's burden' for pink people 'who have been brought up hopelessly, tragically, deceitfully, to believe that they are white', as Ta-Nehisi Coates put it,[23] was first published in 1899 after all.[24] And, as the poem's subtitle, 'The United States and the Philippine Islands', shows, the original target of the unsolicited 'salvation' was not Africa. The promoters of the 'civilizing mission', 'the dual mandate' (and their French and Portuguese versions) also set their sights on Africa long before 1943, admittedly and most importantly.[25] But while it is certainly not being argued that the post-1943 assaults by the West on African freedom, dignity, resources, independence and humanity are any worse than those of any period(s) before it the period stands out as a legitimate focus of forensic study for the following good reasons, among others:

- African co-responsibility for imperialist assaults on the African people is greater, clearer and more easily described and documented than ever before;
- Embedded in the conditions which have made the assaults possible during the period are lessons which can be readily mined to hasten the liberation of Africa and peoples of African descent worldwide;
- Africans and alleged African and 'black-race' weaknesses have been more easily and cynically blamed for the effects of their colonial inheritance and the sins of their puppet masters during the period under review than any other period; and

---

23 Coates, *Between the World and Me*, 7.
24 <http://en.wikipedia.org/wiki/The_White_Man's_Burden>.
25 It would be recalled that Africa had its taste of the 'white man's burden', the 'white saviour complex', European racism and white-race-authority even before Frederick Lugard published his Africa-specific manifesto, *The Dual Mandate in British Tropical Africa*, in 1922. Leopold II of Belgium's *International African Society* or International Association for the Exploration and Civilization of the Congo, established in 1876, is perhaps the most notorious of the tailor-made imperial manifestos for Africa.

- Every extension of imperial domination of the African continent and people is worthy of study as a source of doom and gloom for some of the African people, which also lessens the self-esteem of others and creates unhealthy and abnormal acceptance by too many Africans of their servitude as their lot.

An African reading of the 'decolonization' of Africa

It is a matter of historical record, of course, that the Charles de Gaulle who was to describe the cynical 'transformation of colonisation into cooperation' as an achievement had previously left no doubt about his disdain for African independence: his 1944 declaration as leader of the Free French Forces to a conference of global French occupation-governors in Brazzaville that 'Self-government must be rejected – even in the more distant future' is a matter of record.[26] It is equally indisputable that time, the victory of 'the angels' in the 'Second World War', the participation of *tirailleurs africains* (African rifles) in the liberation of his country and his return to power in free France as Premier of the Fourth Republic did not convert de Gaulle to the cause of African freedom: his scorched-earth treatment of Guinea-Conakry for daring to choose independence over appendage to France in his 1958 referendum which purported to offer that option to France's colonial subjects is enough proof of that.[27] The task, accordingly, is not to prove that the claim (by De Gaulle and his ilk) about colonization having been 'transformed' during the review period was cynical, provocative and designed to muddy Africa's political waters but to keep exposing the dynamics of the continuing colonization of

---

26   Ekwe-Ekwe, 'The concatenation of the African role in the war of 1914–1918 or World War I', 11 September 2014, <http://pambazuka.org/en/category/features/92864>, 693, 11 September 2014, quoting from Hubert Deschambs, 'France in Black Africa and Madagascar between 1920 and 1945', in L. H. Gann and Peter Duiganan, eds, *Colonialism in Africa, 1870–1900, Vol. 2: The History and Politics of Colonialism 1914–1960* (Cambridge: Cambridge University Press, 1970).

27   Other, and worse, examples of the decolonization fraud – and not only from De Gaulle or the French – can be found throughout the book.

Africa and African development for as long as the need remains to empower enough stakeholders in African freedom with the necessary intellectual and forensic tools to see beyond deceptive appearances.

For the benefit of African stakeholders in particular the following examples of African complicity in the continuing colonization of Africa and African development are highlighted:

- General acceptance by the governments and elites of Africa of the 'former' colonial-master countries (and their governments, corporate bodies and other elite types in particular) as 'development partners';
- The pretence that with the decolonization fraud and the internationally recognized 'independences' Africans have become masters of their own destiny;
- African membership of obscene 'voluntary associations' like the (British) Commonwealth, the French Organisation internationale de la Francophonie and the Community of Portuguese Language Countries (lusophonie) after 'independence', which symbolically and effectively grants *post facto* legitimacy to colonization by rewarding 'former' colonizers (and 'mother countries') with the emotional, cultural, commercial, diplomatic, political and other advantages of formal or informal headship of such bodies;
- Similar 'post-independence' affiliation to the former European Economic Community (EEC) through the Yaoundé I and II, the Lome and the Cotonou Agreements and Conventions and follow-up arrangements with its EU successor, with similar symbolic and substantive results;
- The substitution of the language of 'collective self reliance' for Africa's development in the *Lagos Plan of Action for the Economic Development of Africa, 1980–2000* for that of dependency in the New Partnership for Africa's Development (NEPAD) (about which more below);
- Readiness to even consider the EU's trap of New Economic Partnership Agreements (EPAs);[28]

---

28   See, for instance, *The Draft Economic Partnership Agreement (EPA) Between the West African States, ECOWAS and WAEMU (UEMOA) of the One Part and the*

- The networks of French military bases and US and AFRICOM military 'footprints' allowed throughout Africa, for instance;[29] and
- The many African 'boots on the ground' (equivalent of the 'African rifles' and *tirailleurs africains* during the 'First and Second World Wars') in imperialism's so-called war on terror and the African Union's readiness to cover it with its flag.

The above and innumerable other examples of the warped thinking and degenerate African behaviour which facilitated the decolonization fraud and sustain the *presence coloniale* in nominally independent Africa are undeniable. But it is not enough to recognize them for what they are: the need to separate the weaknesses they expose between those borne out of greed, situational necessity (including the instinct of self preservation in unhealthy circumstances) and the material, intellectual, emotional and spiritual enslavement of the ostensible villains, to facilitate their effective and fair revolutionary treatment for the benefit of the African people, should be just as obvious. In this connection and read in conjunction with the material conditions of peoples compelled to live, work and die within the confines of colonial economies and their supporting political structures the following observations by the Walk Free Foundation's *Global Slavery Index Report (2013)* suggest that some, at least, of imperialism's collaborating African villains may be victims of 'physical, spiritual and intellectual (bondage)' in need of liberation, not devils:

European Community and its Member States of the Other Part (after conclusion of negotiations by Senior Officials, February 2014), accessible *inter alia* at <http:// twnafrica.org/ECOWAS%20WA%20&%20EU%20EPA%20draft%20text%20 as%20at%20Feb%202014.pdf> (accessed 20 April 2016).

29   While the French military 'umbrella' in Africa is mostly open, longstanding and known the 'US invasion' of the continent is relatively new and not so well known. For an introduction to the latter see John Glaser, 'The US's Invasion of Africa That Nobody Knows About', *Antiwar.com*, 15 April 2014, <http://antiwar.com/ blog/2014/04/15/the-uss-invasion-of-africa-that-nobody-knows-about/> (accessed 20 April 2015).

victims of ... slavery have their freedom denied and are used and controlled and exploited by another. Modern slavery is not always self-evident as some other crimes ... [It] involves an extreme abuse of power, which is not always immediately apparent but requires understanding the people and the relationships involved.[30]

The 'house-slave' phenomenon, Uncle Tom syndrome and similar examples of collaboration with unjust power beyond the needs of survival on one hand and the many successful and unsuccessful slave revolts in human history against criminal 'authorities' on the other are reminders, however, that servitude does not grant absolute freedom from moral and political responsibility for acts and omissions which amount to collaboration. When, therefore, expectations of private material, political or psychospiritual gain inform personal or group decisions to collaborate with an imperialist power or other slave master it seems illogical to excuse resulting acts and omissions on the grounds of the diminished political and moral responsibility of the culprits. For this reason while 'post-war' US and other imperialist pressures on Africans and others to adopt one form of government or another depending on their interests may be cited by responsive governments and elites to deny their own responsibility for actions and omissions taken in compliance their pleas manifestly do not deserve the sympathetic ears of victims of the collaboration. As a manifestation of cowardice or opportunism failure to resist the pressures – from sources such as the US National Security Council's determination in 1962 that 'when ... in the US interest, to make the local military and police advocates of democracy and agents for carrying forward the developmental process'; the 1968 declaration by Samuel P. Huntington of the US Foreign Policy and National Security Establishment that liberal democracy in the tropics might 'serve to perpetuate antiquated social structure(s)';[31] and, in the opposite direction, the post-'Cold War' sanctions-backed instructions by

---

30 See <file:///C:/Users/hp/Downloads/GlobalSlaveryIndex_2013_Download_WEB1. pdf> (accessed 27 February 2014).
31 The Huntington and US National Security Council quotations are from Prashad, *The Darker Nations*, 141. Prashad's own sources are Samuel P. Huntington, *Political Order in Changing Societies* (New Haven, CT: Yale University Press, 1968) and National Security Council, 'U.S. Overseas Internal Defense Policy', 1 August 1962.

the West to Zimbabwe, but not to, say, Yoweri Museveni's Uganda, Teodoro Obiang Nguema Mbasogo's Equatorial Guinea, Blaise Compaoré's Burkina Faso, Abdel Fattah el-Sisi's Egypt and the many 'friendly' dictatorships across the continent to 'democratize' or else, deserves to be counted, after all, as a veritable sin of commission and omission in itself. The common spectacle in the neo-colonial and globalization eras of brutal, corrupt and incompetent African 'leaders', military and quasi-military dictatorships and 'democratically elected' kleptocracies placing services to imperialism and other foreign interests above loyalty and service to their people – for regime security, material benefits and Western accolades – is, indeed, reminiscent of the conduct of the chiefs and other 'leaders' who partnered the European slave traders and colonialists, not that of helpless slaves.

More depressingly still, the additional fact that Africa as a whole had been turned by 2015 into a constellation of globalized, failed or failing states rotating around the 'former' slave traders and colonial masters, with African complicity, confirms that the essence of the 'partnership' between the Western predators and their African facilitators has remained as it was in the beginning. The following slightly edited report on a mining sector agreement – in the twenty-first century – between Bentsi-Enchill's 'independent' country and a foreign investor is not insignificant in that regard:

> The Chairman of the Mining Review Committee (MRC) ... has revealed that neither he nor the MRC was involved in the negotiations of the Gold Fields mining deal with government.
>
> This is in spite of the MRC's mandate as the negotiating team for government.
>
> The government of Ghana through Parliament agreed to a new development agreement with Gold Fields Ghana Limited which according to the 1992 constitution, is to see Goldfields invest 500 million dollars in its mines.
>
> The new agreement also had a fiscal stability agreement which granted royalty and tax concession to the mining company.
>
> But civil society group, the Third World Network (TWN), subsequently called on government and parliament to disclose details of the agreement because it suspects some illegalities took place, prompting them to write letters to a number of institutions including the MRC.

Huntington, a 'right-wing' crusader, has also served, *inter alia*, as a US National Security Coordinator.

In a statement copied to Citi News,[32] (the MRC Chairman) acknowledged receipt of the letter from the TWN asking the MRC to clarify its role in the development and negotiations of the Gold Fields agreements, but said the MRC was bypassed in the negotiations that produced the Gold Fields Development Agreement.

'In the circumstances, I feel obliged as Chairman of the MRC to state categorically that the MRC was not involved in the development of positions nor the conduct of the negotiations that produced the Gold Fields Development Agreements ratified on 17 March, 2016. Indeed, the negotiations were carried out on the blind side of the committee.'

He further indicated that he did not hear about the negotiations till after they had been concluded.

'As chair of the MRC, I did not get to hear about the negotiations till after they had been concluded even though I was in regular contact with the Ministry of Lands and Natural Resources at all times.'

Despite being sidelined (the MRC Chairman) stated that he still relayed his comments on the deal to government but they were ignored without explanation.

'In spite of information that my detailed comments had been received and favorably considered at the highest levels of government, the agreements remained essentially unchanged and were subsequently ratified by parliament in an expedited process, which dispenses with the standing Order requirement of minimum 48-hour between notice of a motion for ratification and its movement and acceptance – for reasons that are not stated.'

Government should come clean on the deal.

Speaking in reaction to the response from (the MRC Chairman) the Coordinator of the Third World Network … commended (him) for responding to their letter but noted that critical questions pertaining to the deal remained unanswered.

'The question of the legality of the tax and royalty concessions given to Goldfields had not been answered. The request for the disclosure of the docket had not been answered. The request for Parliament's Mines and Energy report that parliament used to justify the agreement had not been answered and the request also for disclosure of who had been involved had also not been answered.'

He further warned that Government's silence on the matter was not in the interest of Ghanaians and urged them to quickly come clean on the matter.

'Silence is not in the interest of the Ghanaian people and I think these agencies, particularly the minister, the minerals commission and parliament and the Attorney General, have the responsibility to come out and clear the air.'

32　A local radio station in Ghana.

The TWN Coordinator reiterated his group's position on the matter to the effect that the fiscal terms agreed between Government and Goldfields were illegal and not economically justified.

'Our first position is that the fiscal terms, that is the tax and royalty concessions given to Gold fields are illegal. They cannot be justified under the terms of the Minerals and Mining Act so there is an issue of illegality.'[33]

The government of Ghana's reported response to the TWN concerns is just as worth quoting for both the quality of the thinking behind its concessions to the investor and the confirmation that the sell-out complained of is not a local aberration:

The Finance Ministry has justified its decision to sign a Stability Agreement with mining firm, Goldfields-Ghana.

Government through parliament last month announced its decision to allow Goldfields-Ghana to pay a fixed tax and royalty rate for the next 11 years.

This decision has, however, not gone down well with some civil society groups and even the committee that was established to review the agreement granted mining firms like, Anglogold and Newmont-Ghana.

But Deputy Finance Minister X tells JOYBUSINESS there was no way government could have declined the agreement.

'As soon as you set one precedent, in the case of Ghana, like Newmont, others doing similar investments will ask for similar equality. Failure to do it will mean they are going away and that is why I said that in taxing petroleum or mineral resources in the extraction industry, you really will have to look at what your sub-region is doing' (the Deputy Minister) said.[34]

Within and outside the West African sub-region it is also not unknown for brutal, corrupt, incompetent and insensitive 'leaders' in 'independent' Africa to feel free to trash their own people; facilitate their continuing dispossession, repression and exploitation by imperial capital; and even risk reprisal attacks on their people from terrorists opposed to the imperialist

---

33   'Gov't bypassed us on Gold Fields deal – Prof Sawyerr', *GhanaWeb*, 26 April 2016, <http://www.ghanaweb.com/GhanaHomePage/business/Gov-t-by passed-us-on-Gold-Fields-deal-Prof-Sawyerr-433792>.

34   'Gov't justifies stability agreement with Goldfields-Ghana', *GhanaWeb*, 26 April 2016, <http://www.ghanaweb.com/GhanaHomePage/business/ Gov-t-justifies-stability-agreement-with-Goldfields-Ghana-434007>.

camp in the 'clash of barbarisms' or what is known in the West and its dependencies as the 'war on terror' – in exchange for guarantees of regime security and 'development cooperation' from their external patrons. *Plus ça change, plus ça reste (vraiment/*truly) *la même chose.*

Decolonization without emancipation: A paradox not unlike 'emancipation without freedom'?[35]

While it may be technically impossible to prove that the 'decolonization' of Africa during the 1943–2015 period failed to free the continent and its people and resources from imperialist domination *because* the people did not care much for their liberation or were all too ready to surrender prime responsibility for it to leaders whose mindset, personal and group interests and political agenda did not necessarily favour *liberation*, as opposed to power transfer to or power-sharing with them, it is the only hypothesis which is consistent with Howard Zinn's observation, which deserves to be called a law, that 'liberation from the top would only go as far as the interests of the dominant groups (permit)'.[36] Indeed, African history from the slave-trade era, general change theory and a retrospective view of the conduct of African leaders during the 1943–2015 period all lead to the irre-sistible conclusion that given a choice between freeing their people from imperialist and other foreign-predator exploitation and aligning with the predators for selfish gain the latter course of action was the 'natural' course of action. As Mafeje observed, recalling the case of the 'former Treason Trialist' who did not see the point in continuing the anti-apartheid strug-gle after the establishment of the Bantustans:[37]

---

35 The phrase 'emancipation without freedom' is borrowed from Zinn, *A People's History of the United States*, 171–210.
36 Zinn, ibid. 171–2.
37 In Mafeje's telling the former 'Treason Trialist' saw the creation of the Bantustans as 'the deliverance of the Black Man from White bondage': 'our moment of deliver-ance, we are going to enjoy riches'. (Mafeje, 'South Africa at Cross-Roads' in Mafeje, *In Search of an Alternative*, op. cit., 73.

(His) was not an isolated case, nor a result of false consciousness. A significant number of erstwhile revolutionaries from all the South African liberation movements joined the governments of the Bantustans in due course and prospered at the expense of the people in the Bantustans. While we might moralise about it, in principle it is no different from what happened elsewhere in Africa. Many of the heroes of the independence movements in Africa turned the same, joined the imperialist exploiters, and made pariahs of their own people.[38]

The underdevelopment and people's poverty-entrenchment effects of their standard betrayals by their so-called leaders are, of course, widely known. Very much underreported are the tell-tale signs of the betrayals themselves, which are, paradoxically, very detectable and verifiable.

At the continental level one of the earliest and strongest indications that 'decolonization' had not emancipated Africa was the adoption by the First Ordinary Session of the Assembly of Heads of State and Government, in July 1964 of the Organization of African Unity (OAU) of Resolution AHG/Res.16 (I) by which the 'state representatives' of newly 'freed' Africa pledged, *inter alia*, to respect the 'national borders' drawn for the continent by the 'departed' colonial regimes for their own purposes and convenience. The excuses offered for the resolution at the time of its adoption, and subsequently were that tampering with those borders would stir up a hornets' nest, jeopardize peace and security on the continent and antagonize the newly 'empowered' black presidents, ministers, bureaucrats, etc., whose interests and egos needed to be satisfied. Such excuses did nothing to dispel the impression in alternative African development and other Pan-Africanist circles that the interests of the African people were not particularly high on the agenda of their 'leaders', of course. With the conscious decision to leave untouched even the most dysfunctional and offensive colonial borders (such as those which divided families and indigenous communities, and complicated and 'delegitimized' traditional cross-border and other intra-African trade) the leaders did worse than confirm their inability to think outside the box: they also confirmed their collective attachment to their colonial inheritance.

---

38   Archie Mafeje, ibid. 73.

The following expressions of attachment to the colonial heritage during the review period were even more vulgar:

- The pilgrimage to London in March 2007 of the then President of Ghana to celebrate the fiftieth anniversary of his country's 'independence', topped by the live telecast to viewers in Ghana of a gala dinner with 'the Queen', as the Queen of Britain and Head of the (British) Commonwealth is referred to in 'anglicized' Ghanaian society and the popular press.
- The no less demeaning visit to Paris by thirteen 'francophone' African heads of state in 2010 to celebrate the fiftieth anniversary of their countries' 'independence' – topped by a working lunch, on 13 July 2010, with the French president and followed, for good measure, by a march past on Bastille Day of military contingents from the thirteen states, in front of their respective Commanders-in-Chief and in salute to the French president.[39]
- The visit to Britain in June 2013 by another president of Ghana to give the British prime minister 'a chance to showcase Ghana as the beacon of democracy in Africa and one of the fastest-growing economies in the world'.[40]

39	Conspicuously absent from these manifestations were President Laurent Gbagbo of Côte d'Ivoire and his army. Coincidentally or otherwise, Gbagbo was subsequently overthrown by armed opponents supported by United Nations and French forces, kidnapped by French forces from a hideout in his 'Presidential Palace' where he had sought refuge from French bombardments and transferred to the International Criminal Court (ICC) in The Hague where he was made to face charges of rape, 'other inhumane acts or attempted murder' and persecution.

40	The state-owned *Daily Graphic* of Ghana dutifully reported David Cameron's patronizing praises for Ghana's 'democratic credentials and economic growth' and 'role in regional security issues'. It further quoted Mr Cameron as '[looking] forward to enhancing [Britain's] cooperation and collaboration with Ghana in the areas of bilateral trade and investment'. Unfortunately for Mr Cameron's reputation in Ghana, his view of Ghana's 'democratic credentials' was not generally shared there and he was dismissed, on the contrary, as a crude and arrogant cynic promoting a puppet or, at best, a conscientious and cheeky dupe touting the virtues of something he does not even bother to know or understand. For a standard Ghanaian assessment of Cameron's

To such unseemly shows can be added the no less impressive spectacle of Frenchified African presidents rushing to Paris to mourn the death in 1970 of General De Gaulle (the father of their countries' 'independence' and author of the sick 'transformation of colonization into cooperation' joke), with some openly weeping and screaming '*notre papa est mort*' (our father is dead!),[41] and the gratitude expressed by some in 'Anglophone' Africa for the Atlantic Charter (for which the British claim co-ownership) and former British Prime Minister Harold Macmillan and his 'wind of change'

'democratic Ghana' see, Baffour Ankomah, 'The Republic of Corruption: Shady deals threaten Ghana's future', in *Africawatch* (the New York-based, Ghanaian-published magazine), Ghana Edition, February 2014. The author backs his damning assessment with quotations from, among others, a prominent academic and traditional chief, the moderator of the Presbyterian Church of Ghana and the Ghana Catholic Bishops Conference. See also the 10 March 2014 edition, No. 19404, of the *Daily Graphic*, which reports a former minister and presidential adviser and sitting member of Ghana's Parliament as '(confirming) that some Members of Parliament (MPs) take bribes to articulate the views of some individuals and organisations on the floor of Parliament' and further revealing that governments of both 'political parties' do also bribe parliamentarians to obtain their support for controversial laws and measures. The paper recalled in this connection that a member of parliament had 'alleged (in 2008) that members of the then Majority side (NPP) had been paid $5000 each by the government to push the Vodafone deal' involving a British multinational telecom- munications company headquartered in London. The leading Ghanaian daily, finally, filled half of its front page on Wednesday, 8 October 2014, with the headline, 'CJ (for Chief Justice) calls for action on corruption: Says situation is at tipping point' (*Daily Graphic*, 19584) Effusions like Cameron's have the merit, however, of putting the subject people concerned on notice that the regime overseeing them has power- ful imperial friends and protectors. The long-term political effects of such notices are, of course, anyone's guess.

41   Note, however, that 'Frenchification', or 'Westernization' with French characteristics, preceded De Gaulle and that the associated France-Afrique concept was an invention of Cote d'Ivoire's and one-time French National Assembly member, Félix Houphouet-Boigny, not the late French General and President. See <http://fr.wikipedia.org/ wiki/Fran%C3%A7afrique#Origine_de_l.27expression> (accessed 25 September 2014), quoting Thomas Deltombe, Manuel Domergue et Jacob Tatsitsa, *Kamerun !, une guerre cachée aux origines de la Françafrique, 1948–1971* (Paris : Éditions La Découverte, 2011), 133 (note 14).

speech[42] for its endorsement of Africa's so-called independence. Gratitude for the colonization and 'decolonization' of their territories by Britain cannot be excluded, after all, from the possible reasons for the presidential celebration of Ghana's golden jubilee in London and the Ghanaian, Nigerian, Kenyan, Sierra Leonean, Tanzanian, Ugandan, Swazi, etc., membership of the so-called Commonwealth.

But there certainly was and remains much more to the bonds between black-empowered Africans and their former colonial overlords, turned 'partners' than astute brainwashing – although, thanks to incessant and ever-broadening British Broadcasting Corporation (BBC) and Radio France Internationale (RFI) propaganda, that remains a potent factor.[43] The Colonial Pact, for one, has been cited as a particularly strong and tangible bond between the *France-Afrique* group of states and their 'mother country'.[44]

---

42 Delivered to the parliament of apartheid South Africa in Cape Town on 3 February 1960.

43 As of 5 December 2015, the BBC had twenty-four-hour relay and partner stations in Angola, Benin, Botswana, Burundi, Burkina Faso, Cape Verde, Cameroon, Central African Republic, Chad, Djibouti, the Democratic Republic of the Congo, Equatorial Guinea, Gabon, Gambia, Ghana, Guinea, Guinea-Bissau, Ivory Coast, Kenya, Lesotho, Madagascar, Malawi, Mali, Mauritania, Mauritius, Mozambique, Namibia, Niger, Nigeria, Rwanda, Seychelles, Senegal, Sierra Leone, Somalia, (Puntland), (Somaliland), South Africa, (Zanzibar), Tanzania, Uganda, Togo and Zambia, counting Africa South of the Sahara only. In addition countries like Burkina Faso, DR Congo, Ghana, Senegal and Tanzania had ten or many more such stations (see <http://www.bbc.co.uk/worldservice/specials/1318_africa_radio_aw/bbc_relay_partners.pdf> (accessed 5 December 2015)). Radio France Internationale was similarly represented on the same date in fifty-nine African countries or territories (<https://en.wikipedia.org/wiki/List_of_radio_stations_in_Africa> (accessed 5 December 2015)). The obvious flipside of this reality is the licence granted by the ruling elites of Africa to the state-owned voices of the 'former' colonial masters to continue to do as they wish to African minds rendered captive and malleable by years of indoctrination and non-stop propaganda designed to make Africa and the world safe for the West in general, the British and French empires in particular, 'market forces' under their control and whatever new 'human rights' the West cares to propagate as its 'civilization' evolves or decays.

44 Key provisions of the Colonial Pact, as highlighted by *New African* (503, February 2011), 13, include: a common currency (the CFA) for countries of the 'former' franc

But there were, and are, more subtle factors behind the apparent paradox of colonial slaves who refuse to be free. Voltaire's very pertinent observation that 'it is difficult to free fools from the chains they revere'[45] suggests itself as a possible solution to the paradox – especially if considered alongside the intoxicating effects of 'intangibles' like the love of Moliere, Descartes, Voltaire, champagnes and other great wines, cognacs and French cuisine – and the 'prestigious' 'Francophone' tag where the alternatives are less prestigious 'tribal' African labels. The now defunct system of 'Commonwealth' trade and other 'preferences' (which was quickly followed by 'cooperation', 'partnership' and 'association' agreements and arrangements when Britain joined the EEC), love of Shakespeare and other English literary greats, the visible and invisible hands of the old Lancaster House agreements which acted as 'independence' conditionalities, the Common Law heritage, formal and informal status of the English language as a passport to 'civilization', the spells cast by the BBC and the British Premier (football) League and many other signs of acceptance that to be 'civilized' is to be 'anglicized' undoubtedly perform similar miracles for the 'Commonwealth-African'-British connection.[46]

It bears repeating in this connection that while even the 'radical' Kwame Nkrumah of the Gold Coast justified his effective partnership

zone with the requirement that the fourteen member states deposit 65 per cent (plus another 20 per cent for financial liabilities) of their foreign reserves in an 'Operations Account' at the French Treasury in Paris; France's first right to exploit any natural resources found in any Colonial Pact country; concessions to French companies in the award of government contracts; and defence co-operation agreements giving France the right to intervene militarily and station troops permanently in the Colonial Pact countries.

45   See <http://www.brainyquote.com/quotes/quotes/v/voltaire136298.html#mkx pKUz4ieB35vhZ.99> (accessed 25 April 2015), for easy reference.

46   The 'oddities' of Cameroonian and Mozambican membership of the (British) Commonwealth, Cape Verdean membership of the Organisation internationale de la Francophonie (OIF) and Ghana's Associate Membership of OIF do not, in themselves, invalidate the observation. Begging with both hands may not be an unjust characterization of the Cameroonian and Mozambican behaviour, much like Ghana's membership of the *Organisation internationale de la Francophonie* (OIF or the International Organisation of *La Francophonie*).

with the British during his Leader of Government Business and early Prime Minister years (1951–1957 years, approximately) as 'tactical action', or dictated by 'pragmatism', that 'partnership', broadened to include the United States and the West in general, continued to the point of keeping Ghana as a colonial-style dependent economy till the very end of his rule in 1966 as president of 'socialist' or 'socializing' Ghana – and for the above reasons and others which have been duly and cruelly exposed by Claude Ake (1996) and others.[47] As Ake also showed, Julius Nyerere's socialistic self-reliant nation-building project for Tanzania and Zambian President Kenneth Kaunda's 'humanist' approach to development were just as compromised by failure to make the decolonization of their respective economies a priority development objective.

Besides the above noteworthy examples of 'radicals' with what Ake (1996) politely called 'a confusion of agendas' and 'improbable strategies'[48] it is also worth remembering that the residues of African nationalism, real and fake, 'Cold War' opportunities and constraints and the gullibility and other weaknesses of large sections of the people facilitated the emergence of an impressive variety of phoney revolutions and revolutionaries on the continent in the immediate independence years. Names and regimes which come to mind in this connection include Alphonse Massamba-Débat (1963–1968), Marien Ngouabi (1968–1977) and Denis Sassou Nguesso, Mark 1 (1979–1992), all of Congo-Brazzaville; Benin's Mathieu Kérékou (1972 to 1991); Madagascar's Didier Ratsiraka (1975–1993); and the People's Democratic Republic of Algeria (from independence in 1962 until it gave up all democratic and revolutionary pretentions and its government reportedly turned to foreign intelligence agencies to secure itself against popular discontent and a democratic vote for 'Islamists'); Ethiopia (from the Derg era until then Prime Minister Meles Zenawi dropped all revolutionary pretentions as well and eventually earned for himself membership of Tony

---

47 See Ake, *Democracy and Development in Africa*. For more of the underlying dynamics see 'The Pitfalls of National Consciousness' in Fanon (1967), Cabral, 'The weapon of theory' in Cabral (1974), Mafeje, 'South Africa at a Crossroads: Liberation or Betrayal', op. cit and Ama Biney, *The Political and Social Thought of Kwame Nkrumah*.

48 Chapters 2 and 3 of Ake (ibid.).

Blair's Commission for Africa); and Somalia, under Siad Barre, the 'scientific socialist' and 'nation builder' whom vocal Somalis accused during his reign of running a clans-based regime which was not above playing clan-against-clan politics for survival.

Further to Samir Amin's observation that colonization was such a 'historic catastrophe' that almost any changes, even within the constraints of phoney independence, were bound to be 'changes for the better'[49] it also seems obvious that the pseudo-radicalism, fake revolutions and the more common failed statehood cases (in which many normal state functions are retained by the 'former' colonial masters or outsourced to them) which have littered Africa since independence were nothing but the tonic fruits of the decolonization fraud which Wallerstein has correctly described as:

> ... political compromise(s) between the colonial powers and the middle-class leadership of the nationalist movements (by which) the former turned over the political machinery to the latter, in return for which the latter implicitly promised to hold in check the radical tendencies of lower-class protest and to leave basically intact the overall economic links with the former (even if the interests of certain Europeans, particularly settlers, were damaged by such a transfer of power).[50]

At the continental level, the decolonization fraud began with the pretence by the OAU/AU that it was ever more than the association of Ayi Kwei Armah's 'idiotic neo-colonial states' it was born to be and has remained,

---

49   Amin's example in this regard is the fact that 'at the time of the end of its colonization, there were nine Congolese educated to university level' whereas 'after 30 years of Mobutu's regime – one of the vilest ever – this figure [had grown] to hundreds of thousands'. Source: Translation from the original French by Alex Free of interview conducted by Christophe Champin of Samir Amin for Radio France Internationale and culled from *Pambazuka News* by *African Agenda* (Vol. 14, No. 1, 2011).

50   Immanuel Wallerstein, 'The Range of Choice: Constraints on the Choice of Policies of Governments of Contemporary African Independent States', in Michael F. Lofchie ed., *The State of the Nations: Constraints on Development in Independent Africa* (Berkeley, CA: University of California Press, 1971), 20. For a similar perspective see, also, T. Hodgkin, 'A Note on the Language of African Nationalism' in K. Kirkwood, ed., *African Papers*, Number One, 1st edition (London: Chatto and Windus, 1961), 22–40; and Prashad, *The Darker Nations*, op. cit.

and was ever in a position to defend the sovereignty and independence of African states.[51] With hindsight, the commitment proclaimed in the *Lagos Plan of Action for the Implementation of the Monrovia Strategy for the Economic Development of Africa* (LPA, 1980) to 'collective self reliance' as a cornerstone of African development also appears all too clearly as phoney from the very beginning, given the alacrity with which it abandoned it under World Bank and other development-partner pressure and replaced it with the New Partnership for Africa's Development (NEPAD) which was nothing if not a blueprint for dependency written as if its authors 'read nothing except World Bank and IMF documents on Africa', as one analyst put it.[52]

The OAU/AU's notorious dependence on donor support, highlighted by the following financial situation report on an organization which claims to defend the sovereignty and independence of African states, is one of the many reasons why it has traditionally acted, in effect, as a subsidiary organ of Obama's 'force multipliers' on African development and much else:[53]

> The African Union has vowed to finance its working budget using mainly domestic resources as it marks its 50th anniversary this week, the deputy chairperson of the continental body's commission has said.
>
> Erastus Mwencha (the Deputy Chairperson) made the comments on Thursday at the AU's headquarters in Addis Ababa, the Ethiopian capital, while addressing a news conference about the union's budget and financial independence.
>
> The financial independence of the AU, launched in 1963 as the Organisation for African Unity (OAU) before being renamed in 2002, has been a source of controversy for a long time, as much of its working budget is financed by foreign donors.

---

51 Articles II.1 (a) of the *OAU Charter* and 3 (b) of the *Constitutive Act of the African Union*.

52 Jimi O. Adesina, 'NEPAD, the post-Washington Consensus', *African Agenda*, Vol. 5, Nos 2, & 3, 2002, 16–17. See also, in the same issue of the journal, Yao Graham 'From Liberation into NEPAD' (cover article), 4–7. Adebayo Olukoshi, 'Africa from Lagos Plan of Action to NEPAD', 8–9 and Ian Taylor, 'NEPAD: Towards the African Century or Another False Start?', 99. 1012.

53 Recall that in President Obama's *Commencement Address at West Point on May 28, 2014* (op. cit.) he specifically counted the World Bank and the IMF as America's 'force multipliers'.

The construction of the new AU headquarters was funded by China and African countries pay for only about 40 percent of the AU's budget. China, the European Union and the US pay for the rest.

The AU has been finding itself in difficult situations since the finances from donors almost always come with strings attached[54]

To self respecting Africans the following write-up on the African Union's Peace and Security Building must be cause for at least equally grave concern:

African Union Commission: Peace and Security Building

Project description
Title: African Union Commission – Peace and Security Building
Commissioned by: German Federal Foreign Office
Financier: German Federal Foreign Office
Country: Ethiopia
Lead executing agency: German Federal Foreign Office
Overall term: 2008 to 2013

Context
Peace and security are priority issues for the whole international community, including the countries of Africa. The African Union (AU) Commission implements a strategy to maintain peace and security throughout the African continent. To support its efforts, the German Federal Foreign Office has donated a specialised, state-of-the-art building with a garden for the AU's Peace and Security Department. Besides hosting the Peace and Security Council, the building will also be home to the Continental Early Warning System, which will enable the Council to monitor critical information on ongoing crises, and help it manage its civil and military operations.

Thanks to its long and successful record in the management of large construction projects in Ethiopia, GIZ International Services has been appointed to manage the design and construction work for the new building in Addis Ababa.

54 *Al Jazeera*, 'African Union seeks financial independence', <http://www.aljazeera. com/news/africa/2013/05/201352412928567270.html> (accessed 27 April 2015).

Objective
The Peace and Security Building provides a plenary hall for the meetings of the Peace and Security Council, a situations room and a military operations room. It also houses the offices of the Peace and Security Department, as well as a library, meeting facilities and space for auxiliary functions.[55]

It may suffice to point out that no self-respecting state or body hands over the financing, construction and equipment of its sensitive premises to, in Thomas Sankara's words, its people's 'enemies of yesterday and today'. It is understandable, however, from an association of 'idiotic neo-colonial states' steeped, like the 'states' themselves, in the politics of 'black empowerment' at the expense of the African people.

'Black empowerment', 'liberation', 'independence', betrayals and all that

'Black empowerment' – or 'power-sharing' by way of the extension of 'white' economic privileges to well-connected 'blacks' who agree to be co-opted by settlers and colonialists as an alternative to independence and government of the people, by the people and for the people – is, as Wallerstein, Mafeje and others have shown, as old as African independence itself.[56] That much can also be deduced from the fact that long before its replication in 'post-apartheid' South Africa raised its profile as a political co-optation and extension programme of embourgeoisement opportunities for selected 'former

---

55 'African Union Commission – Peace and Security Building', <https://www.giz.de/en/worldwide/18903.html>. Original source: Manfred Off (<manfred.off@giz.de>) Also noteworthy is the fact that this German (NATO member state) donation is additional to one built and equipped in the 1990s for the OAU for similar purposes by the US Government.

56 See, for instance, Immanuel Wallerstein, 'The Range of Choice: Constraints on the Choice of Policies of Governments of Contemporary African Independent States' (op. cit.) and Archie Mafeje, 'South Africa at a Crossroads: Liberation of Betrayal?' (op. cit.).

revolutionaries' of the Mafeje-Treason-Trialist variety the phenomenon was recognized in intellectual activist circles as Kenyanization.[57]

Fanon summed up the main deleterious effect of the first 'post-colonial' rounds of black empowerment well when he observed that the resulting 'national bourgeoisie' '(turned) its back more and more on the interior and on the real facts ... and (tended) to look towards the former mother country and the foreign capitalists who count on its obliging compliance.'[58] Most of the current crop of African leaders did not emerge directly from the original black empowerment schemes, of course. But by claiming for themselves and freely enjoying the privileges of black empowerment, adding to the 'sins of the fathers' by aiding and abetting the neoliberal globalization of their territories and peoples and, in particular, aiding and abetting the dispossession of their peoples for the benefit of their external patrons and 'development' and business 'partners', in return for the above-mentioned privileges, they make themselves no better, morally, than the generations before them whom Cabral (1974, op. cit.) denounced as quislings.

The following description of many of them by the astute Ake makes the modern quislings even worse in some respects than their discredited forebears:

> It is often assumed in [their] circles that foreign-made goods are better; and that the major business of Africa, indeed, the only business, is catching up with the industrialized nations. And catching up depends heavily on maintaining relations with these nations and increasing the resource flows from them to Africa. The lack of self-confidence has been obvious in the behaviour of senior officials and even heads of state to relatively minor officials of foreign governments and development agencies; the longing of African leaders for approval in the West; Emperor Jean Bedel Bokassa's longing for long-forgotten and better forgotten French monarchs; and the

57   For a penetrating analysis of its South African and Southern African manifestations see R. W. Johnson, 'False Start in South Africa', *New Left Review* 58, July-August 2009. For some of the facts behind the classification of Kenya's independence as an early case of 'black empowerment' and a virtual term of abuse see Ngugi wa Thiong'o, *Detained: A Writer's Prison Diary*.
58   Fanon, *The Wretched of the Earth*, op. cit, 133.

decision of some African governments to disallow the speaking of African languages and the wearing of African traditional clothes in Parliament.[59]

Nor, for that matter, is the mindset denounced by Ake without its own deleterious consequences. Among these are the promotion of Euro-centrism in Africa by Africans in the name of 'development', 'modernity' or 'modernization' (African implication, in other words, in what Rao has called the 'expansion of cultural imperialism through globalisation'),[60] the insane and interminable 'African' searches for Western solutions to African problems and the related disease of learned helplessness observed in too many African leaders and people and encouraged by their 'development partners' and instructors.[61]

Other costs to the African people of the above-mentioned mindsets and practices include, at the states level:

- The open access of Western governments, capital, armed forces, investors, 'development' NGOs, 'advocacy groups', media, churches and other 'missionaries' to virtually all of Africa and any of the continent's resources they need or demand access to – and on their terms;
- Guarantees that the above-named interests and actors will continue to drive, control and reap the primary benefits of 'African development' as they or their ancestors did in paleo-colonial times;[62]

---

59 Ake, *Democracy and Development in Africa*, 16.

60 Rao, 2008.

61 For further critiques of some of the values, norms and practices which have invaded Africa via globalization see Ferguson, *Predator Nation: Corporate Criminals, Political Corruption, and the Hijacking of America* and Sandel, *What Money Can't Buy: The Moral Limits of Markets*. As a sign of the times *Joy Online*, the online edition of a Ghanaian radio station reported on 8 December 2015 that the Danquah Institute (DI), 'think tank' of one of the two major 'political parties' in Ghana, was to collaborate with the Heritage Foundation – the 'conservative', not to mention the US empire-promoting, Think Tank – to 'promote the politics of ideas' in that country. See 'Heritage Foundation and DI to promote the politics of ideas and values in Ghana', <http://www.myjoyonline.com/politics/2015/december-8th/heritage-foundation-and-di-to-promote-politics-of-ideas-and-values-in-ghana.php>.

62 It is doubtful whether even Ake anticipated the situation where the presidency of a once-proud Ghana would generate the following newspaper story: 'Provide

- Addition of Credit Rating Agencies to the rank of gods to be satisfied by African governments in the formulation of economic policies – even at the expense of the people;
- The effective promotion of the West as Africa's Lord Protectors – under the same sorts of defence-and-security cooperation 'bonds', 'treaties' and other arrangements which led directly to the colonization of some African states initially as protectorates;
- The readiness of African governments to use force, pre-emptive attacks and deception on their own people to ensure that they do not stand in the way of their dispossession, where necessary, for the benefit of 'development partners', business 'partners' and patrons of local 'political' bosses;
- The gratuitous exposure of innocent Africans to terrorist attacks in the clash of barbarisms between the West and Jihadists;
- The effective guarantee – in the absence of the likes of the deposed Kwame Nkrumah of Ghana and the assassinated Patrice Lumumba of the former Congo-Kinshasa and Thomas Sankara of Burkina Faso – that continental Africa will not respond or respond robustly to, for instance, 'the new Jim Crow' phenomenon and racist-police violence against people of African descent in the United States, France's intransigence on the 'reparations' refund to Haiti (see Chapter 2) and affronts to African dignity on the continent itself; and
- The many attempts to import into Africa by hook or by crook norms, values and fashions embraced in the West but offensive to most Africans, under cover of 'human rights' and openness to the age-old insult that

---

African youth with better economic opportunities – Veep' and the following opening paragraph: 'The Vice-President ... has called on the International Monetary Fund (IMF) and the developed world to provide better economic opportunities for African youth to help stem their migration to the western world', *Daily Graphic*, 29 April 2015, 65. The further scandal is that neither the Ghanaian 'political class' nor the rest of its 'chattering classes' as a whole objected to the declaration of African surrender of Africa's economic, governance and development responsibilities to the named external forces.

Africans are incapable of making valid independent moral and value judgements for themselves.

Black empowerment and people's disempowerment in Africa and the Diaspora: The 'post-war' generation of *the rougher methods of an earlier era*

The 'dirty works' catalogued in Ellen Ray and others[63] are nothing if not a sample of the violence and other dirty tricks which imperialism has always employed for its takeover, command and control of other people's human and material resources. Robert Cooper was thus being disingenuous when he appeared to urge the Western Establishment to which he belonged to consider 'reverting' to 'the laws of the jungle' to promote his 'new liberal imperialism'.[64] For, in practice and contrary to his distortion of the history of his valued 'force, pre-emptive attack and deception' in Africa, the assassinations of Mozambique's Edouardo Mondlane and Amilcar Cabral of Guinea-Bissau, accomplished by imperialism before their countries' independence; of Félix-Roland Moumié of Cameroon, accomplished in the year of that country's independence; and the murders of Congo-Kinshasa's Patrice Lumumba and Libya's Muammar Gaddafi, nationalist leaders who would not accept in-dependence in lieu of the real thing, for instance, are evidence enough that imperialism has never spared Africa the 'laws of the jungle'. Correcting the misrepresentation of history in this department is a political, as well as academic, necessity, however.

For, embedded in the kind of historiography which draws the artificial distinction between a so-called new liberal imperialism and imperialism's ancient manifestations, which Cooper and his kind do, are two further and interconnected politically motivated myths:

---

63 Ray and Others (1980).
64 Robert Cooper, 'The new liberal imperialism'.

- the myth that the 'new liberal imperialism' is, unlike its discredited earlier manifestations (including Leopold II's 'civilizing mission') driven by a selfless desire to 'develop', 'democratize' and otherwise 'modernize' a stubbornly backward continent; and
- the use by the United Nations and troop-contributing African states, French armed forces and Blaise Compaoré-backed 'opposition forces' to enforce democracy in Cote d'Ivoire and NATO's 'armed humanitarianism' and 'regime change' in Libya, both in 2011, are morally justified applications of the laws of the jungle in jungle situations, according to the gangster logic espoused by Cooper.

It is easy enough to expose both myths as bogus and fraudulent: for all the verbal gymnastics deployed to whitewash imperialism since the nineteenth century it takes but little effort to recognize the erstwhile wars on 'communism' and Soviet and Chinese 'imperialism', 'the doctrine of humanitarian intervention', 'democracy' and 'democratization', 'African development', 'international justice', 'the war on terror', etc., (all of which preceded the 'civilizing mission' of Leopold II and Company) as no more than the same dubious mission differently cloaked for different times and needs, as Cooper suggests.[65] But as Depelchin and others have shown the distortion of African history by means of 'silences' and outright lies is not an idle sport.[66] In this instance the following ulterior motives in the historiography exemplified by Cooper are easily detectable and particularly relevant:

- to give the impression that 'decolonization' was real and any measures taken to drag Africa back into full-blown or paleo-colonialism (colonialism without the 'power sharing that went with the political compromises described by Wallerstein,) are justified by the mess which the African 'partners' have made of the 'independence' granted them;
- the laws of the jungle ceased to govern relationships between Africa and the West after independence; and

---

65   Cooper, ibid.
66   See, for instance, Jacques Depelchin, *Silences in African History* and Zinn, *A People's History of the United States.*

- the restoration of paleo-colonialism under the new-liberal-imperialism formula is, or would be, good for Africa and 'the world'.

The devil is, of course, partly in the blatant falsehood of all three of the above underlying claims: neo-colonialism is evidence enough that colonialism did not die with 'decolonization'; the evidence presented in Ray and Others (1980) and more, including French solo coup d'état and counter coup d'état making in Françafrique, is enough proof of the falsehood of the second claim; and Amin's indictment of colonialism in Africa quoted above on one hand and the thousand and one reasons why Britain's Tony Blair was right (even for the wrong reasons) to call Africa 'a scar on the conscience of the world' (see Chapter 5 below) should shame those who continue to peddle the nonsense that the recolonization of Africa in any sense is an answer to Africa's problems. Cooper and Blair are, unfortunately, not the only peddlers of this view of Africa, Africans and African development.

Without the nationalism which inclined Gamal Abdel Nasser (Egypt), Kwame Nkrumah (Ghana), Ahmed Ben Bella (Algeria), Julius Nyerere (Tanzania) and a few others of their generation to rock the dependent-development boat, however gently – and the temerity to tap into the once-available Third World support for qualified nationalistic causes, or to exploit the Cold War while it lasted to negotiate improved dependent-development terms for their people, for that matter – the OAU/AU's 'New Partnership for Africa's Development' was, as others have pointed out, a barely disguised re-submission to 'new liberal imperialism', aka neoliberal globalization, after its brief flirtations with the floating ideas of the 1970s: 'self reliance', 'collective self reliance' and a 'new international economic order'. The rejection then and now of even minimal reforms to the colonial division of labour by Africa's 'black empowered' stands out as part of the price the African people have had to pay for the political compromises described by Wallerstein as conditions for black empowerment. But in thus choosing to maintain the surrender of Africa and its development destiny to their 'development partners' the 'black empowered' did worse than entrench the people's disempowerment: they effectively repudiated the African and Pan-African nationalisms which had brought imperialism to the negotiating tables from which they emerged with the political compromises they enjoyed as presidents, ministers, other administrators, technocrats and private-sector entrepreneurs.

Even more indisputably conscientious betrayals of the people and African nationalism at any level which can be cited include the gleeful acceptance by Africa's 'black empowered' of the 'cosmopolitan middle-class' brand attached to them by their Western patrons and praise singers; the psychopathologies described by Fanon and Ake; the commitment of African flags and boots on the ground to the West's 'war on terror'; the first African-American President of the United States' professed belief in 'American exceptionalism with every fibre of (his) being'[67] (a doctrine which places the African people at the risk of the use of military force, 'unilaterally if necessary, when (its) core interests demand it: when (its) people are threatened; when (its) livelihoods are at stake; when the security of (its) allies is in danger');[68] and the second African-American Supreme Court Justice in American history's declared opposition to 'affirmative action',[69] an obvious benefit of the Pan-Africanism-energized US civil rights movement without which his own elevation would have been inconceivable.

Several examples from Pan-Africanism's forgotten history can be cited to illustrate the African people's loss and imperialism's gain from the disdain

---

67   'Remarks by the President at the United States Military Academy Commencement', 28 May 2014. Note the contrast between Obama's affirmation of faith in 'American exceptionalism' and, by implication, the associated doctrine of America's 'manifest destiny', and the forensic examinations of both by Bacevich (*The Limits of Power: The End of American Exceptionalism*), Chomsky (e.g.: *Hegemony or Survival: America's Quest for Global Dominance*) and others. Note, finally, the close resemblance between the doctrine of American exceptionalism and the nineteenth-century British philosopher John Stuart Mill's defence of British imperialism and what Chomsky called 'disgraceful apologetics for terrible crimes'. (*Hegemony*, 45).

68   'Remarks by the President at the United States Military Academy Commencement', ibid. Note, moreover, the many documented instances of the use of US military forces in Africa by or under successive American Presidents, including Barack Obama.

69   <http://en.wikipedia.org/wiki/Clarence_Thomas#Equal_protection_and_affirmative_action> (accessed 30 April 2015) provides a brief introduction to Clarence Thomas' views on equal protection and affirmative action.

and outright betrayals of the movement by those whose rise to empowerment it facilitated.

The seizure of popular singer and civil rights and Pan-Africanist activist Paul Robeson's American passport, the restriction by order of President Truman of his movements to the continental United States and the reason given these executive acts – namely that 'when he travelled abroad he spoke out against colonialism and advocated for African independence (which) was against the best interests of the United States'[70] is one combined measure of the enemy's hostility to Pan-Africanism as an African people's liberation force and extent of the intellectual or moral poverty of African beneficiaries of its once appreciable power who deny or objectively betray it.

The following warning shot which the Jamaican-born Marcus Garvey fired in 1922 at British Prime Minister Lloyd George in response to the massacre by British colonial agents of Kenyan workers in their homeland provides yet another example of political and moral support the African people in Africa once enjoyed from the Diaspora – to the dismay of the imperialist camp:

David Lloyd George, British Premier, Downing St, London

> Four hundred million Negroes through the Universal Negro Improvement Association hereby register their protest against the brutal manner in which your government has treated the natives of Kenya, East Africa. You have shot down a defenceless people in their own native land exercising their rights as men. Such a policy will aggravate the many historic injustices heaped upon a race that will one day be placed in a position to truly defend itself not with mere sticks, clubs and stones but with modern implements of science.[71]

A grateful South Africa's acknowledgement at Nelson Mandela's funeral, in December 2013, of the militant solidarity extended by Cuba ('a country

---

70 Vincent Dowd, 'Singer Paul Robson's granddaughter recalls fight against racism', *BBC News*, 7 May 2014, <www.bbc.com/news/entertainment-arts-27291682> (accessed 14 August 2014).

71 Quoted by Ngugi in *Detained*, 40.

born in the struggle for independence and for the abolition of slavery, and whose children have African blood running in their veins') to the Angolan and South African peoples in their liberation struggles, is yet another reminder of Pan-Africanism's glorious – and freedom-fighting – past.[72] Other examples of the good that Pan-Africanism did for the African people before the 'black empowerment' of some continental and Diaspora Africans disabled it with their attitudes, neglect and even hostility include:

- Jamaica's leadership of the international campaign against apartheid South Africa and credit as the first country to declare a trade embargo against the apartheid republic as early as 1957 (i.e. while the island was still a colony of Britain and thus without full responsibility for its external relations);[73]
- Public and private pressures on the John F. Kennedy and Lyndon B. Johnson regimes by Nkrumah, Nasser, Sekou Toure (Guinea) and Modibo Keita (Mali) among others, to free the African people under their direct control or face the wrath of Africa and her Third World and other internationalist friends;
- The inspiration which the likes of Martin Luther King Jnr, Malcolm X and Kwame Ture (Stokely Carmichael) derived from the examples of Nkrumah's Ghana, leadership and achievements; and

---

72   Cuban President Raúl Castro Ruz's description of his country in his response to the commendation of its contribution to the liberation of South Africa with the rout by its forces in Angola of the then apartheid regime's special-operations forces, thereby '(destroying) the myth of the invincibility of the white oppressor'. For the *Speech of Army General Raúl Castro Ruz, President of the Councils of State and Ministers at the funeral of South African leader Nelson Mandela in Johannesburg on December 10, 2013*. See <http://scottishcuba.org/news-reports/5-nelson-mandela-funeral-speech-by-army-general-raul-castro-ruz> on Mandela's acknowledgement of Cuba's contribution to the anti-apartheid struggle see <http://www.democracynow.org/blog/2013/12/11/nelson_mandela_on_how_cuba_destroyed> (accessed 14 April 2014).

73   Source: <http://www.thediplomaticsociety.co.za/index.php/archive/archive/273-jamaicasouth-africa-relations>.

- The Resolution by the First Ordinary Session of the Assembly of Heads of State and Government by which the OAU 'regretted' 'continuing manifestations of racial bigotry and racial oppression against Negro citizens of the United States of America' and '(urged) the Government authorities in the United States of America to intensify their efforts to ensure the total elimination of all forms of discrimination based on race, colour or ethnic origin'.[74]

But as a product and association of 'idiotic neo-colonial states' the OAU/AU is, not unexpectedly, no stranger to the effective decommissioning of Pan-Africanism as an African people's liberation weapon.

The OAU/AU: Every inch a 'black empowerment' baby

Where global Pan-Africanism has failed to date to take recognizable institutional form of any kind the continental African unity movement gave birth in 1963 to the Organization of African Unity as a mockery of the African nationalist dream of a liberating continental body, and yet another 'force multiplier' in the Obama sense instead. The signs of this are many. And NEPAD is not the worst of them. The signing of an African Union/World Bank *Memorandum of Understanding on Working Together to Support Africa's Development*, in 2008,[75] following a June 2007 call on African states by then incoming World Bank Group President, Robert B. Zoellick to 'integrate' as a means of '(getting) the attention and adequate support of the global economy' and overcoming the difficulty 'for the multilateral organizations and the large-scale financiers of development projects in the developing world to deal with small and fragmented countries such as are in

---

74   Resolution AHG/Res. 15.1 of *Resolutions Adopted by the First Ordinary Session of the Assembly of Heads of State and Government Held in Cairo, UAR, From 17 to 21 July, 1964.*

75   Source: <http://web.worldbank.org/WBSITE/EXTERNAL/COUNTRIES/AFRICAEXT/0,,print:Y~isCURL:Y~contentMDK:21917455~menuPK:258658~pagePK:2865106~piPK:2865128~theSitePK:258644,00.html>.

Africa'[76] is another such sign. In that single act the African Union formally and shamelessly embraced a body on Obama's list of the US' 'force multipliers' which is also known to be closely connected with the US' defence Establishment and its globalization agenda.[77] Not to be ignored either is the fact that the signing of the AU's Memorandum of Understanding with the World Bank and associated developments occurred at the height of 'market triumphalism' and the neoliberal globalization frenzy, confirming the AU's own subscription to the underlying neoliberal ideology.[78] Of the associated developments none is, perhaps, more indicative of the African Union's open renunciation of the most basic of Pan-Africanist scruples – and contempt for the African people – than the establishment of a NATO Liaison Office at its Addis Ababa Headquarters, a gesture which can only be construed as a sign of readiness to collude with an organization which

---

76 Report by the Ghana News Agency on incoming World Bank President Robert B. Zoellick's visit to Ghana in June 2007. For examples of 'assisted' African integration see <http://www.nato.int/cps/en/natolive/news_109824.htm>, <www.nato.int/cps/en/natolive/news_109824.htm>, <http://search.tb.ask.com/search/GGmain.jhtml?searchfor=African+Union%27s+Cooperation+with+the+World+Bank&st=tab&ptb=77C6CFA4-AB0C-4097-8F77-C6F8EEE943E5&n=780c280c&ind=2014062604&ct=SS&pg=GGmain&tpr=tabsbsug&p2=%5EXR%5Exdm006%5EYYA%5Egh&si=COHq4tLıl78CFQHlwgodY3sAWw>, <search.tb.ask.com/search/GGmain.jhtml?searchfor=African+Union%27s+Cooperation+with+the+World+Bank&st=tab&ptb=77C6CFA4-AB0C-4097-8F77-C6F8EEE943E5&n=780c280c&ind=2014062604&ct=SS&pg=GGmain&tpr=tabsbsug&p2=%5EXR%5Exdm006%5EYYA%5Egh&si=COHq4tLıl78CFQHlwgodY3sAWw> and <http://www.au.int/en/partnerships>.

77 See, for instance, Michael Hudson in 'The IMF Forgives Ukraine's Debt to Russia' (<http://thesaker.is/the-imf-forgives-ukraines-loan-to-russia/>), where he points out, *inter alia*, that 'Since 1947 when it really started operations, the World Bank has acted as a branch of the US Defense Department, from its first major chairman John J. McCloy through Robert McNamara to Robert Zoellick and neocon Paul Wolfowitz' and further recalls that 'from the outset, (the Bank) has promoted U.S. exports – especially farm exports – by steering Third World countries to produce plantation crops rather than feeding their own populations', (wrapping up its US export promotion and support for the dollar area in an ostensibly internationalist rhetoric, as if what's good for the United States is good for the world).

78 On 'market fundamentalism' see, for instance, Sandel, *What Money Can't Buy*.

has earned the disgust of African nationalists for, *inter alia*, the murder of an untold number of African heroes;[79] the operational supports it gave to its apartheid South Africa and colonial Portuguese allies in their wars against African liberation movements and the frontline states; and its contemptuous refusal to apologize for its many crimes against the African people, let alone pay due reparations for them. The following newspaper report confirms, moreover, that the reckless disregard for African history, feelings and interests thus displayed at the AU's headquarters was shared at its highest levels:

NATO forces needed in Mali says Boni Yayi

> The African Union's chairman, Thomas Boni Yayi, has called for NATO to send forces to Mali to help fight militant Islamists who have captured the north.
>
> The Malian conflict was an 'international question' and *NATO should intervene just as it had done in Afghanistan*, Boni Yayi said. [My emphasis]
> ...
> Mr. Yayi, who is Benin's president, called for NATO intervention after talks with Canadian Prime Minister Stephen Harper in Ottawa.[80]

The African Union has not been above fronting for NATO and the powers that drive it either. AMISOM (the African Union Mission in Somalia), an offspring of the AU, gives itself and the Union away on that.[81] The authorization from the United Nations (the 'force multiplier') which AMISOM is happy to brandish as its legislative authority and the public admission that

---

79 See, for instance, Ellen Ray, William Schaap, Karl van Meter and Louis Wolf, eds, *Dirty Work 2* and de Mesquita and Alastair Smith, *The Dictator's Handbook: Why Bad Behaviour is Almost Always Good Politics* (New York: BBS Public Affairs, 2011) for examples *before Libya* (2011) of NATO and NATO-backed atrocities in Africa.

80 *Daily Graphic*, 10 January 2013. An African Union Chairman – a sitting Head of State elected by the Assembly of Heads of State and Government of the Union – speaks and acts for his peers and member states during his tenure.

81 See, for instance, <http://amisom-au.org/amisom-background/> and <http://amisom-au.org/amisom-mandate/> (accessed 18 December 2015) for the background and mandate of AMISOM.

it runs on European Union and other Western funds[82] expose it further and without a shadow of doubt as a Western creation funded by the West for the Somali campaign in its war on terror. The support it also receives from America's killer drones and the frequently admitted 'support missions' there of US and other Western special operations forces merely serve to make it even more obvious that it is an auxiliary force under Western command and control. But, with the AU's blessing, NATO and the West's reach in Africa goes far beyond AMISOM and Somalia, making the claim in the *Constitutive Act of the African Union* that it is a defender of the 'sovereignty, territorial integrity and independence of its Member States' fraudulent.[83] The fraud did not begin with the AU, however: the AU lie only repeats the creation myth in preambular paragraph 6 of the *OAU Charter*, that the organization was established and designed to 'safeguard and consolidate the hard-won independence as well as the sovereignty and territorial integrity of (its member) states, and to fight against neo-colonialism in all its forms'.

The fraud and the supporting lies appear to have escaped forensic examination to date not merely because time has venerated them, however. They appear to have benefited more importantly from the fact that both the Nkrumaist and 'radical' wing of the African unity movement and its opposing 'conservative', and 'moderate' wing(s) appear to cherish the myth of the OAU/AU as defender of African independence, sovereignty and territorial integrity, for highly questionable reasons: the former because they provide the much needed fig leaf to cover the fact that in the struggle to unite Africa for change it has been outmanoeuvred by imperialism and its lackeys and the latter because the symbolism of the OAU/AU and the

---

82   According to its official website, <http://amisom-au.org/frequently-asked-ques tions/> (accessed 18 December 2015), 'AMISOM (also) benefits from a UN logisti-cal support package, bilateral donations, and voluntary contributions to a UN man-aged Trust Fund in Support of AMISOM. The European Union (EU) provides the resources needed for the payment of troop allowances and other related expenses, within the framework of the African Peace Facility (APF)'.

83   For other examples of US-Africa military co-operation deemed fit for public disclo-sure see The White House, Office of the Press Secretary, *Fact Sheet: U.S. Support for Peacekeeping in Africa*, <https://www.whitehouse.gov/the-press-office/2014/08/06/fact-sheet-us-support-peacekeeping-africa> (accessed 18 December 2015).

nationalist language it co-opts have the combined benefits of opiates and alibis of the people and many of their leaders.[84] The onus lies squarely and solely on those who take the decolonization of Africa and African development seriously, therefore, to demythologize the OAU/AU.

The open secret that the OAU was designed to frustrate the formation of a continental body pursuing the liberation and freedom agenda of the 'radical', i.e. Casablanca, group of African states articulated most clearly by Nkrumah (with the American-backed Monrovia and French-backed Brazzaville groupings of African states as project implementation agents) is perhaps as good a place as any to begin demystifying the organization.[85] What is less well known but just as important to recall is the fact that the *OAU Charter* itself, with its cynical provision about safeguarding and consolidating the hard-won independence of its member states and protecting them from neo-colonialism in all its forms, was not an African product in any meaningful sense of the word but a document drafted by a US government consultant who can be presumed to have had the US' ubiquitous 'national security interests' in resource rich parts of the world, such as Africa, very much in mind. Those still alive who were privileged to watch Nkrumah live on television as he appended his signature to the *OAU Charter* on 25 May 1963, can confirm that his body language as he did so was that of a vanquished, not a triumphant, campaigner.

Also verifiable and even more damning is the fact that the Emperor Haile Selassie regime of Ethiopia and the John F. Kennedy Administration of America worked together to ensure the adoption by the OAU's founding conference of a *Draft OAU Charter* prepared by a Señor Truco, Chile's

---

84   On page 95 of June Milne's *Kwame Nkrumah: A Biography*, 95 the astonishing but understandable claim is made, for instance, that 'the foundation of the Organisation of African Unity (OAU) in Addis Ababa on 25 May, 1963' was 'a high-water mark in Nkrumah's efforts to establish the political machinery for unification'. 'Moderates' and 'conservatives', on the other hand, seem just content to see the OAU/AU celebrated the way Mafeje's Treason Trialist celebrated the Bantustans.

85   For an overview of Nkrumah's original ideas on African unity see Kwame Nkrumah, *Africa Must Unite* and June Milne, ibid.

representative to the Organization of American States (OAS) at the time, and presented as the Ethiopian Draft, as the definitive *OAU Charter*, in preference to a draft offered by Nkrumah.[86] Nor was that the only original sin. To insure the new organization against 'radical' influences a purpose-built OAU headquarters complex in Accra offered by Nkrumah, a prime mover in the African unity movement, was rejected in favour of the 'temporary' housing of the organization in premises which were originally conceived, constructed and donated by the Americans to the Ethiopian government as a police college campus – in a capital where the ruling aristocracy was reluctant to accept its Africanity, the people had been taught to do the same and the 'black skin' was equated by many with slavery.[87]

The combination of US and allied manoeuvres, Western 'generosity' and African complicity has naturally and predictably saddled the continent and the African people as a whole with a supposed organization *for* African unity and much else which, in practice:

86   Personal communication by a senior African diplomat with direct knowledge of the behind-the-scenes manoeuvres involved and access to related intelligence from various other African sources. This 'intelligence' has been effectively confirmed in writing by Norman J. Padelford in 'The Organization of African Unity', *International Organization*, Vol. 18, No. 3, Summer 1964, 521–42, published by the University of Wisconsin Press Stable, URL: <http://www.jstor.org/stable/2705406> (accessed 29 March 2014) and also at <http://portugalresearchinternship.weebly.com/uploads/2/4/8/8/24883115/the_organization_of_african_unity.pdf> (accessed 19 December 2015). Padelford recalls, in part, that 'Two proposals for an African charter were submitted by Ethiopia and Ghana respectively, together with a Nigerian proposal that the Monrovia ('Group) Charter be accepted as the basis for unity. The Ethiopian plan drew heavily upon the seminal ideas of the Organization of American States (OAS) and was indeed drafted in large measure by Mr Truco, Chile's representative to the OAS, who was asked to be a consultant for the occasion' (526).

87   It may be recalled that, by way of 'consolation', it was decided to hold the Second Ordinary Session of the Assembly in Accra. But that session was duly boycotted by the France-Afrique group of countries which proceeded to stage a 'summit-level' wedding in Paris to coincide with the Accra Summit which was held in October 1965. The OAU's African Union successor, established on 26 May 2001 and launched on 9 July 2002, had to wait until 2012 to acquire permanent headquarters buildings – built at the cost of $200 million by the Chinese as a gift to the beggar Organization.

- Serves as, perhaps, the West's leading Trojan horse on the continent;
- Effectively conflates what is good for the West with what is good for Africa;
- Treats the world order which serves the interests of white race authority as given, immutable and the only possible framework for the peace, security and development of Africa, if not the world, in spite of the mountains of undeniable evidence to the contrary;
- 'Reconciles' with the African people's enemies of yesterday on their terms, in the absence of regrets for past wrongs and in the teeth of their undiminished cynicism, imperial appetites and arrogance;
- Effectively ignores the injustices done to the African peoples of Diego Garcia and other islands of the Chagos archipelago who were expelled from their homelands, and remain exiled in Mauritius more than a thousand miles away, because the British decided and maintain, with typical colonial thinking, that the US' 'need' for a military base in the islands trumps the natives' homeland rights;[88]
- Observes disgraceful silences over the new-Jim-Crow 'in the age of colour blindness' in 'God's own country' (Michelle Alexander, op. cit.), the fact that 'fully 60 percent of all young black men (African-Americans) who drop out of high school will go to jail'[89] and similar bitter fruits of institutional racism in its leading 'partner country';
- Fails or refuses to fight for climate justice with the political, economic and diplomatic weapons which the severity of the deleterious consequences of 'climate change' on the African peoples of Africa and the Caribbean demands, preferring, instead, to rely on the 'climate negotiations' and other mechanisms provided by the United Nations, acceptable to the great polluters;[90]
- Gleefully makes itself a vehicle for neoliberal globalization;

---

88   For an accessible account of this underreported colonial atrocity, see, 'Africa: Stealing a Nation', *New African* 456, November 2006, 10–18. For a fuller account of the process see John Pilger, *Freedom Next Time* (Ealing: Bantam Press, 2006).

89   Coates, 2015, 27.

90   For a critique of the outcome of the 2015 edition of the summit-level 'climate negotiations (dubbed COP 21) see Margaret Kimberley, 'Freedom Rider: Rich Countries

- Is intolerant of 'unconstitutional changes of governments' but tolerant of governments which collude with local and foreign investors to dispossess their people and those which are installed by force of imperialist arms or kept in power by such arms;
- Allows 'the world's radios' – namely the British Broadcasting Corporation (BBC) and Radio France Internationale (RFI), which are none other than the retuned voices of the old and still very active major empires on which the sun never or barely set – the total freedom of Africa's airwaves to make and keep the world safe for British, French and American imperial interests in particular;[91]
- Is not embarrassed to identify itself as an available promotional tool for foreign businesses in Africa, which it unambiguously does when it avows that 'the African Union aims to develop proper partnership with the U.S. to reflect the on-going Strategic Engagement between the two sides, including AGOA';[92]

Subvert Climate Change Talks', *Black Agenda Report*, 16 December 2015, <http://blackagendareport.com/rich_subvert_climate_talks>.

91   While these continuing voices of empire prefer to use their acronyms for both station identification and camouflage their performances give them away to discerning listeners as the mouthpieces of their respective empires, countries and governments they have been since their empire and wartime days in different incarnations. Nor should their consistency surprise: from the advancement and defence of empires through the so-called First and Second World Wars, the Cold War and the 'war on terror' the psychological warfare needs of their employers – and therefore their 'standing instructions' – have never really changed. To put it even more bluntly their job remains, as ever, to do what they can to let the rest of the world see the world the way their respective establishments want it seen, accept the West as a whole as 'the salt of the earth' in the biblical sense and reject serious challenges to its imperialism as 'backward', 'conservative' and even reactionary.

92   See <http://www.au.int/en/sites/default/files/Partnerships.pdf> for the AU's declared partnership intentions with the United States. Note, in view of the AU's specific mention of AGOA, that AGOA is designed to '(support) U.S. business by encouraging reform of Africa's economic and commercial regimes, which will build stronger markets and more effective partners with U.S. firms'. See <http://trade.gov/agoa/legislation/index.asp> (accessed 20 December 2015).

- Lends its flag and uses its good offices to mobilize latter-day *tirailleurs africains* and African rifles for the dubious 'war on terror' waged in Africa by the West;
- Tolerates slavery under its very nose in member-state Mauritania;[93] and
- Debases Pan-Africanism and delights some Diasporan Africans looking for quick bucks by attempting to reinvent it as a business-promotion machine rather than the liberation movement it was meant to be.[94]

While African Union tolerance of the many lamentable regimes which have littered the continent (such as Burkina Faso's Blaise Compaore's and that of Jacob Zuma, who presided over the murderous Afro-phobic violence of 2008 and 2015 in 'post-apartheid South Africa') does not seem at face value to qualify as imperialism's reward for its meddling in African and African Union affairs, it seems illogical not to count it as one when African and African Union acceptance of such regimes cannot possibly be not unrelated to the good standing they enjoyed from the West.[95]

---

93   See, for instance, 'Slavery in Mauritania', <https://en.wikipedia.org/wiki/Slavery_in_Mauritania> (accessed 18 May 2016).

94   For more on this see Chapter 6.

95   With the blessings of his Western patrons Compaoré was, for instance, active as a mediator in regional conflicts. In 2006, he was designated as the mediator of the Inter-Togolese Dialogue which resulted in an agreement between the Togolese government and opposition. He also acted as mediator in some of Cote d'Ivoire's serial crises during his reign, brokering the peace agreement signed by Ivorian President Laurent Gbagbo and New Forces leader Guillaume Soro in Ouagadougou on 4 March 2007. In March 2012, he acted as a mediator in talks between Malian coup d'état makers and other regional leaders. The BBC described him in 2014 as the strongest ally of France and the US in the region and noted that despite his own history of backing rebels and fuelling civil wars in West Africa he used his networks to help Western powers battling Islamist militancy in the Sahel. He served on the International Multilateral Partnership against Cyber Threats (IMPACT) International Advisory Board. Where Zuma's immunity from Western denunciations of the sort heaped on Robert Mugabe, for instance, is concerned the West's need for his goodwill to police the 'political compromise' which 'ended' apartheid, protect Euro-South Africans,

The 'ape syndrome' under globalization and its knock-on effects: Decolonization without emancipation amplified

The 'ape syndrome' or 'apism' – the pandemic which manifests in the widely observed compulsion among typical black-empowered and metropolitan-middle-class Africans to ape 'the West', 'Europe', 'America' or 'the white man' and drive society along the same path in vain attempts to claim or prove to themselves and their handlers that they have graduated from 'black-monkey' to human beings – is not just a problem for the individuals who suffer it: it is a catastrophe which does incalculable harm to communities, nations and the African people as a whole. Nor is it a new, or newly discovered, affliction in Africa.[96] The following are some rough and ready examples of the syndrome from a country which, in living memory, treated 'been to' (for 'has been to England, the United Kingdom or Europe') as a qualification:

- the naming of local league football clubs after some 'talismanic' clubs in Europe (Berekum AC Milan, Bolga Man City and Aflao Bayern Munich among them);[97]
- a street named 'Osu Oxford Street' in the capital city;
- observance of 31 December as the end of an 'old year' and 1 January as the first day of a 'New Year' by people who do not know these Gregorian calendar dates and observances are manmade, not divinely ordered and that there are other manmade calendars besides them, including native ones;

---

advance the West's business interests in 'the rainbow nation' and keep an eye on nest-door Zimbabwe is too obvious and too often admitted a factor to miss.

96   For early insights into these diseases see Kobina Sekyi, *The Blinkards, a Comedy And The Anglo-Fanti, a Short Story* (*The Blinkards* first published in 1915, *The Blinkards, a Comedy And The Anglo-Fanti, a Short Story* republished by Kindle ebook, year not shown), Fanon, *Black Skin, White Masks* (1970) and Ake, *Democracy and Development in Africa* (1960).

97   Stephen Kwabena Effah, 'Ghana's Exotic Football Clubs Revealed', *Unicmag Punica Magazine*, 17 May 2014, <http://infoboxdaily.com/teststage/ghana-s-exotic-football-clubs-revealed/> (accessed 12 May 2016).

- lifestyles, hairstyles, sartorial habits and idols from the ghettoes of America, Europe and the Caribbean of dubious utility and comfort, aesthetic or historical value outside their original homes where they may or may not make sense;[98]
- copycat observance of 'Valentine's Day', 'Mother's Day', 'Father's Day' and other rituals and spectacles of dubious moral or cross-cultural validity;[99]
- the cult of First Ladies, by which noisy wives of collaborating African presidents claim and are accorded Eleanor Roosevelt-like privileges without the authority of local traditions, written and unwritten constitutions or arguable *raison d'état*; and
- elaborate shows of subscription to the superstitions in some Western societies that 'Friday the 13th' is an unlucky day and the first single lady to catch bridal bouquets at wedding receptions will be lucky.

The cult of First Ladies may be particularly offensive where it involves the expenditure of taxpayer and other state resources on persons whose only distinction is that they are the wives of husbands who happen to be presidents

98   Perhaps the most spectacular manifestation of apism in this area is the importation into Africa of the cult of Ras Taferi by continental Africans who should know their idol better than their Caribbean and North American brothers and sisters that their cult figure was no respecter of black people or descendants of slaves generally. Africans in Africa who call themselves Rastafarians can surely not be excused their ignorance of the fact that their 'messiah' imported light-skinned Arabs from Yemen to 'whiten' his ethnic group, the Amharas of Ethiopia – and that His Imperial Majesty (which Ras Taferi became) even refused to take a salute from the very 'black' Colonel Mengistu Haile Mariam when, as garrison commander, he offered his salute to the Emperor on a visit to the Colonel's military region *because the commander was the son of a slave*! For other aspects of ghetto and street culture in some, at least, of the cities of America see Coates, op. cit.

99   It is a mark of the extent of this category of copycatism that the Parliament of Ghana once took time to discuss the observance of Valentine's Day. And under the auspices of the ministry responsible for tourism in that country the Ghana Tourism Authority has deemed it necessary and proper to re-christen 14 February (Valentine's Day, 'a day set aside annually to celebrate love') as National Chocolate Day. Source: <http://www.ghana.travel/events/chocolate_day/>.

or turns presidents and their wives into 'royal couples' in nominal republics. But beyond such abominations, and as a general rule, apism can be deemed to be worse in its deleterious effects than the more traditional dependency and inferiority complexes, in that the power conferred on African administrators by independence is transformed by its sufferers into opportunities to take national and institutional policy initiatives which provide even more scope for the twin evils of dependency and cultural imperialism.[100] A case in point is the situation where university administrators proudly advertise the transformation of their institutions into 'world-class Universities' (i.e. academies comparable to Oxford, Cambridge, London, Harvard and Yale) as their priority development objective, effectively signalling that the universities' future is in the hands of the outsiders who certify institutions of higher learning as 'world-class', 'development partners' and other stakeholders outside the people's influence and control.

In globalized Africa as a whole apism is most visibly expressed in the policy arena through the 'catching-up' development paradigm which allows and encourages local governments to make token gestures to development and leave the real responsibility for development to foreign patrons, as Ake alleged,[101] with resulting catastrophic consequences such as:

- 'the reach of markets, and market-oriented thinking, into aspects of life traditionally governed by nonmarket norms';[102]
- Illicit and inappropriate family law importations by lazy copycat judges on the blind side of their countries' legislatures, not letting the facts of individual cases, equity, logic, simple arithmetic, common sense and decency stand in their way as they do so;

---

100   See V. Krishna Rao, *Expansion of Cultural Imperialism through Globalisation* on cultural imperialism.
101   Ake, op. cit., 7. In the neoliberal era which matured after Ake's publication those 'foreign patrons' have very much included, besides 'donor countries', the World Bank and the European Union and, almost above all, Foreign Direct Investors.
102   Sandel, *What Money Can't Buy*, 7.

- robust un-Africanisms such as the individualism which holds that 'there is no such thing as society';[103] the separation of the development and welfare of individuals from those of society; and the delegitimization of the social ownership of the means of production, distribution and exchange;
- the equation of democracy with 'free and fair' elections and other rituals which guarantee Mkandawire's 'choiceless democracy'; and
- the idea that 'the international community' has a legitimate, if not always welcome, say in previously personal, private and domestic matters in Africa and elsewhere like general lifestyle and sexual orientations, preferences and choices and 'gender' or the division of labour by sex – with all the possibilities of their cooptation by imperialism and cultural imperialists in particular.

'New age' insults, threats and worse to Africa and the African people

Armed with the above and similar developments, the founding 'political compromises' that continue to underpin the 'independence' of most African 'states', the dynamics of African apism and the persistent belief that 'the Africans' lack the right and ability to think and govern themselves and the 'the responsibility to protect' agreed by UN member states at the World Summit to prevent genocide, war crimes, ethnic cleansing and crimes against humanity (which has effectively 'modernized' 'the dual mandate') the Obama White House felt able to patronize Africa with the following proclamation:

---

103   Late British Prime Minister Margaret Thatcher's address to the Zurich Economic Society 'The New Renaissance', 14 March 1977, and in talk to *Women's Own*, 31 October 1987.

While many countries on the continent (of Africa) have made tremendous strides to broaden political participation and reduce corruption, there is more work to be done to ensure fair electoral processes, transparent institutions that protect universal rights, and the provision and protection of security and public goods. Our message to those who would derail the democratic process is clear and unequivocal: the United States will not stand idly by when actors threaten legitimately elected governments or manipulate the fairness and integrity of democratic processes, and we will stand in steady partnership with those who are committed to the principles of equality, justice, and the rule of law.[104]

Worse than patronizing insults from those who have arrogated to themselves the right to determine how Africans should be governed have been neo-Malthusianism-led genocidal plots against the African people hatched within the 'post-war' era if the EIR (Executive Intelligence Review) Special Report quoted below is to be believed:

Investigations by EIR have uncovered a planning apparatus operating outside the White House whose sole purpose is to reduce the world's population by 2 billion people through war, famine, disease and any other means necessary.

The targeting agency for the operation is the National Security Council's Ad Hoc Group on Population Policy. Its policy planning group is in the US State Department's Office of Population Affairs, established in 1975 by Henry Kissinger.

The agency was assigned to carry out the directives of the NSC Ad Hoc Group. According to an NSC spokesman, Kissinger initiated both groups after discussions with leaders of the Club of Rome during the 1974 Population Conferences in Bucharest and Rome.[105]

The following alert by Samir Amin lends one of several measures of credence to the EIR report:

Incontestable quantified data exist which demonstrate that capitalist civilization cannot continue its destructive expansion for long. Preserving the way of life of the

---

104   *US Strategy Toward Sub-Saharan Africa* (Washington, DC: The White House, June 2012, <http://www.state.gov/documents/organization/209377.pdf> (accessed 20 June 2013)).

105   The Haig-Kissinger depopulation policy by Lonnie Wolfe, Special Report EIR (Executive Intelligence Review), 10 March 1981, <http://home.iae.nl/users/lightnet/world/depopulation.htm> (accessed 7 October 2014).

United States alone would lead to pillaging all the resources of the planet for its sole benefit. The energy crisis has already produced military aggression in the Middle East. 'The American way of life is not negotiable,' the president of [the United States] reminds us. In other words, the extermination of the 'redskins' who hinder US expansion will be continued.[106]

Adding even more force to the EIR Report and Amin's concern is the fact that the treatment of African lives by 'big powers' as worthless is not unprecedented. The attempts by the Germans to exterminate the Ovaherero and Khoikhoi peoples of South-West Africa (Namibia) between 1904 and 1907 and the 'world's' deafening silence over them are a case in point which is not rendered less poignant by the fact that other 'dark' lives have been treated as equally expendable when it is in the interest of white race authority to do so.[107] The following are nothing if not further examples of the 'all-lives-are-not-equal' mindset in action:

- The uproar which followed the 9/11 terrorist attacks in the United States – reported to have cost some 3,000 lives – compared with the world's nonchalant responses to, for instance: a) the estimated 60,000 Angolan deaths, between 1975 and 1987, in the sponsored war against that country's then national liberation movement;[108] b) the estimated

106 Samir Amin, *The World We Wish to See: Revolutionary Objectives in the Twenty-First Century* (New York: Monthly Review Press, 2008), 33–4.

107 For more on the South West African episode see George Steinmetz, 'The First Genocide of the 20th Century and its Postcolonial Afterlives: Germany and the Namibian Ovaherero', *The Journal of International Institute*, Vol. 12, No. 2, Winter 2005, <http://quod.lib.umich.edu/j/jii/4750978.0012.201/--first-genocide-of-the-20th-century-and-its-postcolonial?rgn=main;view=fulltext> (accessed 20 October 2013).

108 The *Los Angeles Times*, 18 August 1987, quoting the figure attributed by the official Angolan news agency, ANGOP, to Angolan President Jose Eduardo dos Santos. The standard 'explanation' or 'justification' of the sponsorship of UNITA (National Union for the Total Independence of Angola) and the National Front for the Liberation of Angola (FNLA) as exigencies of the 'Cold War' only adds insult to injury. Without proof of authority from the Angolan people for the 'cold warriors' to fight the Soviets or 'communism on their behalf (directly or by proxy) the premise underlying the 'explanation' of the war on Angolan soil must be seen for what it is: another

3,000 Chilean deaths attributed directly to General Augusto Pinochet's US-backed coup d'état of 9 September 1973 and its aftermath[109] ; c) the costs, provisionally estimated in hundreds of thousands of non-white human lives in the course, and in the wake, of the 'humanitarian' or 'democratic' regime-change operations in Syria and Libya;[110] and d) the hundreds of thousands of mainly landless peasants massacred in Indonesia by General Suharto's pro-Western regime and the subsequent bloody invasion of East Timor;[111]

- 'The world's' conspiratorial silence over the cross-border massacres of innocent civilians in Angola, Mozambique and elsewhere in Southern Africa by the apartheid regime, as it sought to destabilize the 'frontline states';
- The impunity generally enjoyed by state and non-state actors who kill, torture and maim black and other dark peoples for causes approved by white race authority;

---

rationalization of yet another colonial war or another manifestation of the patronizing racism by which 'white race authority' has often asserted the right and duty to force the natives to be 'free' on its terms.

109   According to Chomsky, while the official death toll of the first 9/11 (Chile, 1973) is 3,200 the actual toll is commonly estimated at about double that figure. 'As a proportion of the population, the corresponding figure for the United States would be between 50,000 and 100,000 killed.' Chomsky, *Failed States*, 111. For more on this, see <https://en.wikipedia.org/wiki/1973_Chilean_coup_d%27%C3%A9tat#U.S._involvement> (accessed 26 December 2015).

110   Estimates exist for the casualties of the proxy war against Syria, at least. The Oxford Research Group estimated that some 11,420 children had been killed in the so-called Syrian civil war by late November 2013. See Oxford Research Group, 'Press Release: Major New report Shows 11,420 Children Killed in Syrian Conflict', 24 November 2013, based on an *RT News* report dated 2 March 2011 and retrieved by it on 14 August 2011. *wikipedia*, the free encyclopedia, gave estimates of deaths in the so-called Libyan Civil War as varying from 2,500 to 25,000 for the 2 March to 2 October 2011 period alone. See <https://en.wikipedia.org/wiki/Casualties_of_the_2011_Libyan_Civil_War> (accessed 14 May 2016). *RT News* is the first Russian 24/7 English language news channel.

111   See Chomsky, *Failed States* on Indonesia generally and 'East Timor Retrospective' in Chomsky, *Rogue States*, for aspects of the East Timor saga.

- The 'it was worth it' response by Madeleine Albright on TV in 1996 when, as United States Representative to the United Nations, she was asked for her reaction to the death of 500,000 Iraqi children who, in Saddam Hussein's Iraq, had been deprived of medicines under a long US-led embargo;[112] and
- The striking failure to indict or prosecute as war criminals or perpetrators of crimes against humanity the known authors of the invasion of Iraq which had resulted in an estimated 2.7 million Iraqi deaths by 2013, the human and non-human costs of the carnage and destruction of Libya by NATO and proxy forces in and around 2011, with their long-term human and non-human costs, and similar atrocities against Africans and other 'darker' peoples around the world.[113]

Nor are the regime changers' bombs, bullets, deadly sanctions and nonchalant attitudes to the destruction of 'black' and 'brown' lives the only expressions of contempt for non-white lives observed during the review period. 'Washington-consensus' policies with predictable deleterious effects on the general welfare, health and livelihoods of the African people are obvious other examples of the same 'coloured-lives-don't-matter' attitude. As Susan George (1977) and the Comité d'Information Sahel (1975), among others, have also pointed out, life-destroying famines, malnutrition and undernutrition continued to be visited on Africans, for one, as direct consequences of the workings of the 'looting machine' and its unforgiving operators.[114] The Comité d'Information Sahel (1975), for its part, pointed

---

112 See Chomsky, *Rogue States*, 44 and Graham E. Fuller, 'The Fallacy of "Humanitarian' War', <https://consortiumnews.com/2016/03/20/the-fallacy-of-humanitarian-war/> (accessed 24 March 2016).

113 For details of some of these episodes see Chomsky, *Failed States* and Chomsky, *Rogue States*. On the Iraqi deaths from the US invasion see Gideon Polya, '10th Anniversary of US Iraq Invasion: 2.7 Million Iraqi Deaths', *Countercurrents.org*, 20 March 2013, <http://www.countercurrents.org/polya200313.htm> (accessed 23 July 2014). See also Chomsky, *Imperial Ambitions* on the politics of accountability and impunity in the matter of wars of aggression and associated crimes.

114 This is how Susan George reveals an aspect of the workings of the machine in *How the Other Half Dies: The Real Reasons for World Hunger*, 16: 'Certain of (America's)

to the continuing, and in some cases accelerated, destruction of complex indigenous economic, farming and ecosystems, dispossessions of African peoples and the transformation of hitherto food-self-reliant into 'cash-crop'-producing and food-dependent peoples – for the purpose of satisfying those who have continued to colonize 'African development' in spite of the 'decolonization' of Africa.[115]

Other examples of contempt for African lives and life-support systems during the 1943–2015 years include:

- The dumping in Africa of toxic wastes generated in Europe;
- Degradation of the air Africans breathe, African lands and African water bodies by extractive and other polluting industries working essentially to meet foreign needs and demands for raw materials and profits;
- Illegal and unethical clinical trials by multinational pharmaceutical companies in Africa;[116] and
- The sacrifice of African lives in wars imposed on the African people by the West for its own purposes, notably the 'thirty-year war between the United States and Germany to inherit Britain's defunct hegemony' (Amin, op. cit.), the Cold War, the 'war on terror' and blatant recolonization and punitive wars such as the bogus humanitarian war

---

less subtle spokesmen, like the former Secretary of Agriculture Mr Butz do not hesitate to speak of food as a "weapon"; as a "powerful tool in our negotiating kit". The CIA meanwhile announces (secretly, to its official audience) that increasing grain shortages could give "Washington ... virtual life and death power over the fate of the multitudes of the needy". This is exactly what food has become: a source of profits, a tool of economic and political control; a means of insuring effective domination over the world at large and especially over its "wretched of the earth"'.

115 The very title of the Committee's book, *Qui se nourrit de la famine en Afrique?*, and chapter and section titles such as l'exploitation coloniale, l'exploitation néocoloniale, développement = exploitation and aide = domination give a flavour of its findings.

116 See <http://en.wikipedia.org/wiki/Medical_experimentation_in_Africa> (accessed 13 May 2015) for examples.

in Libya (in and around 2011) and the fake democracy war in Côte d'Ivoire (also in and around 2011).

Just as notable is the fact that like their pre-1943 versions the post-1943 exhibitions of imperialist arrogance, violence and perfidy were emboldened, aided and abetted by African collaborators and unresponsive target audiences. To cite but a few of the more glaring examples:

•   US President Obama and British Prime Minister Cameron were able to issue their scorecards on 'democracy' in Africa; encourage 'good pupils' and admonish and warn 'bad ones'; and instruct African governments and legislatures on the decriminalization of sexual orientations they and their countries have come to endorse and promote, because they could confidently expect attentive ears or at worst nothing but feeble protests in return for their impudence;

•   While, with few exceptions, contemporary empire leaders and agents are too sophisticated to repeat the brashness of General Emile Janssens, the Belgian Commander of Belgian-Congo's Force Publique whose 'before independence = after independence' formula triggered the widespread army mutinies which it took ruthless Belgian-US-UN violence and duplicity to suppress, contemporary lords of the West's empire in Africa have been able to count, as always, on African quislings in the execution of their command-and-control projects based on the same Janssens principle;[117] and

---

117   For some of the evidence in support look no further than the participation of Congolese and Ghanaian quislings in the overthrows of the Congo's Patrice Lumumba and Ghana's Kwame Nkrumah; the rings of French, AFRICOM and other NATO bases and facilities in Africa, hosted by presumably willing African states; the African votes at the UN Security Council which authorized the armed policing of 'democracy' in Cote d'Ivoire and the bogus humanitarianism in Libya; the participation of African foot soldiers in the Ivorian operation as part of the UN's 'democracy' and 'peacekeeping' force; the force-legitimization roles of the African Union and ECOWAS in the Ivorian operation and the rear-base facilities provided by Blaise Compaore's Burkina Faso; Africa's failure to make its protestations that NATO had abused UN Security Council Resolution 1973 (2011) authorizing the protection of

- The reckless submission of most of Africa at the country level to the
  same Washington consensus and World Bank/IMF diktats whose
  reflections in *NEPAD* Jimi O. Adesina (op. cit.) denounced.

African complicity in the domination of the continent by external forces:
The 'elite' factor

The long line of African intellectuals and activists who have dismissed
the West's 'development partners' on the continent as veritable curses
on the people cannot be ignored by self-respecting Africans and non-
Africans who want to know Africa or expect to be taken seriously as
friends of the African people. The many unflattering descriptions of
these 'development partners' – with words like quislings,[118] myopic and
crumb-hungry characters ready to destroy their homelands for their
unthinking profit,[119] naive or opportunistic turncoats[120] and 'mendicant
rulers'[121] flying in their direction – also deserve to wake up all Africans
and friends of Africa, and not because they like the critics but because the
facts speak for themselves and freeing Africa from 'development partners'
of such quality and the underdevelopment they help to sustain requires
acknowledging their insights.

Those facts suggest, unfortunately, that the decadent Equatorial Guinea
which Robert Klitgaard describes may be 'the worst of the worst', as one
of the 'names' he quotes put it,[122] but certainly not entirely *sui generis*. Not

civilians under attack in Libya by serving as the air force of a rebellion against its
duly constituted government count; and the African implication in the so-called
war on terror.

118 Cabral, 1974.
119 Armah, *Osiris Rising*, 1995.
120 Mafeje, 1992, op. cit.
121 Olufemi Taiwo, 'Africa's Mendicant Rulers and their Intellectual Enablers', *Pambazuka
     News*, 5 February 2014 <http://pambazuka.org/en/category/comment/90438>.
122 Robert Klitgaard, *Tropical Gangsters: One Man's Experience with Development and
     Decadence in Deepest Africa* (New York: Basic Books, 1990), 7.

coincidentally, descriptions like 'corporate criminals' Ferguson[123] and Göran Therborn's 'heteroclite aggregate known as the "middle class" ... bearer of no specific relations of production, and (which) harbours no particular developmental tendencies, apart from discretionary consumption'[124] also appear to fit too many of the African collaborators in the 'development' of Africa.

Given the mountains of evidence in support of the above general charges already presented by the likes of Cabral, Armah, Mafeje, Taiwo and, more importantly, exposed on a daily basis by the realities of what may be loosely called 'the African experience', more general observations here about the evils that these gangs have done and continue to do to the African people may be superfluous. But sector-specific examples of how African elites in general and Africa's sectoral, institutional, project and process administrators, in particular, drag their peoples into even more dependency, domination and exploitation (sometimes innocently, naively and instinctively) should provide another measure of the extent and depth of African elite complicity in the continuing underdevelopment of the continent, in the Rodney sense of the term.

The sorry spectacle which African universities make of themselves when they are commissioned *ab initio* or subsequently tasked to achieve 'world-class-university' status is a case in point. It is easy to see how such commissions and ambitions play into the hands of those who have the power to recognize, not recognize or de-recognize such status-conscious universities; how that power may be used in particular to influence, if not determine, hiring, firing and promotion practices in the dependent or 'partner' African universities as well as their research and teaching priorities; and how, the search for and maintenance of 'partnerships' with 'world-class universities' abroad reproduce in vulnerable African academics and university administrators the same dependency and dependency complex which virtually define the 'cosmopolitan middle

123   Charles H. Ferguson, *Predator Nation: Corporate Criminals, Political Corruption, and the Hijacking of America*, Crown Business, New York, 2012.
124   Göran Therborn, 'New Masses? Social Bases of Resistance' in *New Left Review*, 85, January/February 2014, 11.

class' as a whole in Africa. Other dangers are no less real for being even more hidden.

Embedded in the danger of allowing those who control admission to world-class-university status undue influences on research and teaching priorities setting in status-seeking African universities is the hidden danger of exacerbating the African cosmopolitan-middle-class' tendency to transfer their responsibilities for identifying African problems and solutions to external 'partners'. A sitting African Vice Chancellor's briefing in May 2016 to an audience, which included the author, about his university's world-class-university-status ambitions, partnerships promotion for cutting-edge research towards this goal and the expected local benefits from such partnerships, citing the rollback of malaria, a 'tropical disease', as an example of how the opening of 'world-class universities' can benefit local populations, illustrates some of the dangers to higher education, scientific research in 'less advanced countries' and society at large from apism perfectly. For it is impossible to dissociate apism and the related craving for world-class-university status from the rush to the conclusion that the rollback of malaria in an African country in the twenty-first century requires collaboration with world-class-university-based pharmaceutical researchers abroad when the records clearly show that the 'Italian National Disease', as malaria was once called, was actually eradicated in Italy through vector control using known pesticides, not through collaborative high- or low-tech research.[125] In this particular instance valuable human and material resources are almost certain to be wasted on researching a problem and solutions which have been long settled by knowledge and successful practice. Just as regrettably, such misguided focus on non-issues and issues in which prestigious partners happen to be interested, for their own reasons, can mean the neglect or mistreatment of genuine local problems unknown to, outside the priorities of or misunderstood by friendly world-class universities and donors. Other discernible costs and risks of this particular brand of apism include:

---

125   See, for instance, Frank M. Snowden, *The Conquest of Malaria: Italy, 1900–1962* (New Haven, CT: Yale University Press, 2006 and <http://www.jstor.org/stable/j. cttinpf5o>).

- The stunting of intellectual and technological development in Africa by educational, scientific, cultural and technological dependency as imported thoughts and solutions systematically displace or prevent the flowering of local ones, especially in areas of special interest to Western scholars and their constituencies; and

- The risk that the interests of collaborating 'world-class universities', their teaching and research staff and their constituencies – and those of Africans ready and willing to partner them – will come to trump those of the African people in the study of African problems and solutions.

The developmental states in Africa which exhibited their developmentalism in the early independence years through 'industrialization by import replication' masquerading as 'industrialization by import substitution' have hardly, if ever, been accused before, and directly, of apism. But where, for instance, 'new nations' chose to industrialize by establishing factories to produce locally what used to be imported – ignoring more economically and environmentally sustainable, socially desirable and developmentally beneficial alternatives – the ape syndrome cannot escape blame for the insanity.[126] Thanks, moreover, to the sorts of power elites and their intellectual and commercial associates described by Fanon, Cabral, Armah, Mafeje, Taiwo, Ake and others, the insanity cuts across policy and management decisions in virtually all the sectors which account in sane societies for the satisfaction of the people's needs as well as their growth and development.

---

126 An obvious example is where governments chose the establishment of 'vitamin c'-producing factories over the farming of vitamin-c-rich fruits, promotion of their consumption as fresh fruits and the conservation of surpluses for future consumption as a health promotion and/or economic and industrialization strategy, avoiding the burdens of dependency on imported machines, inputs and manufacturing licences and need to export even more raw materials to earn the foreign currencies to run the local 'vitamin c' factories and harvesting the benefits of rural development, jobs and income opportunities creation opportunities and self-sustaining industrialization, etc., instead as strategic gains from the latter option.

The 'mass' factor

There is no shortage of 'explanations' of 'poverty' in Africa. And they are conveniently and mostly based on the African people's alleged backwardness. The colonial enterprise and colonial development needed such 'explanations' and the 'empowered' Africans who followed have based their own mission statements and legitimacy on versions of the old colonial mantras – carefully adjusted to limit the tag of backwardness to the African poor and remove it from themselves. Pulling no punches, however, one prominent Ghanaian academic and traditional chief has had a word of caution to 'elite' and 'masses' alike in his country which may be relevant to fellow Africans outside its borders:

> We need a revolution in this country, and unless we can do that, what is happening will keep on happening and we won't have any future because we have reached a point in our country where people try to lie to make profit. I saw a fleet of V8s tooting their horns around, at very top speed.
>
> About four of them were empty. I looked at them and I could see my wealth being drained up by very stupid people who you and I are more intelligent than. We pay them, we elect them to serve us and they come and sit on us. And you are busy dividing yourself into NDC and NPP, for what?
>
> When somebody is corrupt, you find one party defending him, and another party says no. So even corruption we can't get the mind that this is bad and so we should not do it? So if we can't govern a country in truth, then what are we doing?[127]

While the scholar-chief's own ire was obviously directed at the 'useful idiots' and the 'very stupid' and inconsiderate 'politicians' they support equally reprehensible 'fellow tribesmen', co-worshipers , favourite sons and daughters, patrons, etc., have been known to benefit from similar self-defeating indulgence from similarly misguided followers. The contributions of ordinary Africans to their impoverishment do not end there, moreover. Fear of freedom arising from their own dependency and inferiority

---

127 'Fraud is high in Ghana, we need a revolution', *Ghana Web*, <http://www.ghanaweb.com/GhanaHomePage/economy/artikel.php?ID=290538>, citing as source, *Joy Online*, General News, 31 October 2013. Also quoted by *Africawatch* in its February 2014 edition, 21.

complexes every bit as damaging as those suffered by 'their elites' has also been frequently observed as a factor which leads significant sections of them to serve a *status quo* hostile to them – as mercenaries. Other contributing mass disorders include opportunism and popular versions of queue jumping (on the backs of 'tribe' and other differentiating criteria); poor-on-poor violence; reckless and mindless alienation of potential allies outside their own class and communities; and the superstition which traces their man-made misery to supernatural causes and allows their enemies to escape responsibility for their roles in the manufacture and maintenance of their poverty. Desperate and increasingly deadly attempts to flee poverty or seek 'greener pastures' via treacherous trans-Saharan journeys, across the Mediterranean and the Red Seas and to Afro-phobic South Africa as neoliberalism, political repression and class wars against the poor on the continent continue to take their toll have also exposed a regrettable reluctance, inability and failure of the African poor to mobilize and fight back in the face of internal and external aggression.

At the psychological and cultural levels it is also sadly true that while 'normal' people and cultures resist psychological and cultural aggression too many Africans, 'ordinary Africans' very much included, act as if they cannot succumb to cultural imperialism fast enough.

Destiny or choice? The African people between continuity and change

In the face of all of the foregoing the African people seem to have but one simple choice: allow the underdevelopment of their continent and their impoverishment to follow their course, with their active or passive complicity, or take on the responsibility of writing Africa's own history in the manner envisioned by Patrice Lumumba[128] by, *inter alia*:

---

128   Patrice Lumumba, 'Letter from Thysville Prison to Mrs Lumumba'.

- Responding positively to Thomas Sankara's famous call on them to imagine and invent their own future;
- Accepting that they cannot entrust their freedom and development to the elites 'elected' for them by their 'former' colonial masters, the 'international community' or 'partnerships' between the two;
- Investing in their own liberation through the relevant political, ideological, technical and management education, training and short-term sacrifices for long-term gains;
- Ensuring that as their revolutions progress their gains are not nullified by their traditional enemies employing the *force, pre-emptive attacks* and *deceptions* recommended by Robert Cooper, for instance; hijacked by 'allies', wolves in sheep's clothing and turncoats of the sort that sold out past liberation struggles on battlefields or through negotiations, for the personal and group benefits of black empowerment – or confiscated by *Animal Farm*-style Napoleons from within their own ranks;
- Ensuring that internal disagreements and conflicts are not exploited by their enemies to roll back change and reverse gains;
- Freeing themselves from the complexes of inferiority and dependency which led 'radical' and populist governments in the past to go back to the 'traditional development partners' or chase non-traditional ones for 'development ideas', economic, social and business models, 'aid', loans, technology, investors, tourists, etc.;
- Promoting innovative thinking and problem solving ideas and talents; and
- Restoring self-esteem and modernizing their localities, communities and continent not as an act of submission to other people's modernities and diktats but as revolutionary and evolutionary responses, as necessary, to their evolving physiological, social and psycho-spiritual needs in challenging environments.

Pan-Africanism: A movement in need of rehabilitation, for the sake of the African peoples of the continent and the Diaspora

Resurgent Pan-Africanism in the immediate 'post-war' years – fuelled in large part by popular anger about the ill treatment of African ex-servicemen discarded with contempt by colonial masters who had used them for their colonial-war victories – was an undeniable factor in compelling the imperialist powers to accept that the paleo-colonial business model in which virtually all the benefits of imperialism were reserved for 'white skins' (to the exclusion of aspiring 'black-middle-class' types) was no longer sustainable in Africa and parts of the Caribbean. The movement's ability to help create and tap into allied nationalisms and anti-imperialisms (such as Third World nationalism and Afro-Asian people's solidarity) and its ability to exploit the political and diplomatic weapons of the 'Cold War' to the African people's advantage were indisputable additional headaches for imperialism while they lasted. But, for all the promises and achievements of the immediate 'post-war' years, the year 2015 ended the 1943–2015 period as perhaps one of the worst years – and certainly a most humiliating one – for Pan-Africanism as an African people's liberation movement.

In that year, the African Union, the much touted embodiment of the continental African-unity component of Pan-Africanism, demonstrated how unfit it is for purpose with its deafening silence over the resurgence in South Africa of Afro-phobia, the virulent and sometimes deadly strain of xenophobia which targets African immigrants, including from countries to which 'black' South Africa owes much for its 'deliverance' from apartheid.[129] But perhaps worse than the near-total silence of the African

129 The *BNL Times* of Malawi reported, by way of example, that thousands of people from Zimbabwe, Somalia, Democratic Republic of Congo, Ethiopia and Zambia, among other African countries, were driven out of their homes in violence linked to the April 2015 outbreak alone and as many as four and perhaps six people died in that attack. See <http://timesmediamw.com/k30-million-set-aside-for-xenophobia-victims/> (accessed 14 April 2015).

Union's member states on the issue[130] was the African Union Commission's pathetic response to it, as reflected in the following press release:

Directorate of Information and Communication

Press Release N°102/2015
Xenophobic attacks on foreign nationals in South Africa
    Washington DC, USA – 18 April 2015: The Chairperson of the African Union Commission, Dr Nkosazana Dlamini Zuma has described the attacks of foreign nationals in the province of KwaZulu Natal in South Africa as 'unacceptable', calling an immediate halt while expressing once again her deep concerns regarding the attacks on foreign nationals. (Sic)
    'Whatever the challenges we may be facing, no circumstances justify attacks on people, whether foreigners or locals. It is unacceptable,' she lamented. [Italics in original]
    While calling for an immediate halt to the attacks, the AU Commission welcomes the interventions from the South African government, including the deployment of the Inter-Ministerial committee to KwaZulu Natal to engage with those affected and with local communities, as well as the deployment of more police to provide protection and keep law and order.
    The AU Commission Chairperson decried the incidents as particularly unfortunate, as celebrations of Africa month approaches. 'On 25 May we remember the founding of the Organization of African Unity, which played such a critical role in mobilizing international solidarity for the end of Apartheid' she added.
    The challenges faced by South Africa, poverty and unemployment, are challenges faced by all countries on the continent and we must work together to address these, and build a better future for all Africans.
    The AU Commission Chairperson appealed for dialogue in and amongst communities, to address the challenges and find peaceful solutions.[131]

Remarkable features of the above statement include the failure to propose sanctions on the 'post-apartheid' state for allowing the Afro-phobic mayhem to happen; failure to take any note of the fact that the flames of

---

130   Nigeria, for one, had the decency to at least recall its High Commissioner and his Deputy from that country over the Afro-phobic attacks.
131   See 'Communiqué of the AUC Chairperson on the Xenophobic Attacks on Foreign Nationals in South Africa', 16 April 2015, <http://www.peaceau.org/en/article/xenophobic-attacks-on-foreign-nationals-in-south-africa#sthash.1SgexeRv.dpuf>.

the 2015 edition of the Afro-phobic violence were fanned by the King of the Zulus, no less, and a son of the sitting President of South Africa;[132] commendation of the South African government for what was seen by many outside the African Union as its pathetic response; and effective endorsement of the xenophobes' narrative about African immigrants taking South African jobs – without pointing out the obviously many more rest-of-Africa jobs exported to South Africa via the destruction of many consumer-goods industries there by South African substitutes.

At the Global African Family level the headline catastrophe has to be the farce which was first announced as the 8th Pan-African Congress and subsequently staged in Accra, Ghana, from 5 to 7 March 2015, as 'the first session of the 8th Pan-African Congress, with the second session to be convened by May 2016'.[133] The Accra gathering was not an ordinary farce, however: it doubled as a sick joke at Pan-Africanism's expense with the following features, among others:

- It was opened by a state president who seemed so star-struck by the British Broadcasting Corporation (BBC), the official and unapologetic voice of Britain and perhaps the West's unofficial Propagandist-in-Chief, that only a year before the Accra Conference he presided over a Ghanaian *state funeral* for a dead broadcaster whose only discernible claim to the distinction was, to quote the president, his '*rise to the lofty*

---

132   On this see, Adetokunbo Mumuni, 'Nigerian NGO asks ICC to probe Zulu King for xenophobic attacks' *Pambazuka News*, 723, 23 April 2015, <http://pambazuka. org/en/category/features/94535> and Bandile Mdlalose, 'Bitter boy who shames his father and his people', *Pambazuka News*, 724, 30 April 2015, <http://pambazuka. org/en/category/features/94605>.

133   Another gathering of Pan-Africanists, also calling itself the 8th Pan-African Congress (PAC) , had taken place over a year before, from 14 to 16 January 2014, in Johannesburg, South Africa – implying that one group or another, or both groups, was taking the name of the Congress in vain. But the comedy of one-number-two-separate-events raises a different set of issues.

heights of being one of the lead presenters of BBC TV and radio in the UK' [my emphasis];[134]

- In his capacity as Commander-in-Chief of his country's Armed Forces the host president of the Accra Conference had had his troops air-lifted to Mali by the British Air Force in February 2013, to support 'the war on terror' there – barely two years after the same Air Force had participated in the overthrow of the government of Libya, a sister African state, in what was, all too obviously, a recolonization act;

- In the same Commander-in-Chief capacity – and barely two weeks after the Accra Conference – the official host of the Accra 'Pan-African Congress' hosted and presided over an AFRICOM-sponsored military exercise (codenamed Exercise Obangame Express 2015) 'designed to improve regional cooperation, maritime domain awareness (MDA), information-sharing practices and tactical interdiction expertise to enhance the collective capabilities of Gulf of Guinea nations to counter sea-based illicit activity';[135]

- At the time of the Accra Conference the host country was actively seeking IMF 'bailout', thus placing itself under the tutelage of one of the 'force multipliers' named by Obama (Obama 2014, op. cit.);[136] and

- As if to complete its mockery of Pan-Africanism the guest of honour at the Opening of the Accra Conference was none other than the same Boni Yayi who, as President of the African Union, had sent an SOS to NATO in 2013 to come over to Africa to save Mali!

---

134   'Tribute' by the President of Ghana at the State Funeral for Komla Dumor, 22 February 2014, <https://www.dropbox.com/s/bb8nxzysmrjyh2m/Komla_Dumor_Funeral_ Brochure_Download.pdf> (accessed 15 April 2015). The programmed reading of a Tribute in the broadcaster's honour by the British Broadcasting Corporation (BBC) just before the President's Tribute on the supposedly Ghanaian State Occasion may not be insignificant in this regard either.

135   See 'Naval officers from 22 Countries Begin skills Training', *Daily Graphic*, 19 March 2015. AFRICOM was also implicated in the 2011 NATO coup d'état in Libya.

136   <citifmonline.com> (*Ghana Web*, General News, 5 August 2014) (accessed 5 August 2014). See also 'IMF Speaks: Asks Ghana to Strictly Implement Measures for Bailout', *Daily Graphic*, 15 April 2015.

Nor were the culprits cited above alone in mocking Pan-Africanism or desecrating its hallowed name. President Yoweri Museveni, named in the Accra Conference resolutions as Patron of the '8th Pan-African Congress', and retired Major General Kahinda Otafiire, its Convener and International Preparatory Committee (IPC) Chairman, were President of Uganda and Commander-in-Chief of its People's Defence Force and Uganda's Minister of Justice and Constitutional Affairs, respectively, when that country sent troops to fight alongside AFRICOM and other NATO forces in Somalia in the American 'war on terror'.

But the farce in Accra was preceded by another layer of infamy. Prior to that spectacle a first '8th Pan-African Congress' was held in Johannesburg in 2014 which proudly 'billed itself as the anti-continentalism Congress' and advocated 'an African unification of sub-Saharan states and peoples, excluding 'the Arab-African states in the north of the continent (which) were only geographically African, not African-first'.[137] By its 'tribalism' the Johannesburg Group of so-called Pan-Africanists discredited itself and insulted Pan-Africanism by, among other things:

- Pretending to be more Pan-Africanist than the universally acknowledged Pan-African legend, Kwame Nkrumah, who never ceased to proclaim that 'If in the past the Sahara divided us, now it unites us and an injury to one is an injury to all' and lived as he preached by entering an arranged marriage with Madam Fathia Nkrumah, née Rizk, originally of Egypt, chosen for him by President Nasser himself;[138]
- Denying the undeniable contributions of the likes of Mohammed V of Morocco, Gamel Abdel Nasser of Egypt and Ahmed Ben Bella of Algeria to the erstwhile African liberation and unification movements;

137 Source: David L. Horne, *The 8th Pan African Congress, A Pan African Step Forward: A Preliminary Report*, <https://www.google.com.gh/?gws_rd=cr,ssl&ei=-EsuVcyF Js6HPaqqgPAB#q=The+8th+Pan+African+Congress+POSTED+BY+PETA+L ONG+5PC+ON+FEBRUARY+02%2C+2014+A+Pan+African+Step+Forward :+A+Preliminary+Report+by+David+L.+Horne%2C+Ph.+D+++++>.
138 June Milne, *Kwame Nkrumah*, 80.

- Denying the equally undeniable fact that Algerians, Egyptians, Libyans, Moroccans and Tunisians contributed more than any Ivorian or Gabonese or Malawian, for instance, to the African liberation struggles in Rhodesia, South Africa and South West Africa;
- Further denying by implication that the all-embracing African-unity Pan-Africanism it contemptuously dismissed as 'continentalism' was crucial in getting the French to halt the nuclear tests it conducted in the Sahara in the early 1960s, with its environmental and human health implications in parts of Africa north and south of the Sahara, and that the much-needed US government support for Ghana's Volta River Project was obtained from a hesitant Kennedy Administration, thanks to support for US participation from most of the African governments canvassed, not least from Nkrumah's ally, President Nasser;[139] and
- Essentially aligning its members with Africa's traditional divide-and-rule masters.

In the face of the continuing and expanding misery of the African people at the end of the post-1943 period it would be frivolous to place the need to expose and neutralize abuses and abusers of Pan-Africanism at the centre of the challenge of decolonizing Africa and African development. But such abuses are living reminders that even practising quislings appreciate Pan-Africanism as a sleeping giant and source of legitimacy worth tapping; of the truth that while 'those who do not learn from history are doomed to repeat it', it is also true that inconvenient facts are often distorted, suppressed or forgotten; and of the fact, finally, that African history, ancient and modern, is in part a history of quislings colluding with external predators for political, material and other benefits.

These reminders do not disclose the full extent of the painful lessons from African history and the African people's circumstances, however. Some more lessons and food for thought follow.

---

139   Kwesi Armah, on 'The US and the Volta Hydro-Electric Scheme of Ghana' (180–3) in Kwesi Armah, *Peace Without Power* (Accra: Ghana Universities Press, 2004) plus personal communication.

CHAPTER 2

Haiti as Food for Thought

> Haiti did not fail. It was destroyed by two of the most powerful nations
> on earth, both of which continue to have a primary interest in its cur-
> rent condition.
>
> — HILARY BECKLES[1]

A study in programmed state failure

Imperial historiography and the inconvenient truths that will not go away

Haiti has been portrayed by imperialist and racist historiographers and
other commentators, openly and by innuendo, as a desperately poor country
which has nothing but chronic mismanagement, corruption by bungling
and brutal dictators and the racial inferiority of its black-majority population to blame for its plight.[2] The real facts and consequences of Haiti's
underdevelopment history which imperialist and racist scholars seek to
bury are, of course, undeniable. Below are some of them:

---

1   Hilary Beckles, 'The Hate and the Quake', *African Agenda*, *The Barcados Advocate*,
    19 January 2010 and <http://www.globalresearch.ca/haiti-the-hate-and-the-
    quake/17191> (accessed 21 May 2015).

2   For an *original* version of the convenient narrative see 'Haiti, the First Black Republic:
    An Object Lesson for White South Africans' (author unnamed) and Dr William
    Pierce, 'The Lesson of Haiti', both published by the Racial Nationalist Library in
    <http://library.flawlesslogic.com/haiti.htm> (accessed 20 December 2015).

The World Food Programme (WFP) reports that, as of January 2015:

1) Two and a half million Haitians lived in extreme poverty. Haiti was the poorest country in the northern hemisphere.
2) Two out of three Haitians lived on less than US$2 per day.
3) 10 per cent of the richest Haitians possessed 70 per cent of the country's total income.
4) 50 per cent of urban Haitians were unemployed.
5) Shocks induced by climate change threatened over 500,000 Haitians every year.
6) Although agriculture was an important sector of Haiti's economy, the country failed to produce enough food, and imported more than 50 per cent for its population's needs. It imported 80 per cent of its main staple: rice.
7) 90 per cent of farmers depended on rain for their harvest as only 10 per cent of the crops were irrigated.
8) One hundred thousand children under five years of age suffered from acute malnutrition, while one in three children was stunted or irreversibly short for their age.
9) Less than 50 per cent of households had access to safe water and only 25 per cent benefitted from adequate sanitation.
10) One-third of Haitian women and children were anaemic.[3]

Various other sources indicate that on average and even prior to the 2010 earthquake:

• Life expectancy was between fifty-two and fifty-four years; 10 per cent of Haiti's infants died before they reached the age of four; almost one third of the population was either ill or underweight; the adult literacy rate was 53 per cent; the gross domestic product (GDP) was less than $8 billion per annum; the average salary was around $70 a

---

3   World Food Programme (WFP), *10 Facts About Hunger in Haiti*, January 2015, <https://www.wfp.org/stories/10-facts-about-hunger-haiti> (accessed 3 January 2016).

month; the country had the lowest per capita income in the western hemisphere, and unemployment was rampant;

- Haiti was ranked 146 among 177 countries in the UN Human Development Index for 2007/2008 – a normal, pre-2010 earthquake year;[4]
- The land of natural beauty that Haiti once was had become a country of severe deforestation, denuded mountains and brown waters which was subject to hurricanes, flooding and other climate-related disasters; and climate change had become a major challenge to survival, livelihoods and development;
- Only about 10 per cent of the rural population had access to electricity and less than 8 per cent to potable water; school facilities were woefully inadequate; and
- Many young Haitians saw migration to the Dominican Republic (with which Haiti shares the island of Hispaniola) as their only escape from desperate poverty and were willing to risk life itself to seek economic refuge in North America or Europe.[5]

While these facts are clearly indisputable there can be no denying either that there is '(a veritable) rubble of imperial propaganda, out of both Western Europe and the United States' designed to cover up the fact, exposed by Hilary Beckles and others, that 'Haiti did not fail' but 'was destroyed by two of the most powerful nations on earth', which 'could not imagine their world inhabited by a free regime of Africans as representatives of the newly emerging democracy' and 'continue to have a primary interest in its current condition'. To grasp the *real* lessons from the plight of Haiti and Haitians – as opposed to the myths peddled by the imperialist and racist propaganda machine and its cover-up managers – the following inconvenient facts about

4   For 2014 it was ranked (at 0.483) the lowest of the ten lowest performing countries on the Index, for 'America, North'. Source: <https://en.wikipedia.org/wiki/List_of_countries_by_Human_Development_Index#America.2C_South>.

5   For more of the relevant facts and sources see, *Poverty in Haiti*, Wikipedia, the free encyclopaedia, <https://en.wikipedia.org/wiki/Poverty_in_Haiti> and 'Rural Poverty in Haiti', <www.ruralpoverty.org/country/home/tags/haiti>.

Haiti's underdevelopment and impoverishment history must be recounted as often as is needed to separate the facts from the offerings of those who, to adapt Naomi Klein, would 'erase' and 'remake' the history of Haiti for their imperialistic and racist purposes.[6]

Stubborn rubble, defiant truths

The portrayal of Haiti by Samuel Huntington – the former US Department of State consultant, Coordinator of Security Planning for the National Security Council in the Jimmy Carter White House, adviser to the apartheid regime in South Africa in the 1980s and author of *The Clash of Civilizations* – as 'the neighbour nobody wants' and 'truly a kinless country', two centuries after the destruction of Haiti began, deserves to be acknowledged as high-profile confirmation that that country remains as 'undesirable' to the 'masters of the universe' as it ever was. The not-unrelated pronouncement by Pat Robertson, the televangelist and 'Man of God' – namely that Haiti's misfortunes were God's 'punishment for making a pact with the devil' (presumably for enshrining the religion of their ancestors in the Haitian constitution)[7] – raises impertinence to celestial levels. There can be no more reckless and pretentious reaffirmation of the belief in the circle to which he belongs that 'God' is 'white'; that there is no *legitimate* God but the 'white' or 'white-man's God; and the multiple disasters which have befallen Haiti and Haitians since their attempted escape from French colonial slavery have been visited on them by a ruthless 'white' or 'white-man's God who abhors diversity!

---

6   See, in particular, the 'Blank is Beautiful' (Introduction) and 'The Torture Lab' (Chapter 1) of Klein, *The Shock Doctrine*.

7   Both quotations from Marlene Nourbese Philip, 'Letter to Haiti' (February 2010). Note also the coincidence of Robertson's beef with the apartheid-championing Pierce's condemnation of Haiti in 'The Lesson of Haiti' (op. cit, an abridged version of a magazine article first published in 1997), as a nation where 'the barbaric rites of voodoo, a survival of the population's African heritage, still flourishes'.

Ex-President Bill Clinton's reported call on Haiti '(to) shake off her history' is of a different cynical kind.[8] As Nourbese Philip (ibid.) points out, the history of Haiti includes the footprints of Toussaint L'Ouverture: the 'black-man ... who refused to be slave', as the African-American poet and writer, Ntozake Shange, described him.[9] But it also includes the imprints of Francois 'Papa Doc' Duvalier (the brutal local dictator beloved of imperial caricaturists) and the legacy of over two centuries of brutal and manipulative Franco-American dictatorship and exploitation under various pretexts. While Clinton appears to have avoided specifying which portions of Haitian history he wanted the Haitian people 'to shake off' – and which, if any, he wanted them to remember – the stench of an 'erase'-and-'remake' the history of Haiti to suit purposes he approved of in his demand is unmistakable.

Judging, moreover, by the facts which imperial scholars, policymakers and storytellers routinely bury the persistent traumas from the theft of their ancestors which took the Haitian people to the 'New World' in the first place must be high on Clinton's list of Haitian history to be shaken off.[10] Beyond and beneath the necessary distinction drawn by Nourbese Philip between Haitian history as the footprints of Toussaint L'Ouverture on one hand and the imprints of Francois 'Papa Doc' Duvalier on the other, moreover, is the fundamental one to be drawn between the Haitian people's consistently frustrated attempts to take their destiny into their own hands and the history of French, Franco-American, American and 'international community' frustrations of their will through the power of sanctions, invasions, naked robbery, debt bondage, regime change, development games and psychological warfare. Both strands in the history of Haiti require relentless forensic examination – if the real lessons of Haiti's history are not to stay buried by 'blank' (as in 'Blank is Beautiful') or under the rubble of apartheid and apartheid-like ideologues.

---

8   Quoted by Nourbese Philip, ibid.
9   Quoted by Philip in ibid.
10   For more on this see the *Caribbean Reparatory Justice Program: Ten Point Action Plan* issued by the Caricom Reparations Commission, copy accessible, among others, at <http://pambazuka.org/en/category/features/91378>.

The following are some of the stubborn truths within the two strands of Haiti's underdevelopment history which call for the recommended forensic examination.

The price of blackness and being the neighbour Huntington's kind 'do not want' and never wanted

There can be no denying that its Africanness, or blackness, accounts in large part for the trials and tribulations of Haiti throughout its 'post-liberation' history. It is no idle speculation, either, that the natural beauty of Haiti which led the French to nickname their former colony of Saint-Dominque *'La Perle des Antilles'* ('The Pearl of the Antilles'), 'provocative acts' like the provision in its 1805 Constitution that 'any person of African descent who arrived on its shores would be declared free and a citizen of the republic'[11] and the independence declaration by Jean-Jacques Dessalines (Haiti's second liberation war hero after Toussaint L'Ouverture) that 'never again shall a colonist or a European set his foot upon this territory with the title of master or proprietor'[12] made the free-Haiti project of its founding fathers an affront to 'white race authority', father of the modern 'international community'. Indeed, 'white race authority' did not hide its abhorrence of the prospect of a free and independent black nation – in Haiti or anywhere else in their world.

The following recollections by Howard Zinn of the position of the 'international community' on black nationhood, or the danger of it, in the century in which Haiti became a 'fugitive-slave colony' is apposite in this regard:

11   Quoted by Beckles, 'The Hate and the Quake'.
12   Quoted in Clayton Goodwin, 'Why Haiti is Poor', *New African*, 492, February 2010, 39. Goodwin also cites Haiti's 'slave revolt' as an inspiration to the revolutionary movements that liberated Central and Latin America 'and countries further afield', confirming the concern the imperial powers had about Haiti as an 'evil influence'.

The Cleveland administration said a Cuban victory might lead to 'the establish-ment of a white and a black republic,' since Cuba had a mixture of the two races. And the black republic might be dominant. This idea was expressed in 1896 in an article in *The Saturday Review* by a young and eloquent imperialist, whose mother was American and whose father was English – Winston Churchill. He wrote that while Spanish rule was bad and the rebels had the support of the people, it would be better for Spain to keep control ...

A grave danger represents itself. Two-fifths of the insurgents in the field are Negroes. These men ... would, in the event of success, demand a predominant share in the government of the country ... the result being, after years of fighting, another black republic.

The reference to 'another' black republic meant Haiti, 'whose revolution against France in 1803', continues Zinn, 'had led to the first nation run by blacks in the New World'. Still recalling the open racism around the time of Haiti's aborted escape from colonial slavery Zinn quotes the following words from the Spanish minister to the US Secretary of State:

In this revolution, the Negro element has the most important part. Not only the principal leaders are coloured men, but at least eight-tenths of their supporters ... and the result of the war, if the Island can be declared independent, will be a seces-sion of the black element and a black Republic.[13]

The reason for the programmed failure of Haiti as a nation-building project should, in the circumstance, be self-evident. The execution of the plot – from the nineteenth century to date – is a matter of record.

Recapturing the 'fugitive slave', keeping country and people subdued and useful

The facts clearly show that the response of France and its North-Atlantic allies to Haiti's self liberation was to treat the ex-colony as a fugitive slave. As Beckles tells part of the story:

---

13   Quotations and comments by Zinn (A People's History of the United States: 1492-Present), 303.

The French refused to recognize Haiti's independence and declared it an illegal pariah state. The Americans, whom the Haitians looked to in solidarity as their mentor in independence, refused to recognize them, and offered solidarity instead to the French. The British, who were negotiating with the French to obtain the ownership title to Haiti, also moved in solidarity, as did every other nation-state in the Western world.

Haiti was isolated at birth – ostracized and denied access to world trade, finance and institutional development.[14]

Haiti survived the punitive sanctions for twenty-one years – but at a price: its failure to integrate economic liberation into its national liberation agenda before and after its battlefield victory made its 'independence' hollow and doomed to succumb to the economic warfare by the enemy which surely followed. The resulting French counteroffensive and damaging Haitian climb down, as recounted by Beckles, were as predictable as they had been preventable:

> [French] officials arrived in Haiti and told the Haitian government that they were willing to recognize the country as a sovereign nation but it would have to pay compensation and reparation in exchange. The Haitians, with backs to the wall, agreed to pay the French.
>
> The French government sent a team of accountants and actuaries into Haiti in order to place a value on all lands, all physical assets, the 500,000 citizens who were formerly enslaved, animals and all other commercial properties and services.
>
> The sums amounted to 150 million gold francs.[15] Haiti was told to pay this reparation to France in return for national recognition.
>
> The Haitian government agreed; payments began immediately. Members of the cabinet were valued because they had been enslaved people before independence.

14   Beckles, op. cit.

15   In 2001, this was estimated by some financial actuaries to be equivalent to US $21 billion and, according to others, to US $22 billion. Note, also, that on the bicentenary of Haiti's independence in January 2004, the then President, Jean-Bertrand Aristide, officially demanded the return of the 'reparations' money from France. After initially rejecting the demand, France, in the person of President Jacques Chirac, promised to set up a commission to study the possibility of restitution after Aristide's threat to take the case to the International Court of Justice. Aristide was overthrown in a US- and French-backed coup d'état the following month – on 29 February 2004. The commission and the restitution appear to have been quietly forgotten by France and by Aristide's Western-installed successors.

Thus began the systematic destruction of the Republic of Haiti. The French government bled the nation and rendered it a failed state. It was a merciless exploitation that was designed and guaranteed to collapse the Haitian economy and society.

Haiti was forced to pay this sum until 1922 when the last instalment was made. During the long 19th century, the payment to France amounted to up to 70 percent of the country's foreign exchange earnings ...

In the years when the coffee crops failed, or the sugar yield was down, the Haitian government borrowed on the French money market at double the going interest rate in order to repay the French government.[16]

But, the project for the humiliation and underdevelopment of the now recolonized country had only just begun.

Widening and deepening the underdevelopment of recaptured Haiti: The US contributions

But Haiti's principal tormentors were not content with the initial round of humiliation and robbery. As Beckles (ibid.) recalls, 'when the Americans invaded the country in the early twentieth century, one of the reasons offered was to assist the French in collecting its reparations'. The US invasion of Haiti in 1915 began what US Marine Corps Major-General Smedley D. Butler (one of the most decorated US war heroes of his time) was to describe candidly as follows:

I spent 33 years and 4 months in active military service. And during that period, I spent most of my time being a high-class muscle man for Big Business, for Wall Street and for the bankers. In short I was a racketeer, a gangster for capitalism ...

I helped [turn] Haiti and Cuba [into] a decent place [for] the National City Bank boys to collect revenues. I helped in the raping of half a dozen Central American republics for the benefit of Wall Street. The record of racketeering is long ...[17]

16 Beckles, 'The Hate and the Quake'.
17 Contribution to the November 1935 edition of *Common Sense* magazine, quoted by Goodwin, 'Why Haiti is Poor', 40. The General's post-retirement denunciation of his mission in Haiti is consistent with the view he propagates in retirement of war in general as a racket. For more of his anti-war views see Smedley Butler, 'War Is A Racket', A speech delivered in 1933, by Major General Smedley Butler, USMC,

General Butler's post-retirement candour on Haiti and other American
invasions does not appear to have set a trend for subsequent US com-
manders of invasion forces and their Commanders-in-Chief, however, as
these have generally preferred to stick to the exceptionalist and messianic
rhetoric of the likes of Belgian King Leopold II (butcher of the Congo),
John Stuart Mill (the nineteenth-century British philosopher and notorious apostle of 'humanitarian intervention')[18] and US Founding Father and
pioneer American exceptionalist John Adams.[19] More unfortunately for
Haiti, the Butler-led 'armed robbery and rape' of Haiti, to borrow from
Bentsi-Enchill, was only the beginning of the direct and sustained US
contribution to the underdevelopment and impoverishment of the 'the
neighbour nobody wants'. The following is Elombe Brath's summary of
some of the United States' post-Butler crimes against the Haitian people:

> The US supported the dictatorships of Dr François 'Papa Doc' Duvalier and his
> son, 'Jean Baby Doc' Duvalier, whose combined regimes started in 1957 and ended
> in 1986, when the Haitian people elected Jean-Bertrand Aristide, a former Catholic
> priest and a friend of the poor. But US officials under President George Bush (Senior)
> did not want Aristide to run in 1986, preferring rather a former World Bank official,
> Marc Bazin. Aristide refused to heed their advice and ran anyway, winning convinc-
> ingly (over 67.5% of the vote) in Haiti's 'first free elections'. Washington grudgingly
> accepted Aristide's victory but again advised him to appoint Raoul Cedras as his

---

<http://www.informationclearinghouse.info/article4377.htm> (accessed 26 May
   2015).
18   On how Mill promoted imperialism as a gift from enlightened England to 'barbarians'
     like the Indian victims of its colonial crimes see Chomsky, *Failed States: The Abuse
     of Power and the Assault on Democracy* (2006); Chomsky, *Hegemony or Survival:
     America's Quest for Global Dominance.* (2004); and Eileen P. Sullivan, 'Liberalism
     and the Imperialism: J. S. Mill's Defence of the British Empire', *Journal of the History
     of Ideas*, Vol. 44, No. 4, October/December 1983.
19   Jefferson's 1813 boast that '(America's) pure, virtuous, public spirited, federative repub-
     lic will last forever, govern the globe and introduce the perfection of man'] , quoted
     by Perry Anderson, is regarded by some as the foundation of American exception-
     alism. For more on the 'menace' of American exceptionalism see Perry Anderson,
     'American Foreign Policy and Its Thinkers', *New Left Review*, 83, September/October
     2013, 7, citing Robert Kagan, *Dangerous Nation: America and the World 1600–1900*
     (Berkeley, CA: Atlantic Books, 2006).

military commander. He did and seven months later Cedras organised a coup d'état against Aristide while he was travelling in the US soliciting economic assistance. It was later discovered that the CIA was behind the coup.

Cedras' junta was aided by the dilatory tactics of the American administration which kept Aristide at bay in the US for four years. The CIA then attempted to discredit him by 'leaking well-crafted fake medical files presenting him as mentally incapable', as one reporter put it. Later, Washington instructed the coup leaders it was time to leave. Aristide was thus allowed to return to Haiti in September 1994, escorted by 20,000 US troops and a contingent of UN peacekeepers. His return was in exchange for his promise to back-off from liberation theology but work to reconcile rich and poor. He was, thus, confronted with the difficult choice of respecting his commitments to Washington or betraying the hopes of his voters.[20]

Clinton's version of this episode in the flaunting of US power in Haiti differs from Brath's in but one and only one material respect: the difference lies in the fact that while Clinton presents the US and UN forces in Haiti as nation builders who made themselves graciously available to fulfil '... a commitment to help rebuild the infrastructure through the Army Corps of Engineers there, and do a lot of other things', Brath portrays them as an imperial constabulary whose mission was to ensure Aristide's compliance with the terms and conditions of his restoration.[21] Bolstering Brath's account of events is an interview Clinton gave to *Haiti Liberté* in which he spoke with the authority of a colonial master, and without a hint of irony, of how '*we*' (an obvious reference to himself and his administration) '*restored*

20 Elombe Brath, 'Aristide's Ouster, African Lessons'. For a supporting general account of how the US did it and some of the instructive details which are missing from the above extract from Brath's see Chomsky, *Failed States*, 153–4. Details like the roles of the US Agency for International Development (USAID), the National Endowment for Democracy and AIFLD (the AFL-CIO affiliate) and USAID's huge 'Democracy Enhancement' project which was 'specifically designed to fund those sectors of the Haitian political spectrum where opposition to the Aristide government could be encouraged' in undermining Aristide's democratically elected government and the sabotage by the first Bush and Clinton regimes of the OAS blockade of the Cedras junta designed to force a return to democracy on the Haitian people's terms would no doubt interest students of US-style 'democracy promotion' in Haiti and beyond.

21 Chomsky, on his part, talks simply and bluntly of 'Clinton's invasion' (*Failed States*, 109).

President Aristide (to the Presidency of Haiti)' [my emphasis].[22] But that assertion of imperial authority did more than confirm that the troops in question were an imperial constabulary and not a construction brigade: it also confirmed the increasingly open secret that the US invasion of Haiti in 1915 marked the transition of Haiti from the *de facto* French colony it became when it 'negotiated' its return to the *status quo ante* 'liberation' to an American dependency.

That transition was effectively acknowledged by Clinton himself, when, in addition to revealing his king-making activities there, he reportedly 'apologised (in March 2010) for forcing Haiti to drop tariffs on imported, subsidised US rice during his time in office (as President of the United States) … (wiping) out Haitian rice farming and seriously (damaging) Haiti's ability to be self-sufficient'.[23] Clinton's admission that the devastation of Haitian rice production and food security he thus engineered 'may have been good for some of (his) farmers in Arkansas'[24] would not surprise students of imperialism, of course. But by the same token Kim Ives' dismissal of Clinton's 'apology' in both a US Senate Foreign Relations Committee testimony in March 2010 and the interview with him as 'a lot of bluff' from 'Slick Willie' is difficult to fault.[25]

22 From a Bill Clinton-Kim Ives of *Haiti Liberté* interview granted by the former in his new capacity as UN Special Envoy to Haiti and republished by Amy Goodman in Amy Goodman, "'We Made a Devil's Bargain": Fmr President Clinton Apologises for Trade Policies that Destroyed Haitian Rice Farming', 1 April 2010, <http://www. democracynow.org/2010/4/1/clinton_rice> (accessed 4 April 2010).
23 *Democracy Now!*, "'We made a Devil's Bargain'", ibid.
24 Amy Goodman, ibid.
25 Quotation from Ives from Amy Goodman, ibid. Note, also, that by Clinton's own admission in the same testimony and interview those same policies were propagated in other 'poor countries' from 1981, the year in which the World Bank-led Western campaign for the OAU to drop collective food self sufficiency as an African development goal started in earnest with the publication of the World Bank's 'Accelerated Development in Sub-Saharan Africa: A Plan for Action' (commonly referred to as the Berg report)! To his credit Clinton volunteered in the same interview that the policy reflected the thinking of 'Bob Zoellick … the head of the World Bank'.

Haiti and the international development octopus: 'Development' as extended colonization

The involvement of United Nations forces in what was, by all accounts, a US operation is yet another example of 'the world body' acting in cahoots with imperialism against the interests of an African people.[26] To some informed Caribbean observers UN Secretary-General Ban Ki-moon's appointment of ex-President Clinton (Haiti's nemesis during his presidency of the United States) as his Special Envoy to Haiti in 2009 spoke for itself in that regard.[27] But any doubts about the UN's wilful complicity in the renewed Clinton-led assaults on the Haitian people's interests were emphatically dispelled when Ban Ki-moon went out of his way to charge Clinton to '[mobilize] international support for Haiti's economic recovery and reconstruction'. It is a measure of the UN's shamelessness that the 'economic recovery and reconstruction' recipe Ban Ki-Moon was promoting was none other than the selfsame neoliberal 'plan of death' which first surfaced in Haiti under Baby Doc Duvalier, was duly rejected by the Haitian people and re-imposed

---

26 The first dramatic demonstration of this fact on African soil was arguably the UN's' complicity in the overthrow and murder of the Congo's first democratically elected Prime Minister at the dawn of Africa's 'newly restored independence'. For proof and details see Kwame Nkrumah, *Challenge of the Congo: A Case Study of Foreign Pressures in an Independent State*, International Publishers, New York, 1967. In this episode insult was added to injury as Nkrumah was forced to watch the commander of the Ghanaian UN contingent permit Ghanaian troops to be used to prevent Patrice Lumumba from using his own radio station to broadcast to his own people. President Obama's declaration in his 2014 West Point Commencement Address that NATO, the United Nations, the World Bank and the IMF are 'force multiplier(s)' which serve '(to reduce) the need for unilateral American action and increase restraint among other nations' should go further to banish any illusions about the United Nations in this regard.

27 President Obama's appointment of the selfsame Bill Clinton as US envoy to Haiti was seen as 'a matter of concern' by Clayton Goodwin, for one. See Clayton Goodwin, op. cit., 41.

on them by the Clinton Administration with the consequences over which Clinton was to shed his crocodile tears.[28]

Not surprisingly, in the circumstances, Haiti's post-2010-earthquake orders from the 'international community' – in the shape of the donor-driven and UN-backed *Action Plan for National Recovery and Development of Haiti* adopted in March 2010 – retained the 2006 World Bank/IMF-driven Poverty Reduction Strategy, with its emphasis on setting capital free in Haiti to pursue profit to the neoliberals' content. As the planners avowed:

> *The Plan focuses primarily on activities financed by public aid for development since it is the outcome of a meeting held by donors* ... [The Plan] still leaves plenty of room for other actors in the business and private sectors and NGOs who are essential players in Haiti's renewal ... [It also] puts forward a macro-economic framework based on growth and a series of measures to facilitate wealth creation by the private sector.[29] [My emphasis]

By the planners, own admission:

> In the past, Haiti fully met the food needs of its population, [but] this is no longer the case ... Haiti [now] uses about 80 per cent of its export earnings just to pay for food imports, [rendering the country] less food [secure and] the population in general very vulnerable to natural disasters and to fluctuations in the price of basic commodities on international markets.[30]

But standing logic on its head, and as faithful as ever to the neoliberals' prioritization of 'wealth creation by the private sector' over 'outdated' development objectives, such as food security for the people through their improved physical access to food, the Plan entrusted Haiti's recovery and development to the same alliance of international and local agents which

---

28   For more on 'the plan of death' and how the Clinton Administration manoeuvred to re-impose it of the Haitian people see Ashley Smith, 'How the NGOs are Profiting off a Grave Situation: Haiti and the Aid Racket', *Socialist Worker*, 14 January 2010, <http://socialistworker.org/2010/01/14/catastrophe-in-haiti> (accessed 26 April 2014).

29   Introduction to the *Action Plan for National Recovery and Development of Haiti*, 5. That 'private sector' is, of course, essentially foreign.

30   Section 4.2.1 of the *Action Plan*, 22.

had transformed the previously food-self-sufficient country into a food-inse-
cure one before the quake.[31] Also consistent with the planners' dedication
to the logic of the absurd was their capacity to ignore the fact that the US
$11.5 billion said to be needed for the Plan's implementation – to be sought
and granted on the basis of the notorious neoliberal conditionalities – represented about half the estimated US $21 to US $22 billion in restitution
which France continues to owe to Haiti. Preferring a conditionality-loaded
'macro-economic framework based on growth and a series of measures to
facilitate wealth creation by the private sector' to the recovery of the US
$21 to US $22 billion due to Haiti from France for its post-earthquake disaster and development management may or may not have been designed
to keep it as a 'decent place for racketeers'. But whatever the intentions of
the 'recovery and development' planners, the measures they commanded
to 'facilitate wealth creation by the private sector' appeared to have served
the interests of major humanitarian industry operators as well as the private
contractors whom Fenton accused of going to post-earthquake Haiti 'to
grab the loot like vultures'.[32]

Haiti, disaster management and the humanitarian aid industry

The humanitarian aid industry which did not generally behave more honourably than their 'development aid' counterparts before the January 2010
earthquake did not do so in its aftermath either. On the contrary, the captains of the industry proved themselves to be every bit as patronizing,
manipulative and exploitative as their counterparts in the commercial

31 Note, not coincidentally, how the resulting decreased food security for the people of
    Haiti serves the interests of the promoters of food as a 'weapon', a 'powerful negotia-
    tion tool', etc., as per the declarations cited by Susan George in *How the Other Half
    Dies* (op. cit.)
32 Anthony Fenton, 'Haiti: Private Contractors Like Vultures Coming to Grab the
    Loot', *IPS*, 19 February 2010, <http://www.ipsnews.net/news.asp?idnews=50396>
    (accessed 27 February 2010) and Ashley Smith, 'How NGOs are Profiting off a Grave
    Situation: Haiti and the Aid Racket'.

'private sector'. Furthermore, the following boast or indiscretion by Ken Merten, the US Ambassador to Haiti, on 12 February 2010, confirms that some humanitarian aid bodies (otherwise known as non-governmental organizations or NGOs) are government agents in disguise:

> In terms of humanitarian aid delivery ... frankly, it's working really well, and I believe that this will be something that people will be able to look back on in the future as a model for how *we've been able to sort ourselves out as donors on the ground* and responding to an earthquake.[33] [My emphasis]

The ambassador's claims are revealing in another respect. As evidence before him led Smith to conclude some ambassadors, at least, believe it to be their duty not only to lie abroad for the good of their countries but for that of their fake NGOs as well. The following are some choice responses to Ambassador Merten's propaganda claims conveyed by Smith:

> The UN Office for the Coordination of Humanitarian Affairs (OCHA) reports that 'more than 3 million people – one in every three Haitians – were severely affected by the earthquake, of whom 2 million need regular food aid. Over 1.1 million people are homeless, many of them still living under sheets and cardboard in makeshift camps. The government of Haiti estimates that at least 300,000 people were injured during the quake.'
>
> So far, the relief effort has only managed to provide 270,000 people with basic shelters like tents. More than 1 million people still have little access to food and water and have to scrape by to find sustenance. Even worse, because the relief operation is so inefficient, Haitians report that some of the food spends so long at the airport that it is rotten by the time it gets to the hungry.[34]

Bill Quigley, Legal Director of the US-based Centre for Constitutional Rights (CCR), began his demolition of the ambassador's bogus claims as follows, according to Smith (ibid.):

---

33   Ambassador Ken Merten, quoted by Ashley Smith, op. cit. Smith, who is generally very critical of the games the NGOs played in Haiti, does, however, acknowledge the sincere and efficient interventions of Partners in Health and a few other NGOs.

34   Ashley Smith, ibid.

What? Haiti is a model of how the international government and donor community should respond to an earthquake? The Ambassador must be overworked and needs some R & E. Look at the facts.

The respected medical NGO, *Médecins Sans Frontières* (MSF or 'Doctors without Borders') was equally unimpressed by the humanitarian aid industry's performance, also according to Smith, who quotes a disappointed MSF as complaining:

> It's hard to believe that four weeks after the quake ... so many people still live under bed sheets in camps and on the street ... One can only wonder how there could be such a huge gap between the promise of a massive financial influx into the country and the slow pace of distribution. MSF is concerned that with the onset of the rainy season, we'll be facing new medical emergencies, when people who are living without shelter come to us with diarrhoea or respiratory infections.

The 'humanitarian-aid' community also appeared to have allowed paranoia – or worse – to stand in the way of respect for the people they were ostensibly in Haiti to serve and the quality of the service itself. Quoting an unnamed friend, Smith refers, in this connection, to a colour-coded security zoning map used by all the larger NGOs in Port-au-Prince which succeeded in both conveying their disrespect for the people they claimed to be serving and building inefficiencies into their operations:

> Port-au-Prince (was) divided into security zones: yellow, orange, red. Red zones [were] restricted; in the orange zones, all of the car windows [had to] be rolled up, and they [could not] be visited (by NGO personnel) past certain times of the day; even in the yellow zone, aid workers [were] often not permitted to walk through the streets, and [spent] much of their time riding through the city from one office to another in organizational vehicles.

Smith continued:

> the creation of these security zones [was] like the building of a wall, a wall reinforced by language barriers and fear ... [The fear], much like violence, [was] self-perpetuating', and was offensive on several counts: 'when aid workers [entered] communities radiating fear, it [was] offensive; the perceived disinterest in communicating with the poor majority [was] offensive; driving through impoverished communities with windows rolled up and armed security guards [was] offensive'.

While the treatment of the Haitian people as 'pariahs' and savages, *in their own country*, is obvious from the above quotation the efficiency costs of the paranoia are not so evident from it. It must be added, therefore, that the efficiency costs included, according to Smith, the tendency of the bulk of the aid to remain in stores – awaiting the *UN* and *US military escorts* deemed essential while people in the camps suffered and their patience waned.

Vulgar and rewarded self-promotion was another feature of the humanitarian industry, according to Smith, citing the following example:

> The big NGOs which [were] getting the bulk of the money [saw] the crisis as an enormous opportunity to raise funds and their profile. Thus, instead of a centralized and logical relief effort, something only a sovereign state could provide, the NGOs [were] competing with one another, literally branding areas they [served] with their logos.

The resulting spottiness and chaos in the distribution of relief items caught the attention of the authoritative British medical journal, *The Lancet*, which reportedly complained about the NGOs 'jostling for position, each claiming that they [were] doing the most for earthquake survivors' – and even claiming credit for 'spearheading' the relief effort when 'in fact, as [could be seen] only too clearly, the situation in Haiti [was] chaotic, devastating and anything but coordinated.'[35] The games played by the large NGOs in Haiti are not unknown elsewhere, unfortunately, according to Smith, who has studied these creatures. It is his general observation, for instance, that:

> Polluted by the internal power politics and the unsavoury characteristics seen in many big corporations, large aid agencies can be obsessed with raising money through their own appeal efforts. Media coverage as an end in itself is too often an aim of their activities. Marketing and branding have too high a profile. Perhaps worst of all, relief efforts in the field are sometimes competitive, with little collaboration between agencies, including smaller, grassroots charities that may have better networks in affected countries, and so are better placed to immediately implement emergency relief.

Another unsavoury large-NGO practice observed by Smith in post-quake Haiti is the exploitation of international clout to enrich some NGOs and starve others of resources. 'Most of the privately raised funds [were]

---

35   Smith, op. cit, citing *The Lancet*, Vol. 375, No. 9718, 13 March 2010, 891.

funnelled to NGOs that [had] a chequered history in Haiti, not ones with a real commitment to invigorating Haitian self-organization', according to him. In support of his contention he cited CCR's Bill Quigley's observation that of the more than $644 million in donations to NGOs for earthquake relief in Haiti over $200 million went to the Red Cross, which had only 15 people working on health projects in the country before the earthquake, while a mere $40 million or so went to Partners in Health which had 5,000 people working on health before the disaster.

Further arguing that the welfare of ostensible beneficiaries was not the prime consideration in donations to NGOs for disaster relief in Haiti or anywhere else, Smith points out that:

> The US policy of bypassing the Haitian state to fund NGOs is nothing new ... this has been the US practice in the Third World since the turn to neoliberalism in the 1970s. The U.S. has used IMF and World Bank structural adjustment (programmes) to force Third World governments to privatize government industry, cut wages and government (programmes), lower trade barriers, and open economies to U.S. trade and investment. At the same time, the U.S. and corporate donors started funding NGOs to address the social crisis created by neoliberal policies.[36]

In a similar vein, Smith quotes Harvey as follows:

> The rise of advocacy groups and NGOs has ... accompanied the neoliberal turn and increased spectacularly since 1980 or so. The NGOs have in many instances stepped into the vacuum in social provision left by the withdrawal of the state from such activities. This amounts to privatization by NGO. In some instances, this has helped accelerate further state withdrawal from social provision. NGOs thereby function as 'Trojan Horses for global neo-liberalism'.[37]

---

36 For corroboration Smith cites evidence provided by Peter Hallward in *Damming the Flood: Haiti, and the Politics of Containment* (New York and London: Verso Books, 2010) which further shows that the NGOs are non-governmental in name only and reveals that, generally, the US Agency for International Development (USAID) and counterpart 'aid' agencies in other 'donor' countries provide 70 per cent of their funding and corporate bodies and individual contributions account for the remaining 30 per cent.

37 David Harvey, *A Brief History of Neo-Liberalism* (Oxford: Oxford University Press, 2007), 177. Harvey refers readers, in turn, to T. Wallace, 'NGO Dilemmas: Trojan

Indeed, Smith, Harvey, Mike Davis and other critics of the big-brother NGOs expose them as soft tools for imperialism. Davis, in particular, is reported by Smith as arguing that the NGOs:

> Play a role very similar to the one that missionary religious institutions played in the earlier history of empire. They provide moral cover ... a civilising mission of helping the hapless heathens ... for the powers that are plundering the society. And just as religious institutions justified imperial war, many NGOs, abandoning their traditional standpoint of neutrality in conflicts, have become advocates of military intervention.[38]

In Haiti itself Smith accuses the NGOs of worsening poverty, no less. He recalls, by way of example, the testimony of another Haiti watcher, Timothy Schwartz, who is said to show, in *Travesty in Haiti*,[39] how CARE International, which claimed that its mission in Haiti was to provide food aid to 'the poorest of the poor', not only failed in this mission but actually exacerbated the food crisis. Still drawing on *Travesty in Haiti* Smith continues:

> When the US implemented its 'plan of death' in Haiti, which undercut peasant agriculture and flooded the market with subsidized US products, it caused a food crisis. Peasants were no longer able to find a market for their produce, and were therefore thrust into poverty, often unable to meet their own food needs because of their collapsed standard of living. They then became dependent on food aid.
>
> USAID, in turn, funded CARE International to feed the impoverished peasants. The NGO began to distribute US crops as food aid, during both bad and good harvests, further undermining Haitian peasants' ability to compete for the market.[40]

Horses for Global Neoliberalism?', *Socialist Register*, 2003, 202–19 – and, for a general survey of the role of NGOs, to M. Edwards and D. Hume, eds, *Non-Governmental Organisations: Performance and Accountability* (London: Earthscan, 1995).

38   Smith, op. cit., relaying a Mike Davis view of NGOs in Mike Davis, *Planet of Slums: Urban Involution and the Informal Working Class* (London: Verso, 2006).

39   Timothy Schwartz, *Travesty in Haiti: A true account of Christian missions, orphanages, fraud, food aid and drug trafficking* (Charleston, SC: BookSurge Publishing, 2008).

40   Ashley Smith, 'How the NGOs are Profiting off a Grave Situation'.

While also confirming Brath's narrative (in 'Aristide's Ouster', op. cit.) on how the US neoliberalized Haiti and turned it into 'the most neoliberal economy in Latin America and the Caribbean', Smith saw beyond the economic aspects of the US imposition and claimed that it was also aimed at preventing the emergence of people's power by the crushing of *Lavalas*, the mass movement of Haitian workers and peasants which had sprung up to defend the poor against the 'plan of death' and had succeeded in getting Jean-Bertrand Aristide elected president in 1990 on an anti-neoliberal-reform platform.[41]

But instances were also reported of active poverty-harvesting or vulturism by the established NGOs. One such example was the establishment by NGOs of fake orphanages to shelter the children of the elite in boarding-house facilities while vulnerable real orphans were sold abroad.[42] Another example of NGO duplicity and assault on the Haitian poor, cited by other Haiti watchers, was the displacement of 'an extensive disaster preparedness system following the Cuban model' put in place by the first Aristide government by NGOs dispensing charity to promote the political and commercial interests of external paymasters.[43] With over 10,000 NGOs (by one World Bank count) doing everything in Haiti from garbage collection to health care and food production in a chaotic patchwork of services, ordinary Haitians could also be forgiven for reportedly deriding their displaced and incapacitated state as the 'Republic of NGOs'.[44]

Worse still, Smith provides evidence – and supporting arguments from other observers –that some, at least, of the NGOs active in Haiti

41 Smith, ibid.
42 Ibid.
43 'Haiti Needs Solidarity, not Charity', Amanda Zivcic interview with Marilyn Langlois, *Pambazuka News*, 11 March 2010, <http://www.pambazuka.org/en/category/features/62924> (accessed 11 March 2010). As Langlois puts it, 'most major NGOs in Haiti are not really meeting the needs of the people. They tend to be well connected with major big business and the US/UN occupiers, with well-paid staff and a carefully crafted image of doing a few projects here and there, as long as the recipients of their largesse don't get political and vocal about calling for the return of Aristide and Haitian democracy'.
44 Smith, op. cit.

were 'in the business of poverty, not its eradication, and they ... prolifer-
ated in lockstep with the collapse in the Haitian standard of living.' In yet
another damning example of such practices Smith quotes the following
from *Travesty in Haiti*:

> The world's largest multinational charities – CARE, CRS, World Vision and ADRA –
> executed the political will of institutions, governments and lobbyists that had iden-
> tified Haiti's comparative advantage as low wages – i.e. poverty – and in doing so,
> these charitable organisations dedicated to helping the poorest of the poor wound
> up working to make the people of Haiti even poorer.

'International security assistance': A Haiti-coloured view

'American exceptionalism' – heart of the 'rhetoric of the nation's calling'
and other American self-idolatry claims by missionaries and managers of
the American empire[45] – is, of course, no more than the appropriation for
America's purposes of the same part-cynical, part-self-adulating messianic
ideology invented by America's English, French and Portuguese forebears
to mystify *their* imperial power and resource grabs abroad and hold on
to previous acquisitions in their times. But the people of Haiti and other
victims of 'American exceptionalism' can be forgiven for seeing the diaboli-
cal side of the ideology, especially, but not exclusively, when it is expressed
with American power and its 'force multipliers'. For their history, from the
US occupation in 1915 to date, is one of subjugation through unforgiving
and unbroken applications of Robert Cooper's *force, pre-emptive attack*
and *deception*.

The invasion that launched the occupation was, itself, executed 'by
genuinely Marine Corps methods', as Major (later General) Smedley Butler

---

45   On this see, for instance, Perry Anderson, 'American Foreign Policy and Its Thinkers';
      Andrew Bacevich, *The Limits of Power: The End of American Exceptionalism*; Anders
      Stephanson, *Manifest Destiny: American Expansionism and the Empire of Right*, Hill
      and Wang, New York, 1995; and Chomsky, *Hegemony or Survival: America's Quest
      for Global Dominance*.

who led it, subsequently confirmed.[46] There may or may not be any lessons to be learnt from those methods, the fact that it was American troops who employed them or Butler's admission. But the fact that an invasion which was initially advertised as 'reparations'-collection assistance to the French transformed itself into a launch pad for re-inventing Haiti as 'a decent place [for] the National City Bank boys to collect revenues', as Butler also confessed, for contesting France's previous privileges as sole proprietor of neo-colonized Haiti and for eventually turning it into a *de facto* American colony in which France is only allowed some of the cultural and other influences usually observed in Francophone states provides an early demonstration of the fact that even among 'allies' 'international security assistance' is not always what it seems.[47]

But since America's 'democracy promotion' policies and practices – from Latin America through Iraq to Côte d'Ivoire and many countries in between and a presumably still standing US National Security Council document – combine to give militaries (American and local) a role in 'democratization' and 'development' in general 'when it is in the U.S. interest' (see Chapter 3) the way Butler's occupation army accomplished its mission in Haiti has to be of more than passing interest to all concerned. Butler's army:

> dissolved the National Assembly ... (blaming it on) the assembly's refusal to ratify a US-designed constitution that gave US corporations the right to buy up Haiti's lands – regarded by the invaders as a 'progressive' measure that Haitians could not comprehend. A Marine-run plebiscite remedied the problem: the constitution was ratified by a 99.9 percent majority, with 5 percent of the population participating. Thousands of Haitians were killed resisting Wilson's invaders, who also reinstituted virtual slavery, leaving the country in the hands of a vicious National Guard after

---

46   Chomsky, *Failed States – The Abuse of Power and the Assault on Democracy*, 153.
47   As evidence of France's retained cultural influences in still Francophone Haiti recall the television images of Haitian children singing and dancing to the tune of *Sur le Pont d'Avignon*, the French song about the Pont d'Avignon (the Bridge of Avignon) that dates back to the fifteenth century, on the ruins of a school block crushed by the 2010 earthquake.

nineteen years of *Wilsonian idealism*. Horrors continued unabated, along with US support, until Haiti's first democratic election in 1990.[48]

But 'international security assistance' has cost Haiti and its people more than their democracy and sovereignty. The following allegations by Marilyn Langlois provide another dimension of the price the people of Haiti have had to pay for US-UN military occupation:

> Immediately after the (2010) quake, a Doctors Without Borders airplane carrying a medical field hospital was denied landing at the Port-au-Prince airport five times by the US military.

It is a matter of speculation whether such acts of military occupation cum 'international security assistance' cost Haitian lives. But speaking in March 2010 Langlois had this to say about the US-UN occupation forces and human lives in Haiti in the modern era:

> There has been massive resistance to the past six years of UN occupation, with often lethal consequences, as on multiple occasions blue-helmet-clad 'peacekeepers' invaded poor neighbourhoods populated by vocal demonstrators in pre-dawn hours, killing unarmed men, women and children with impunity.[49]

Thinking through Haiti: More food for thought

Haiti may be the oldest living black 'state' but is certainly not the first black nation ever or the first black entity with national ambitions or pretentions in the so-called New World: the latter distinction belongs to Palmares (or Quilombo dos Palmares), the nation of escaped slaves and others in colonial Brazil which existed from 1605 until its suppression in 1694. The

---

48   Chomsky, *Failed States*, 153.
49   Both quotations are from 'Haiti needs solidarity, not charity', Interview of Marilyn Langlois. Langlois was a board member of the California-based Haiti Emergency Relief Fund (HERF) which was formed shortly after the 29 February 2004 coup d'état as an offshoot of the Haiti Action Committee. Its activities include political advocacy and consciousness raising about Haiti.

continent of Africa itself is littered with former states, stateless societies and other polities which have since been totally or partially eclipsed by the contraptions of European imperialism dismissed by Ayi Kwei Armah as 'idiotic neo-colonial states'. Haiti *may*, therefore, be unique as the oldest black state, bar none, in the *modern* sense of the term.

But thinking Haitians, Africans and humanity in general must sometimes wonder whether 'successful' or 'lucky' escape from the fate of Palmares, for example, is, itself, cause for celebration if the 'living state' ends up like Haiti or as another 'idiotic' neo-colonial state many of whose 'citizens' are desperate to flee from by hook or by crook. In less abstract terms, Haitians, Africans, and thinkers of all colours and nationalities may well wonder whether Afro-Brazilians are better or worse off than they would have been as citizens of Palmares – or better or worse off than their Haitian counterparts. Those, it would be observed, are issues about the legitimacy and functional value of 'citizenship' for 'ordinary Africans' who do not make the 'black-empowerment' grade in independent Africa and the Caribbean, Dzidzienyo and Oboler's Latin America[50] and the America described by Michelle Alexander[51] where a 'black lives matter' movement has also been deemed necessary by many black people.[52] But beyond idle speculation and unproductive agonizing, thinking through Haiti can be employed as a vehicle for mobilizing the energies of Africans in Africa and the Diaspora towards the achievement of Pan-Africanism's historic dream: dignity for Africans and people of African descent wherever they may be.

Integration or liberation? Lessons from Haiti

The OAU/AU's substitution of *NEPAD* for the *LPA* and enthusiasm for the neoliberal globalization of Africa and Haiti;[53] the individual and

50　Dzidzienyo and Oboler, *Neither Enemies nor Friends*.
51　Alexander, *The New Jim Crow*.
52　'Black lives matter' is, of course, the name of the activist movement which was started in the African-American community in 2013 to campaigns against violence toward black people.
53　Note the AU's endorsement of the 'plan of death', highlighted below.

collective acceptance by African states of NATO, AFRICOM, the French Armed Forces and other unreconstructed imperialist forces as the continent's defence shields;[54] and the many other indications that African states are happy to go along with the transformation of neoliberalism from an economic ideology into a development one and to pass on their responsibilities for 'development' and 'security' to the West and the market forces and NGOs it controls are signs enough of black-empowered Africa's failure to learn the most important lesson of Haiti's history – namely that it is unsafe and insane (and when done for reasons of self-interest criminal) for Africans to place the 'security' and 'development' of the people, territories and resources they are entrusted with under the umbrella of 'those who for 500 years nationalized and refined armed robbery and rape (and) globalized pillage and serial genocide against the African people'.

In the global jungle predators unite but their victims divide, make themselves available for subjugation, rape, humiliation and mass murder as isolated targets – or are thrown to the wolves by their own kind

It is easy enough for Africans and people of African descent across the globe who are aware of the hostility which greeted the battle-won independence of 'black' Haiti *in the nineteenth century* to be outraged by Samuel Huntington's reported characterization of it as 'the neighbour nobody wants' and 'truly a kinless country' – *in the twenty-first century*. But if impotent rage is to give way to positive action it must be followed by introspection as well as critical thinking, given, especially, the fact that Huntington

54   Indeed, in 'How to Disappear Money, Pentagon-Style' (*TomDispatch*, 24 May 2016, <http://www.tomdispatch.com/post/176144/tomgram%3A_william_hartung%2C_how_to_disappear_money%2C_pentagon-style/>), William Hartung disclosed that the United States alone enjoyed 'staging areas', 'cooperative security locations', 'forward operating locations', and 'other outposts' in Burkina Faso, Central African Republic, Chad, Ethiopia, Gabon, Ghana, Kenya, Mali, Niger, Senegal, the Seychelles, Somalia, South Sudan, and Uganda, among other places for a total of 60 such sites in 34 countries as of late 2015, in return, presumably, for covering the 'co-operating' countries or regimes with its 'security' umbrella.

was able to taunt Haiti as 'a kinless country' despite the existence in Africa of over fifty nominally independent black or African 'states' and no less than fifteen black-majority states in the Caribbean. Critical thinking would also reveal that in describing Haiti as 'the neighbour nobody wants' Huntington was reflecting the same *united* Western attitude to independent black nationhood which first surfaced in modern forms with the rejection of Palmares (or Quilombo dos Palmares) in the seventeenth century, Haiti in the nineteenth and repeated rejections of Aristide's and the people's two unsuccessful 'revolts' (in the twentieth and twenty-first centuries), as the following examples of white race authority's relentless opposition to 'black' and 'brown' nationhood in four successive centuries will show:

- In 1791 George Washington sent troops along with $750,000 to help the French suppress a slave revolt in Haiti;
- When Belgian King Leopold II, 'the butcher of Congo', pursued his nefarious activities in 'his' 'Congo Free State' – which effectively displaced or subordinated the pre-colonial political entities in the region, including the Kingdom of Kongo (1390–1914) –the imperialist camp was unanimous in congratulating and hailing his civilizing work in Africa's interior;[55]
- NATO, 'the free world' and the 'leader of the free world' supported Portuguese colonialism in Africa and apartheid South Africa at different times or concurrently with arms, logistics, diplomatic cover and covert operations against national liberation movements – all under the pretext of fighting 'terrorism', 'communism' or Soviet or Chinese 'imperialism';[56]

---

55 Prashad, *The Darker Nations*, 18. For more on Leopold II's escapades in the 'Congo Free State', see Baffour Ankomah, 'The Butcher of Congo', *New African*, October 1999.

56 In *Back Channel to Cuba: The Hidden History of Negotiations between Washington and Havana* William M. LeoGrande and Peter Kornbluh (Co-authors) (The University of North Carolina Press, 13 October 2014) report, for instance, that then-US Secretary of State Henry Kissinger considered launching airstrikes against Cuba after Fidel Castro sent troops to support the national liberation movement and oppose apartheid

- The overthrow and murder of ex-Belgian Congo's democratically elected Prime Minister, Patrice Lumumba, were effected jointly by the US and Belgium, with the United Nations providing cover and logistic support;
- The EU and American sanctions against Zimbabwe – using the pretext of election-rigging and human rights abuses in that country to cover the underlying reason: unacceptability to Britain of a land reform initiative designed to correct the wrongs of the seizure by British settler colonialists of native lands while they held colonial power;[57]
- US and UN assistance to France in the restoration of Côte d'Ivoire to full informal French colony status as a response to a brief period of 'caretaker-President' Laurent Gbagbo's rebelliousness and NATO's regime-change operations in Libya culminating in the overthrow and murder of its then leader, Muammar Kaddafi, both in 2011 and both under cover of dubious UN Security Council resolutions; and
- The effective use of the US' 'force multipliers' named by Obama in his May 2014 *West Point Commencement Address* – and others, such as the EU, the International Criminal Court, the BBC (which often sounds like the voice of America)[58] and RFI, some of the so-called advocacy and human-rights NGOs (which sound and behave like another Estate of the Realm and 'force multiplier') and the African Union, acting collectively as 'the international community' or tailor-made coalitions – to prosecute the US' globalization agenda and discharge such other 'exceptionalist' responsibilities as it may please it to assume.

The contrast between the unity of imperialist forces and the rush among their victims to distance themselves from one another – for safety or

---

South Africa's destabilization force in Angola in 1976. See, also, Chomsky (2000) and (2004).

57   For a brief on this episode see Connie White, 'Sanctions on Zimbabwe: Africa Under Attack', 20 January 2003, <connierw@earthlin.net> (accessed 18 June 2015).

58   Assertion based on the blanket coverage by the BBC of US leaders' pronouncements, activities and tours around the world, the use of serving and former US functionaries and 'think tanks' as 'independent' and 'expert' commentators and background providers and obvious pro-US slants on news selection, presentation and editorializing.

'preferential treatment' – could not be sharper. And, once again, Haiti's experience provides food for thought – and backhanded support to Huntington's sneer that it is a kinless country, despite an impressive litter of some seventy African and Afro-Caribbean states on the planet. For examples of such support one needs go no further than the following episodes:

- The near-total success of the Franco-American campaign for the boycott by heads of state and government of 'independent' states of the Global African community of Haiti's bicentennial celebrations on 1 January 2004 (with South Africa's Thabo Mbeki as the sole exception);[59]
- The affirmative votes of all three African UN Security Council members for the resolutions which were used to cover armed meddling by white race authority in Côte d'Ivoire and Libya in and around 2011;
- The lackadaisical African support to Zimbabwe in the face of the West's economic war on it for daring to give back to native Zimbabweans lands seized from them by settler colonialists empowered by British colonialism;
- The idiotic call in *Barbados Underground*, the online newsletter, on October 19, 2014 for a ban on travellers from all of Africa – on account of an Ebola outbreak in three (3) unfortunate West African countries;[60]
- All-too-frequent outbreaks of Afro-phobic violence and other forms of Afro-phobia against African cross-border migrants;[61] and

59 Brath, 'Aristide's Ouster, African Lessons', op. cit., 16.
60 'Impose Ban on Travellers from Africa NOW!', *Barbados Underground*, <http://barbadosunderground.wordpress.com/2014/10/19/impose-ban-on-travellers-from-africa-now/> (accessed 20 October 2014). The *Barbados Underground* call may be a stab in the back and 'unpatriotic' (from the Pan-Africanist point of view), as well, from a publication which ought to know, as Horace Campbell points out ('Ebola, the African Union and bio-economic warfare: Health questions and the challenges for Africa', *Pambazuka News*, 697, 8 October 2014, <http://pambazuka.org/en/category/features/93093>), that the three West African countries which were at the epicentre of the Ebola-disease may have been victims of 'bio-economic warfare'.
61 Examples outside South Africa include Ghana's disgraceful Aliens Compliance Order of 1969 (which appears to have targeted resident Nigerian traders, mainly, to

- The gratuitous, obscene and divisive attack on Africans in Africa in the same online publication as a people 'doing an excellent job of genocide on themselves'.[62]

The 'trading-with-the-enemy' trap

It is easy enough, with a bit of intellectual effort and political imagination, to understand that Haiti did not have to walk into the trading-with-the-enemy trap which cost it the independence and dignity it had won on the battlefield. The conclusion is based on the not unreasonable assumption that while their 1791–1804 liberation war lasted, the people of Haiti lived and fought the French and their allies without needing to trade with them. The further fact that the Haitian people survived their enemies' blockade for another twenty-one years after the war only strengthens the conclusion that it had been within the Haitian people's power to avoid the capitulation to enemy forces which has remained their undoing since – and that they could have done so by keeping their economy on a war footing during the immediate war years and for as long as it took to match and complete their political independence with economic independence. The Haitian people's repeated failure to fight the US-imposed 'plan of death' as resolutely as their ancestors had fought and won their national liberation war also raises obvious political and research questions about the changed national character of a people whose ancestors fought a long anti-slavery and anti-colonial war (1791–1804) with relatively basic means and against no less formidable odds. The collapse of continental and territorial nationalisms of virtually any

make room for then Prime Minister K. A. Busia's aspiring Ghanaian petty trading constituency); Nigeria's expulsions of 'ECOWAS aliens' in 1983 and 1985; and the Afro-phobic violence against Rwandans in Zambia in 2016, after false accusations of the implication of Rwandan migrants in ritual murders which had *not* taken place, according to a Zambian police spokeswoman. Other culprits include Cameroon, Côte d'Ivoire and Gabon.

62   Robert D. Lucas, 'Dispelling a Myth About EBOLA', <http://barbadosunderground. wordpress.com/2014/10/14/dispelling-a-myth-about-ebola/>.

kind in Africa – including the independent territories and societies which still pride themselves on their anti-imperialist past – raises similar sets of questions. But there are obvious and not-so-obvious differences between Haitian and continental African circumstances which make the latter's addiction to 'trading with the enemy' even more perverse than the former's. For, the first remarkable fact about Africa's initial 'trading-with-the-enemy' misadventures is that unlike Haiti, which started life as a slave colony in any case, Africa did not have a prior history of trading with the enemy before 'international trade', in the forms of the slave trade and the subsequent imperial division of labour, turned it into a patchwork of slave and vassal states. Nor did Africa need or initiate the 'unequal exchanges' which have always characterized 'trade' with Europe and its New World outposts. As Rodney pointed out, 'the first significant thing about the internationalization of trade in the fifteenth century was that Europeans took the initiative and went to other parts of the world ... and if any African canoes reached the Americas (as is sometimes maintained) they did not establish two-way links. What was called international trade was nothing but the extension overseas of European interests.'[63] The cascading consequences of 'international trade' for Africa included, moreover, not only the loss of sovereignty and dignity (along the lines of post-liberation Haiti) but also food insecurity and the lowering of other quality-of-life indicators for the mass of the people – not unlike Haiti after 'the plan of death'. One proof of the latter is provided by the following summary by Rodney of some of the findings of a global study of hunger by Josué de Castro, the Brazilian scientist:

> (de Castro's) study convincingly indicates that 'African (diets) (were) previously more varied, being based on a more diversified agriculture than was possible under colonialism. In terms of specific nutritional deficiencies, those Africans who suffered most under colonialism were those who were brought most fully into the colonial economy: namely, the urban workers.[64]

63 Walter Rodney, *How Europe Underdeveloped Africa*, 85.
64 Rodney, ibid. 259. Rodney does not provide the details of the study concerned. But based on information from <http://en.wikipedia.org/wiki/Josu%C3%A9_de_Castro#The_Geography_of_Hunger> it is assumed that he was referring to Josué de

Needless to add that based on de Castro's and similar nutrition studies the often repeated or insinuated arguments for keeping Africa within the vicious trading-with-the-enemy circle can be rejected out of hand. When it is conceded, additionally, that good nutrition is a function of economic as well as physical access to the right kinds of food in the right amounts de Castro's observations about how the African people fared better before than after colonization must also expose the insistence on tying Africa's development to the imperial division of labour determined by the 'early developers' as cynical, ignorant or worse.[65]

Imperialism in Haiti as verification of the charge that imperialism knows no law beyond its own interests

Few would deny that the following examples of the treatment of Haiti by France and the United States add weight to the charge that imperialism is shameless and knows no law beyond its own interests:

• The violent French and North Atlantic reactions to the Haitian people's victory in 1804;

• The treatment of the Haitian people when they finally 'chose' integration over liberation in the face of the economic war on them following their victory in the armed struggle;

• The killing by the thousands of Haitians who resisted the US invasion of their country in 1915;[66]

Castro's book, *The Geography of Hunger* (originally published in the US in 1952 and republished by the Monthly Review Press, also in 1952, as *The Geopolitics of Hunger*). See also <http://int.search.tb.ask.com/search/GGmain.jhtml?searchfor=The+Geo politics+of+Hunger&st=tab&ptb=77C6CFA4-A80C-4097-8F77-C6F8EEE943 E5&n=780c280c&ind=2014062604&ct=SS&pg=GGmain&tpr=tabsbsug&p2= %5EXR%5Exdm006%5EYYA%5Egh&si=COHq4tLıl78CFQHlwgodY3sAWw>.

65 For a book-length critique of aspects of the toxic trade myth see Chang, *Bad Samaritans: The Myth of Free Trade and the Secret History of Capitalism.*

66 Chomsky (2006), 153.

- Employment of the Duvalier father and son dictatorships, with their *tonton macoutes*, as agents of indirect American rule;[67]
- The landing in the 1960s of US marines in Haiti during the regime of Papa Doc Duvalier under express orders to help keep him in power, 'so he can serve out his full term in office, and maybe a little longer if everything works out', as the US Colonel who led the operation is reported to have said;[68]
- US sponsorship of Raoul Cedras' coup d'état against President Aristide and the support given to his junta by the Bush I and Bill Clinton regimes, in violation of OAS sanctions;[69]
- The engineered change of Haiti from a rice self-sufficient to an import-dependent country – in the name of a policy of '(relieving) them of the burden of producing their own food', which also happened to be 'good for some of (Clinton's) farmers in Arkansas', in his own words;[70]
- The abduction and forcible removal of President Aristide by the French and the Americans in February 2004 not only from office but from the land of his birth;
- The manoeuvres by which Woodrow Wilson's invasion force succeeded in imposing on Haiti the US-designed constitution that gave US corporations the right to buy up Haiti's lands;[71]
- The breathtaking combination of shamelessness and cynicism which enabled a President Bill Clinton to speak in one and the same interview of 'when we restored President Aristide' after the first US-sponsored coup d'état against him and claim, when asked about his second restoration after the US and France had forced him into exile, that 'that

---

67   For a write-up on the *tonton macoutes* – a special operations unit within the Haitian paramilitary force created in 1959 by François 'Papa Doc' Duvalier as a veritable instrument of state terror – see <https://en.wikipedia.org/wiki/Tonton_Macoute> (accessed 21 June 2015).
68   Brath, op. cit.
69   Chomsky, *Failed States*, op. cit, 153–4.
70   *Democracy Now!*, '"We made a Devil's Bargain"'.
71   For details see quotation from Chomsky (2006), op. cit., 153.

(was) up to the Haitians, including those that (weren't) demonstrating' for his return';[72]

- Conspicuous refusal by the French and the Americans to recognize 'term limits' for themselves as effective rulers of Haiti, contrary to the doctrine of term limits the Americans in particular prescribe for those who are not 'essential royals' or 'good bad guys'; and
- The French refusal of justice to the Haitian people on the reparations debt owed to them.

Thinking through Haiti must necessarily involve determining, in the light of experiences elsewhere in the African and Third Worlds, whether the ruthlessness, shamelessness and single-minded pursuit of imperialist interests at the expense of the interests and very lives of the Haitian people are unique to that country or observable elsewhere. Considering, moreover, the openly racist grounds advanced in the early nineteenth century for the rejection of an independent Haiti – and any 'black state', for that matter – among the comity of nations; the humiliating and debilitating conditions subsequently imposed on it to allow it the indignity of 'flag and anthem' 'independence' while the 'former' colonial master and its allies kept it as a dependency, in the true sense of the word; the power retained by Haiti's historical tormentors to make and unmake its 'governments' and 'its' food and development policies; and the ability of the likes of Huntington and Pat Robertson to taunt it as a kinless country, one nobody wants and worshiper of an unapproved God non-Haitian people of African descent would seem to have a moral, political and intellectual duty to mainstream Haiti's problems as Pan-African problems.

It goes without saying, in this context, that justice to Haiti on the reparation issue deserves to be placed on the agenda of self-respecting Africans and people of African descent everywhere as a Pan-African project.

72 *Democracy Now!*, "'We made a Devil's Bargain'", op. cit.

From colonies, trust territories and protectorates to new partnerships
for Africa's security (NEPAS): Old wines in new bottles?[73]

After NEPAD (the New Partnership for Africa's Development), NEPAS
seems logical enough. NEPAD is official. NEPAS has been germinating
for some time and seems to have fruited in the unmistakable forms of
AU-AFRICOM cooperation on many fronts; AU-NATO collaboration
in the 'war on terror' in Mali; the French military bases across Africa; the
African Union Mission in Somalia (AMISOM); the signing on 8 May
2014 of an agreement formalizing the status of the NATO liaison office
to the African Union Headquarters in Addis Ababa; provision by the US
army of logistics and funding for the Nigeria-led war on Boko Haram,[74] etc.

There is, of course, nothing new about Western armed forces in Africa.
Their use in the conquest, occupation, 'protection', 'policing', and robbing
of Africans across the centuries is, of course, legendary. Their roles in Haiti,
Algeria, Kenya, the robbery of the people of Diego Garcia and other islands
of the Chagos archipelago of their homeland (as *New African*, No. 456 of
November 2006 put it), the violent regime-change operations in Côte
d'Ivoire and Libya, though memorable and by no means pardonable, are
not necessarily the worst of their kind. Nor were these other operations all
dressed up or mistaken in their African theatres as designed for the protection of the host or target populations. But some, such as the episode below,
were – and ended up, by chance or design, as preludes to colonization by
that or other names:

---

73 For a related discussion see Nick Turse, 'The Terror Diaspora: The U.S. Military
    and the Unraveling of Africa', <http://www.tomdispatch.com/blog/175714/nick_
    turse_blowback_central> (accessed 25 January 2016). See also the spread of America's
    defence shields in Africa, as reported in 'How to Disappear Money, Pentagon-Style',
    op. cit.
74 On the last manifestation see Daniel Flynn 'U.S. army to provide equipment, intel-
    ligence to fight Boko Haram', *Reuters*, 17 February 2015, <http://www.reuters.com/
    article/2015/02/18/us-nigeria-violence-usa-idUSKBN0LL0W320150218> (accessed
    20 February 2015) and 'US to fund Nigeria-led force to fight Boko Haram', *Daily
    Graphic*, 17 June 2015.

The majority of the Gold Coast's fortresses were under British control by the early 19th century. Seeking a peaceful environment in which to conduct trade for raw materials, Britain viewed Ashanti efforts to assert dominance as a threat to Britain's commercial interests and began to intervene in local conflicts. The Ashanti, on the other hand, saw British interference in its conquered territories as infringement on its sovereignty and fought back. During a confrontation in 1824, the Ashanti army routed a British force and killed its commander, Charles MacCarthy, the colonial governor of Sierra Leone. In 1826 the Ashanti launched an offensive against British coastal positions. They suffered high casualties and were turned back by an alliance of British and Danish troops in a fierce battle on the plains near Accra. The Ashanti signed a peace treaty with Britain in 1831. The subsequent peace coincided with a period of increased European Christian missionary work in the region.

In 1844 the British signed a political agreement with a confederation of Fante states. Known as the Bond of 1844, the agreement extended British protection to the signatory states and gave Britain a degree of authority over them. In subsequent years, additional coastal and interior states signed the Bond. Britain bought all of Denmark's Gold Coast territory in 1850 and purchased the Dutch fort at Elmina in 1872[75]

The upshot of the manoeuvring and treatying is that the Fantes became colonial subjects by treaty and the Ashantis by conquest. The Northern Territories were to be added to Britain's trophies in that part of the world as a British protectorate in 1902. Those who lived through the sophistry until 1957 (year of the colonial Gold Coast's rebranding as independent Ghana) and well beyond also knew, however, that the modes of Britain's acquisitions of its various possessions in the Gold Coast –and their formal designations – mattered less in the lives of the colonial subjects within the various provinces than the division of labour organized for them in the service of British interests. But even without personal experience of life in the Gold Coast it would take extraordinary naivety – or cynicism – to argue that the specializations of the Gold Coast colony and parts of Trans-Volta Togoland in the production and supply of administrative and technical staff to man the colonial services, of the then Ashanti province in the production of commodities required by Britain and British-approved export destinations and of the Northern Territories as 'labour reserves' were done for the good

75   <http://www.countriesquest.com/africa/ghana/history/the_british-ashanti_wars. htm> (accessed 31 May 2015; author and other publication details not specified).

of the natives concerned. Across Africa as a whole none can seriously argue, either, that the other colonial types identified by Samir Amin by 'mode of colonial exploitation' were cast by imperialism in their respective roles for their own good.[76] What is indisputable, on the other hand, is the role of force, disguised in many cases as 'security' or 'policing' assistance or cooperation, in establishing and maintaining Africans and various African territories within the colonial-neo-colonial-international division of labour.

Regardless of this history and its lessons, African leaders continued to place their countries and the region under the 'protection' of the West, as of the year 2015. Britain's BBC informed Africans and the world on 29 May 2015, for example, that 'Spain (had) agreed to host a US rapid reaction military force to deal with crises in Africa, Europe and the Middle East'.[77] And the African people paid the price, as usual: the low-intensity traditional conflicts between Somali nationalism and Kenyan and Ethiopia nationalisms were transformed into deadly guerrilla or 'terrorist' wars between Somalia's al-Shabab fighters and Ethiopian and Kenyan armies with deadly spill-over effects on ordinary people, courtesy of the sponsored Kenyan and Ethiopian invasions of Somalia and the engineered conflation of traditional Somali nationalism with Islamism –for the benefit of the US, and therefore Western, 'war on terror'.[78] The issue is for how long the African people will allow 'their leaders' to get away with such recklessness!

Separating the effects of 'the hate' from those of 'the quake' in damage assessments and response strategies

As Hilary Beckles observed in his post-2010-Haitian-earthquake think piece:

---

76   Samir Amin, 'Underdevelopment and Dependence in Black Africa.

77   <http://www.bbc.com/news/world-europe-32929930>.

78   For a scholarly perspective on some of the issues see Osman Abdi Mohamed, 'Beyond the Dominant Terrorist Narrative', *The Thinker*, Vol. 64, Quarter 2, 2015. For an all-African perspective see *Pambazuka News*, 757: *Terrorism as Empire's New Tool*, 15 January 2016.

The sudden quake [came] in the aftermath of summers of hate. In many ways the quake has been less destructive than the hate. Human life was snuffed by the quake, while the hate has been a long and inhumane suffocation – a crime against humanity.[79]

Amy Goodman also definitely hit the nail on the head when she pointed out that 'earthquakes alone do not create disasters on the scale ... experienced in Haiti (in 2010)', and added the following man-made causes of the 'natural disaster':

Loans from the World Bank, the International Monetary Fund (IMF) and the Inter-American Development Bank (IDB) imposed 'structural adjustment conditions on Haiti, opening the economy to cheap U.S. agricultural products. Farmers, unable to compete, stopped growing rice and moved to the cities to earn low wages, if they were lucky enough to get one of the scarce sweatshop jobs. People in the highlands were driven to deforest the hills, converting wood into saleable charcoal, which created an ecological crisis – destabilizing hillsides, increasing the destructiveness of earthquakes and causing landslides during the rainy season.[80]

Nourbese Philip's note, from her knowledge of indigenous Caribbean culture, on how contemptuous rejection of the Haitian people's native knowhow and the imposition on them of an inappropriate modernity added greatly to the loss of lives when the earthquake struck throws even more light on problem. As she put it:

There was a time when our Caribbean houses kept faith with wood, whether one-room homes –some call them chattel house – or larger, more graceful estate houses. Time was when the thatched Ajoupa bequeathed us by Taino, Arawak and Carib would have swayed to the groans of the earth as she eased her suffering, opening herself along her wounded fault lines to the ever blue skies, the constant love of the sun, to release all her pent up grief for us, birthing we don't yet know what. Time was when hands steeped in skills of building homes brought from a homeland a slap, kick and a howl way, across a rolling ocean, would have gently patted mud over wattle, weaving branches to create cool interiors, shaping shelters from the earth that would not, could not, betray the safety in home to crush, obliterate, to fall down around our ears.[81]

---

79   Beckles, op. cit.
80   Goodman, 'Haiti, Forgive Us'.
81   Nourbese Philip, 'Letter to Haiti', *New Legon Observer* 4/1, 25 February 2010, 13.

Continental Africa has had its own share of empire-made disasters masquerading as natural disasters. Below, for instance, is how the authoritative Comité d'Information Sahel saw the devastating famine of the 1970s in that region of Africa:

> Africa's ... famine disaster cannot be attributed solely to bad weather. It is as much, if not more, the result of colonial 'development' policy which successor independence regimes have continued. What development? It is a process of the development of regional disparities, of urban development at the expense of the rural areas, of privileges for some, of profiteering by transnational corporations and their local allies and, on the opposite side of the coin, of the impoverishment of the peasantry, soil degradation, the marginalization of food cultivation and the rise in unemployment.[82]

In more recent times 'the severe drought in the Horn of Africa, which ... caused the death of at least 30,000 children and affected some 12 million people, especially in Somalia, (is said to have been) a direct consequence of weather phenomena associated with climate change and global warming'.[83] The only thing that may be worse than such preventable man-made disasters is failure to learn from them!

The hate, the quake and Africa's shame

Continental Africa's failure to bond more directly and closely with its own Diaspora meant, *inter alia*, that when the quake struck in 2010 its responses were all too obviously based on misinformation from the rubble of imperial propaganda about the quake itself and the 'hate' which has been the Haitian people's lot throughout their existence. Not surprisingly, therefore, 'Africa' offered them pity, rather than solidarity, in the wake of the quake.

---

82   Comité d'Information Sahel, *Qui se nourrit de la famine en Afrique?* (Paris: François Maspero, 1975), 15 (unofficial translation by the author).

83   Julio Godoy, 'Africa: Global Warming behind Somali Drought', *IPS*, 26 August 2011, <http://www.ipsnews.net/2011/08/global-warming-behind-somali-drought> (accessed 30 April 2014).

The condolence letter sent by the Chairman of the Commission of the AU to the Secretary-General of the United Nations following the quake was, in the circumstance, as ill-informed as it was scandalous in its claim that:

> The earthquake hit Haiti at a time when the country was making progress in the social and economic fields, with the support of the United Nations and other members of the international community. [84]

The AU Commission took the opportunity of the earthquake to cover itself in infamy twice, in fact. While the message to the UN quoted above endorsed 'the plan of death' by implication a direct AU message conveying its 'heartfelt condolences to the people and Government of Haiti and (assurance) of AU solidarity in this moment of enormous suffering and hardships' failed to join the continental body to the Haitian people's struggle for the recovery of the reparations debt owed them by France and which they needed after the quake more than ever for their reconstruction and development.[85]

Senegalese President Abdoulaye Wade's offer to resettle interested Haitians in his country and appeal to other African countries to 'make room for victims of Haiti's earthquake to restart their lives on the continent from where their ancestors were snatched as slaves' was, in the circumstances, more fitting.[86] But even he would not, or could not, use the occasion to offer the militant solidarity of his country with the Haitian people on the reparations issue or call for continental action on it. The charitable, but not-so-flattering, view of Africa's failure or refusal to take up the reparation issue is that it is off their radar because 'the international press', the 'world's radios', the 'human rights organizations' and 'the world' (on which Africa appears to depend for its worldview) have kept it so. But it would be just as reasonable to read into it

---

84   African Union Commission, 'Haiti earthquake', 14 January 2010, <http://appablog. wordpress.com/2010/01/14/Haiti-earthquake-chairperson-of-the-african-union-commission-auc-condolence-letter/> (accessed 18 August 2014).

85   See <http://www.normangirvan.info/wp-content/uploads/2010/01/au-the_press_ release.pdf> for the full text of the AU solidarity statement.

86   *AFP*, 'Resettle Haitians in Africa: Senegal President', 17 January 2010, <http://www.the freelibrary.com/Resettle+Haitians+in+Africa%3A+Senegal+president-a01612121133> (accessed 18 August 2014).

the moral cowardice or impotence of continental and 'national' leaders who cannot afford to antagonize France, a 'world power' and their 'development partner', on a subject it wishes the world to treat as taboo.[87]

By the same token it is difficult to see how Africans, other people of African descent across the world and, indeed, decent humanity at large can continue to treat the issue of 'reverse-reparation' for Haiti as a non-issue or a taboo subject without objectively identifying with the French position on it.

Unkindest cuts: Treatment of Haitians and people of Haitian descent in neighbouring Dominican Republic

When Samuel Huntington wrote that Haiti was 'the neighbour nobody (wanted)' there is little or no indication that he thought he spoke for the Dominican Republic, the state Haiti shares the island of Hispaniola with as well. The state-sponsored 'xenophobia' against people of Haitian descent in the Dominican Republic, including Dominican citizens, described below suggests, at the very least, that 'Haitians' are 'neighbours' or 'others' the Dominican Republic does not want, regardless of their status:

> The (Dominican apartheid) policy, resulting from a 2013 Constitutional Court ruling ... stipulates that Haitian-descendant Dominicans lacking documentation of their citizenship or immigration status are to be treated like first-generation Haitian migrants, subjected to arrest and deportation across the eastern border to Haiti.
>
> Without precise census data, it is difficult to know exactly how many people of Haitian descent live and work in the Dominican Republic (DR). Minority Rights Group International places the figure anywhere between 700,000 and 1 million, of which 250,000 were born and raised in the Dominican Republic.

87 *Al Jazeera* reports pointedly on this issue that during the first ever visit by a French President to France's former slave colony – an under four-hour whistle stop in February 2010, a month after the quake, that is – then French President Nicolas Sarkozy claimed that '(France was) staring at history in its face, (France) (had) not discarded it and (France) assume(d) responsibility', but when asked by *Al Jazeera* about the issue of reparations for Haiti's post-independence payments to France he appeared dismissive': 'non, non, non ...', he said. See <http://www.aljazeera.com/news/ameri cas/2010/02/20102171611239534477.html> (accessed 31 May 2015).

The vast majority are undocumented workers who came to find employment on sugar plantations, in household labour or in construction jobs, often encouraged by Dominican companies and the Dominican military.

In response to popular outcry and international pressures, the administration of President Danilo Medina in 2014 passed a law amending the court policy, which allows Dominicans born to undocumented Haitian migrants to begin a new 'path to citizenship' by handing in their birth certificates and registering for temporary visas. Many prominent Dominican leaders praised this reform, including New York state Sen. Adriano Espaillat, himself a first-generation immigrant to the U.S.

But most Dominico-Haitians are denied state certificates at birth by racist and xenophobic bureaucrats. This maltreatment is so rampant that – even amid the present panic to remain legally in the country – only 300 people have received visas out of an estimated 250,000 who attempted to apply.

The new regulations not only threaten mass deportations in the near future, but they also lay the basis for a codified apartheid state. In all likelihood, many thousands of Haitian descendant workers will remain in the country. Employers depend on them for cheap, unprotected labour in order to threaten other Dominican workers with dismissal when they fight for higher pay and more rights.[88]

Unpleasant and discriminatory as the situation which Dorian Bon describes obviously is, the 'apartheid' label may be something of a verbal overkill. More importantly, the mixed-race Dominican Republic is definitely not alone in treating other black or mixed-race peoples, especially of African descent, as unwanted neighbours. As noted above Ghana, Nigeria, Cameroon, Côte d'Ivoire, Gabon, South Africa and Zambia, to name but a few, have been just as guilty or worse.

In place of the shame, impotent rage, AU-like pathetic pleas for 'understanding' and calls for solidarity (based on skin colour or common African ancestry) which have tended to greet outbursts of Afro-phobia in too many pockets of the African world, results-oriented Pan-Africanists may wish to explore possibilities for converting the latent community of people of common skin colour or common African ancestry into a global community or commonwealth in which class and nationality are no barriers to

---

88   Dorian Bon, 'Dominican apartheid: Made in the USA', 23 June 2015, <http://social istworker.org/2015/06/23/dominican-apartheid-made-in-the-usa> (accessed 23 June 2015).

co-prosperity, community welfare and common defence. Africans would not be the first to invent or re-invent a race or community for themselves. A future Pan-African community – or even race – may wish to distinguish itself, however, as the first or among the first of its kind to forswear hegemonistic, supremacist or aggressive ambitions of any kind.

CHAPTER 3

Democracy versus the People: African Edition[1]

Democracy is government of the people, by the people and for the people.

— ABRAHAM LINCOLN

Freedom in capitalist society always remains about the same as it was in ancient Greek republics: Freedom for slave owners.

— VLADIMIR ILYICH LENIN

A democracy is a system in which you are free to do whatever you like as long as you do what we tell you.

— NOAM CHOMSKY[2]

1   It would be evident to those familiar with President Dwight D. Eisenhower's famous Military-Industrial Complex Speech (available at: <http://coursesa.matrix.msu. edu/~hst306/documents/indust.html> (accessed 4 July 2015)) and other relevant literature that the victims of the 'democracy fraud' are, in the first place, those who are directly short-changed by it (wherever they may be and whether or not they are aware of the fraud) as well as all who innocently extol actually existing oligarchies and kleptocracies, for instance, as 'democracies' in the Lincolnian sense. The literature of special interest includes, Chomsky, 'Secrets, Lies and Democracy' (134–205) in *How the World Works*; Chomsky, *Failed States: The Abuse of Power and the Assault on Democracy*; Dan Hind, T*he Return of the Public*; Naomi Klein, *The Shock Doctrine*; Charles H. Ferguson, *Predator Nation*; Colin Leys, *Market-Driven Politics: Neoliberal Democracy and the Public Interest* London: Verso, 2003); Sharon Beder, *Free Market Missionaries: The Corporate Manipulation of Community Values* (London: Earthscan, 2006); and Colin Leys, *Total Politics: Market Politics, Market State* (Monmouth: Merlin Press, 2008)

2   Chomsky, *Imperial Ambitions*, op. cit., 79.

Gunboat and fraudulent democratization: Another
dependent development project for the benefit of the
developer

Notwithstanding legitimate questions about Abraham Lincoln's own democratic credentials, based on his use of the words 'the people' few would
openly question the democratic ideal set out by the sixteenth President of
the United States in the above quotation. It is, indeed, a measure of the
problem of democracy in 'the global village' that it is promoted in target
countries by those whose 'you-are-free-to-do-whatever-you-like-as-long-
as-you-do-what-we-tell-you' philosophy and practice make government of
the people, by the people and for the people impossible for peoples they
choose to impose on: their practice of undermining the will of the people
when it proves inconvenient, sometimes using so-called 'democracy promotion' agencies as we saw in Haiti is, indeed, one measure of how 'democracy'
has been used to 'disenfranchise' people of the wrong skin colour or class.
Lenin's observation about 'freedom' quoted above and Amin's on the contradiction between globalization and democracy were thus merely stating
the obvious.[3] What ought to matter more to genuine democrats, however,
is not what is genuine or fake democracy or freedom by the standards of
Lincoln, Lenin, Amin, Chomsky or anyone else but what is said and done
in democracy's name – and how they impact on a people's ability to govern
themselves and for themselves. That notwithstanding, logic, not Lincoln
or Amin (ibid.), makes government of the people, by the people and for
the people incompatible with government to suit the tastes or serve the
interests of outsiders, no matter who they are or what cloaks they wear. But
the 'contradictions' are particularly sharp when the 'democratizing' agents
or 'democracy police' have the history and posture in Africa that the West
has – and are easily understood if regarded as the twists and turns of an

---

[3]   Samir Amin, 'Mondialisation et démocratie, une contradiction majeure de notre
        époque', *Recherches Internationales*, 55 (1999).

imperial power which knows no law beyond its selfish interests but also knows how to vary its orders as new circumstances demand. Thus understood there should be no mystery about the same power which determined in 1962 that 'a change brought about through force by non-communist elements may be preferable to prolonged deterioration of government effectiveness ... (and added that) it is U.S. policy, when it is in the U.S. interest, to make the local military and police advocates of democracy and agents for carrying forward the developmental process'[4] threatening brimstone and fire on 'those who would derail the democratic process (in Africa)', as the Obama White House did fifty years later through the selfsame National Security Council.[5] The following observations by de Mesquita and Smith resolve the 'contradictions' in even more concrete terms:

> Almost every US president has argued that he wants to foster democracy in the world. However, the same US presidents have had no problem undermining democratic, or democratizing, regimes when the people of those nations elect leaders to implement policies US voters don't like ...
>
> Undermining democracy was the story behind US opposition to the Congo's first democratically elected Prime Minister, Patrice Lumumba. He was elected in June 1960 and he was murdered on January 17, 1961, just half a year later. Lumumba ran into difficulty with the Western democracies because of the policies he adopted; not because he usurped power. He spoke out vehemently against the years of Belgian rule over the Congo. In a speech during Congo's independence celebration less than a week after his election as prime minister, Lumumba announced, 'Nous ne sommes plus vos singes' [We are no longer your monkeys] ... The massive bulk of evidence today points to US and Belgian complicity in Lumumba's murder. Later the United States would become closely associated with the Congo's (that is, Zaire's) Mobutu Sese Seko who, unlike Lumumba, was neither democratic nor pro-Soviet.[6]

---

4 National Security Council, 'U.S. Overseas Internal Defense Policy', 1 August 1962. Quoted in Prashad, *The Darker* Nations, op. cit. 141 from Gabriel Kolko, *Confronting the Third World: United States Foreign Policy, 1945–1980* (New York: Pantheon, 1988), 133.

5 *US Strategy Toward Sub-Saharan Africa* (Washington, DC: The White House, June 2012), op. cit.

6 Bruce Bueno de Mesquita and Alastair Smith, *The Dictator's Handbook: Why Bad Behaviour is Almost Always Good Politics* (2011), 191–2.

With so much cynicism packed into the above history – not to mention the fact that in Africa and elsewhere some 'brutal dictators' and others who 'derail democratic processes' are sanctioned and even overthrown by the global democracy police and its 'pro-democracy' agents while others of the same category are quietly or loudly celebrated – the conclusion seems irresistible that 'democracy' is not what it used to be and is now a born-again tool selectively employed by born-again civilizing missionaries pursuing the same interests which unite the authors of the US National Security strategy documents of 1962 and 2012. For reasons which should be obvious to students of African elite collaboration with imperialism and indeed slavery itself this conclusion cannot be said to be invalidated by the fact that the born-again civilizing missionaries are partnered in their democratization fraud by the black empowered and cosmopolitan middle classes of Africa. But for those who wish to see a peoples-empowering and therefore truly democratic Africa awareness that the globalizers' 'democracy' is 'bogus and fraudulent' should be a defence against yet another Trojan ideology and movement.

The 'new democracy': The dual-mandate trail, primitive and neoliberal imperialism and the logic of the absurd

It is perhaps not within the competence of non-initiates to fully understand the mindset and the 'logic of the absurd' which enabled white race authority to grant itself the right and responsibility it has enjoyed since colonial times to make and unmake governments in Africa and the Diaspora.[7] What is obvious to all and undeniable is the fact that while the authority's armed intervention in Côte d'Ivoire in and around 2011 to settle its post-2010

7   It is conceded upfront that no distinction is recognized here between the traditional 'dual mandate', the 'white man's burden' and the 'civilizing mission' and the 'modern' 'right and duty to interfere' (*le droit d'ingérence*) which has been employed to justify the new imperialism's' 'humanitarian and 'democratic' interventions.

election dispute in favour of France's darling there was possibly the first to be presented as an act of democracy policing it is certainly not the first or sole act of imperial government reshuffling and application of 'the logic of the absurd' in nominally independent Africa.[8] Examples of similar conduct before the Ivorian drama include:

1. The overthrows of Kwame Nkrumah's government in Ghana in 1966,[9] of Milton Obote of Uganda's government in 1971[10] and Jean-Bertrand Aristide (twice);
2. The 1983 US-led invasion, counter-revolution and regime change in Maurice Bishop's Grenada; and
3. The many assassinations, coup d'états and other Western interventions in Africa exposed in Ellen Ray, William Schaap, Karl van Meter and Louis Wolf, eds, *Dirty Work 2*.[11]

In the neoliberal age the dual-mandate trail, old-fashioned and Robert Cooper's 'new liberal imperialism' and various applications of the logic of the absurd have tended to appear more often than not in cloaks of democratic and humanitarian righteousness, however. The case of Zimbabwe – where so-called targeted sanctions, psychological pressure, diplomatic isolation, travel bans and crude meddling in domestic politics have been employed in the name of democracy but for the unmistakable purpose of disrupting a lands restitution programme over which a war of national liberation had been fought – is, perhaps, the perfect example of what Robert Cooper must have meant by 'deception' in 'new liberal imperialism's tool kit. Not far behind, however, have been other applications of the 'before independence = after

---

8   For a review of how the 'logic of the absurd' was employed in Côte d'Ivoire see Pierre Sané , 'Cote d'Ivoire : The Logic of the Absurd?', *Pambazuka News*, 520, 10 March 2011, <http://pambazuka.org/en/category/features/71588>.
9   See John Stockwell, *In Search of Enemies: A CIA Story*, New York, W.W. Norton and Company, 1978.
10   Pat Hutton and Jonathan Bloch, 'How the West Established Idi Amin and Kept Him There', in Ellen Ray, William Schaap, Karl van Meter and Louis Wolf, eds, *Dirty Work 2*.
11   Bruce Bueno de Mesquita and Alastair Smith, op. cit.

independence' (*'avant l'indépendance égal après l'indépendance'*) principle
such as the threats by David Cameron and Barack Obama to cut off aid to
Uganda and Ghana (and other African countries thereafter) if they did not
treat the American declaration that 'gay rights are human rights and human
rights are gay rights' as binding on themselves.[12] Needless to add that a whole
army of acknowledged and unacknowledged 'force multipliers' – ranging
from the World Bank, the IMF and the EU through a variety of so-called
'development' and advocacy NGOs, 'the World's Radios' to Credit Rating
Agencies, etc., and the 'idiotic neo-colonial states' – do their best to ensure
that the use of imperial armed forces to police the new global order and its
'democracies' is kept to the absolute minimum.

*Keeping the 'political compromise' active in the era of 'the new liberal
imperialism'*

It seems safe to assume that those who benefit from the frailties and services
of Africa's 'idiotic neo-colonial states' and 'crumb-hungry Africans ready to
destroy (Africa) for unthinking profit'[13] know as well as Cabral did that 'in
spite of their armed forces, the imperialists cannot do without traitors.[14] It
is just as obvious from their actions that these beneficiaries also know that
the 'traitors' who man the 'looting machines' need and demand carrots and
sticks for their services.[15] The following, in consequence, appear to be what
may be described as unwritten supplements to the political compromise
described by Wallerstein for the age of neo-colonialism and globalization:

12   Quoted by Ernesto Londoño in 'America's Global Campaign for Gay Rights', 26
      May 2016, <https://www.google.com.gh/?gfe_rd=cr&ei=htpIV8yROM2IOs3m
      qLgL&gws_rd=ssl#q=America%E2%80%99s+Global+Campaign+for+Gay+Ri
      ghts> from a declaration by then US Secretary of State, Hillary Clinton in Geneva.
13   Armah, *Osiris Rising*, op. cit.
14   Amilcar Cabral, 'Guinea and Cabo Verde Against Portuguese Colonialism' in Amilcar
      Cabral (1974), op. cit, 14.
15   On 'the looting machine' see Tom Burgis, *The Looting Machine: Warlords, Tycoons,
      Smugglers and the Systematic Theft of Africa's Wealth* (New York: Public Affairs, 2015).

1. The outsourcing of routine military aspects of policing the 'world' and local looting machines to local militaries and their officers and men whose benefits include sweeteners like lucrative overseas training, modern weapons and logistics, lucrative international 'peacekeeping' and war-on-terror assignments, political influence for top brasses and, in some cases, illicit business and self-enrichment opportunities;

2. Insulation of cooperating 'governments' and 'opposition' 'politicians' from effective local sanctions – no matter how corrupt, incompetent and brutal they may be – as long as they perform to the satisfaction of their external patrons; and

3. External partnerships and patronage for established and aspiring non-political sector members of the cosmopolitan middle class such as business men and women, industrialists and members of the 'liberal professions' with international career or 'world-class' recognition ambitions.

Destroying African lands and peoples for 'unthinking profit': A case study from the 'non-political' sector

The following lamentation in the online magazine, *MG – MODERN GHANA* may or may not be wholly factual: it has not been independently verified. But it is published below, in full and unedited, except for slight changes to hide identities where necessary and appropriate, because third parties familiar with corruption in their corners of globalized Africa have passed it as consistent with their own observations and otherwise familiar with the phenomenon:

Ghana, The Begging Millionaire – Africa, The Begging Trillionaire

Recently, I witnessed in dismay a tirade by a white man in the first class cabin of a mid-size airplane, admonishing another first class passenger, a Ghanaian male, for 'begging' for his seat. 'What is wrong with you Africans? All you do is beg, beg, beg for everything!! You can beg all you want; I am not going to give you my seat'. Tempers finally cooled down, and the aircraft took off. Unfortunately,

I was sitting next to this white man who, a few minutes ago, had insulted my whole race. With nothing else to do, I turned and asked him 'what was all that about'? Apparently, the Ghanaian man was travelling with his 'wife'; they had been seated in 1st class on separate rows, and apart. The man had asked this white man to exchange his seat, so the couple could be close. The white man had refused, but the Ghanaian man had persisted with numerous 'I beg you'; which eventually took the white man to his boiling point. 'So what would it have cost you to exchange your seat?' I asked. His response, the essence of this chapter was this: 'I booked my flight the last minute, and got the last 1st class seat available, this one. This means it was also available to this man, if only he had asked to be seated close to his wife. He did not, but now comes "begging" for what WAS DUE HIM in the first place.' 'That still shouldn't get your collar up', I said. 'You may be right; unfortunately, I have just finished a month long negotiations with your Ministers and Government officials over your god given mineral rights, and what my gold mining company should pay.'

'I come to your country, see all this poverty everywhere, with wealth right under your feet. Your own government gives only foreign companies the rights and privileges to rape and steal your country blind. For a few thousand dollars, your government officials allow these foreign companies to walk away with: (a) Perpetual tax holidays, (b) Duty free imports, (c) Bloated capital and operational investment costs, (d) under-declared mineral output, (e) minimum wages for local employees doing all the work, but FAT salaries and expense accounts for foreigners who do almost nothing; (f) exaggerated cost of shoddy school blocks and boreholes instead of meaningful royalty to local land owners and communities; (g) destruction of local farm lands with pitiful resettlement payments; (h) pollution of local drinking water; (i) destruction of local infrastructure, etc.

'My bosses had counselled me at a briefing before my departure. I was asked to read your Osageyefo's "Neo-Colonialism". Then I was told: "be prepared, and the first, to offer the negotiating team, (a) a few thousand dollars each; (b) a center, or a 6-room school block, or a few bore holes for the community. And there will be no mention of the usual above 10% royalties, or an actual government oversight of our operations, or adequate resettlement compensations, etc.' (Sic)

'I did not believe my bosses since I, a mere high school graduate, was coming to deal with officials with Masters and Doctorate degrees. Imagine my shock and disappointment when these officials, instead of demanding what is INTERNATIONALLY ACCEPTABLE COMPENSATIONS AND ROYALTIES for their country and communities, only accepted the 3% royalties, and with ALL KINDS OF GIVEAWAYS, and then came to me later BEGGING me to deposit "something" in their foreign accounts (numbers written on pieces of paper). I do not want to hear the phrase "I beg you" again.'

'The irony here is that these so called educated people, after negotiating away the country's wealth, and depositing their "somethings" into foreign banks, turn round to go and BORROW their own money from the IMF, World Bank, or "Donor" countries/ "Development Partners". Do you remember the number of PhD beneficiaries, and the destinations of the Mabey & Johnson kickbacks?[16] It amazes me that your intelligentsia, Ministers and Presidents, who have studied, or have travelled overseas still don't get the idea that "THERE IS NO FREE LUNCH". THERE ARE NO "DONOR COUNTRIES" OR "DEVELOPMENT PARTNERS". THE FOREIGN MINING COMPANIES TAKE YOUR MINERALS FOR NEXT TO NOTHING, DEPOSIT THEIR HAUL INTO THEIR BANKS, AND THEN TURN ROUND TO LOAN THE SAME TO OUR GOVERNMENTS, AGAIN WITH REDICULOUS (sic) CONDITIONS. SUCH AS "NO SUBSIDIZED" BASIC EDUCATION'.

'Surely, companies like Anglogold and Newmont are contributing to our economy', I offered.

'At what price? Have you been to Obuasi recently to see the devastation and destruction of once a beautiful city? Newmont has over 740 sq. km concession in Ahafo; what did the Ahafo's get in return for Newmont's ANNUAL revenues of over $750,000,000? Almost NOTHING!!'

'This is exactly what your first President was talking about in "Neo-Colonialism."'
'Have you read that book?', he asked me. I was ashamed to answer 'No'. 'I don't blame you; none of your "Educated" officials at the negotiating table had read it. That book ought to be a must-read textbook in your schools and colleges, so that you can understand how foreign companies and governments strive to rob you blind, just as before. Only this time, their methods are cloaked in one-sided "agreements" with the connivance of your "Educated" Managing Directors, Ministers, and Presidents.' 'How can you accuse our officials of complicity?', I asked defensively. 'Has your media asked why ... can you imagine these foreign companies, under the watchful eyes of your govt. officials, paying the indigene 5 pesewa (GhC 0.05) ground rent for their acre of concessional land after they have hauled away GhC 1,000,000 from the same acre?'

'THE BIG COMPANIES ... ARE NOT EVEN ASHAMED TO CONNIVE WITH YOUR GOVT OFFICIALS TO SIDESTEP PAYING THE INCREASED 5% ROYALTY. THEY ARE PAYING THE 5% BASED ON ANCIENT GOLD PRICE OF $300.00/OZ INSTEAD OF THE CURRENT WORLDWIDE PRICE OF $1500.00/OZ., SHORTCHANGING YOUR PEOPLE $75,000,000

---

16 The bridge-building firm, Mabey and Johnson, is said to have been the first major British company to be convicted of foreign bribery. Many of its contracts were reportedly supported, financially, by the British taxpayer. See David Leigh and Rob Evans, 'British firm Mabey and Johnson convicted of bribing foreign politicians', *The Guardian*, 25 September 2009, <http://www.theguardian.com/business/2009/sep/25/mabey-johnson-foreign-bribery> (accessed 1 July 2014).

in the process. Unfortunately, your negotiating officials are happy to giggle to the foreign banks with their thousands, accompanied in some cases by (dubious honours).'

'Even the Chinese are getting in on the act, albeit ILLEGALLY. They are threatening communities with guns and firepower, AND YOUR MILITARY LOOKS ON UNCONCERNED. Your media is just as bad. With buffet lunches or dinners and a few Cedis in their pockets, your print media become the propaganda machines of these mining companies. They tout the few boreholes and the 6-room schools, but leave out the callous treatment of local employees and residents, and the destruction of the environment. The airwaves are SILENT on all this. WACAM IS THE LONE VOICE FOR THE PEOPLE. Why don't your media SUPPORT WACAM by broadcasting and educating the masses, especially the officials that (a) THE UNITED NATIONS DOES NOT APPROVE OF FOREIGN COMPANIES ROBBING THE INDEGENES FULL BENEFITS OF THEIR GOD GIVEN MINERAL AND OIL DEPOSITS. (b) Before Rawlings, foreign mining companies in Ghana could not hold more than 40% interest in their partnership with the government; now the Ghana govt. holds ZERO percent, while they hold 100%; and therefore do not account to any authority.'

'A 50% annual return on investment (ROI) for the first 7 years is generally considered EXCELLENT. Foreign mining/ oil companies in Ghana and the rest of Africa, are PERPETUALLY hauling away over 400% return on their investments, without any regard to the plight of the indigenes.'

I feigned sleep, so he stopped talking. I was actually reflecting on all that he had said. I realized that YES, we had become too 'give me, give me'; 'I beg', 'I beg you'; 'My Christmas box'; 'Give us something for water'.

I am reminded by this my brother's analogy (sic). His cat will 'meow' for some food, usually crumbs, in his bowl outside. The bowl of food will attract the resident mice. One would think the cat would opt for the juicy mice, NOO. He would lay there and watch the mouse eat all his food, and then come back 'Meowing' for more crumbs.

WE WATCH OUR OFFICIALS GIVE AWAY OUR GOLD, OIL, BAUXITE, DIAMOND, ETC FOR THEIR MEAGRE KICKBACKS, WHILE WE WALLOW IN POVERTY. IT IS TIME WE WAKE UP FROM OUR SLUMBER, AND TAKE WHAT IS RIGHTFULLY OURS AT THE NEGOTIATING TABLE. AT THAT TIME, WE CAN TELL OBAMA AND CAMERON TO TAKE BACK THEIR GAYS AND AID.[17]

It is, perhaps, best to let the story speak for itself.

---

17   Nana Kofi, 'Ghana, The Begging Millionaire – Africa, The Begging Trillionaire', *Modern Ghana*, 2 February 2012, <http://www.modernghana.com/news/375003/1/ ghana-the-begging-millionaire-africa-the-begging-t.html>.

'Butlerism' without Butler: Another man's account of racketeering for capitalism in a neoliberized African 'democracy' under orders from a 'force multiplier'

The following observations by Craig Murray, former Deputy British High Commissioner to Ghana, on IMF-led 'energy-sector reforms' in 'the first African country south of the Sahara to achieve independence from colonial rule' suggests that '(racketeering) for capitalism' did not end with Butler and the US military occupation of Haiti he began in 1915:

Just ten years ago,[18] Ghana had the most reliable electricity supply in all of Africa and the highest percentage of households connected to the grid in all of Africa – including South Africa. The Volta River Authority, the power producer and distributor was, in my very considerable experience, the best run and most efficient public utility in all of Africa. Indeed it was truly world class, and Ghana was proud of it.

Obviously the sight of truly successful public owned and run enterprise was too much of a threat to the neo-liberal ideologues of the IMF and World Bank. When Ghana needed some temporary financial assistance (against a generally healthy background) the IMF insisted that VRA be broken up. Right wing neo-liberal dogma was applied to the Ghanaian electricity market. Electricity was separated between production and distribution, and private sector Independent Power Producers introduced.

The result is disaster. There are more power cuts in Ghana than ever in its entire history as an independent state. Today Ghana is actually, at this moment, producing just 900 MW of electricity – half what it could produce ten years ago. This is not the fault of the NDC or the NPP. It is the fault of the IMF.

Those private sector Independent Power Producers actually provide less than 20% of electricity generation into the grid – yet scoop up over 60% of the revenues! The electricity bills of Ghana's people go to provide profits to fat cat foreign corporations and of course the western banks who finance them.

Indeed in thirty years close experience the net result of all IMF activity in Africa is to channel economic resources to westerners – and not to ordinary western people, but to the wealthiest corporations and especially to western bankers.

Not content with the devastation they have already caused, the IMF and the USA are now insisting on the privatisation of ECG, the state utility body which provides

18   Murray was writing in June 2015.

electricity to the consumer and bills them. The rationale is that a privatised ECG will be more efficient and ruthless in collecting revenue from the poor and from hospitals, clinics, schools and other state institutions.

Doubtless it will be. It will of course be more efficient in channelling still more profits to very rich businessmen and bankers. I suspect that is the real point.[19]

Murray's concerns are understandable, and can be easily appreciated by the many in Ghana who suffered planned power cuts and other assaults for the years leading up to 2016 and were bemused by rumours which persisted into that year of the privatization or commercialization of the state electricity power distributor. But they do not go to the heart of the many problems raised by the influence in Ghana and Africa, for that matter, of 'the neoliberal ideologues of the IMF and the World Bank'. Nor do they absolve the local 'power elite' through which that power is transmitted much too readily. Among the issues thus too carelessly ignored or brushed aside are:

- The source and extent of the power of the neoliberal ideologues and authoritatively outed force multipliers to 'ruin Ghana', as the title of his piece suggests, and intoxicate Africa, as Adesina (op. cit.) and many others have suggested;
- What that power says about who really rules Ghana and Africa; and
- How to understand, characterize and respond to the governance system which parades in neoliberalized and globalized Africa as democracy.

19   Craig Murray, 'IMF and USA set to ruin Ghana', <https://www.craigmurray. org.uk/archives/2015/06/imf-and-usa-set-to-ruin-ghana/>. Also available at <http://graphic.com.gh/features/opinion/45619-imf-and-usa-set-to-ruin-ghana-craig-murray-writes.html> and <http://www.ghanaweb.com/GhanaHomePage/NewsArchive/IMF-USA-set-to-ruin-Ghana-former-British-Ambassador-366270>. All three URLs were accessed on 3 July 2015.

Beware the Westocrats' 'democracy'

Westocracy and Westocrats defined

Following Chomsky's interpretation of 'democracy' as propagated by the West in countries it targets for 'democratization' a safe working definition of that 'democracy' would be a system in which target countries are free to govern themselves the way they like as long as they follow the template dictated by the West. Westocrats are Westocracy's crusaders.

The Westocrats at large and over time

When President Obama declared in his *West Point Commencement Address* that 'the United States will use military force, unilaterally if necessary, when our core interests demand it: when our people are threatened; when our livelihoods are at stake; when the security of our allies is in danger' he was not, in fact, making new US 'foreign policy', despite the impression he sought to give to the contrary.[20] As a public declaration that the United States knows no law beyond its own interests that 'principle', policy, 'doctrine' or posture is at least as old as President Bill Clinton's 1993 warning to the United Nations that the United States will act 'multilaterally when possible, and unilaterally when necessary'. Pre-Obama declarations in the same vein include then US Ambassador to the United Nations, Madeline Albright's declaration of the same 'principle' in 1994 and then US Secretary of Defence William Cohen's repetition that the US was committed to 'unilateral use of military power' – to defend vital US interests, which include, 'ensuring uninhibited access to

---

20   His offending words were 'First, let me repeat a principle I put forward at the outset
     of my presidency', which is how Obama reaffirmed this long-established 'principle'
     of US imperial policy in his *West Point Commencement Address*.

key markets, energy supplies and strategic resources', and indeed anything that Washington might determine to be within its 'domestic jurisdiction'.[21] US practice is even older still, as Chomsky argued in the following summary of the evidence he considered:

> In the internal record (the Clinton/Albright/Cohen positions) are assumed from the earliest days of the post-war order (in that) *the first memorandum of the newly formed National Security Council (NSC1/3) called for military support for underground operations in Italy, along with national mobilization in the United States, 'in the event the Communists obtain domination of the Italian government by legal means'.*[22] [My emphasis]

The corresponding US practice goes even further than Chomsky realized, as the following recollections by Mesquita and Smith show:

> Hawaii's Queen Liliuokalani was overthrown in 1893. Her sin? She wanted Hawaii and Hawaiians (no doubt including herself) to profit from the exploitation of farming and export opportunities pursued by large American and European firms operating in Hawaii. As these business interests organised to depose her, the United States sent marines ostensibly to maintain peace from a neutral stance, but in fact it made it impossible for the Hawaiian monarch to defend herself ...
>
> And then we ought not to forget the overthrow of democratically elected Juan Bosch in the Dominican Republic at the hands of the American military in 1965. His offence: he liked Fidel Castro. Or Salvador Allende in Chile, Mohammed Mosaddeq in Iran ... and the list goes on.[23]

21   Chomsky, *Rogue States*, 4. The quotations are taken by Chomsky from: Bill Clinton, speech before the UN General Assembly, Sept. 27, 1993; William Cohen, *Annual Report to the President and Congress: 1999* (US Dept. of Defence, 1999), cited by Jonathan Bach and Robert Borosage, in Martha Honey and Tom Barry, eds, *Global Focus* (New York, St Martin's Press, 2000), 180.10. Madeleine Albright's statement that the US will act 'multilaterally when we can and unilaterally as we must' in areas '(US strategists) recognize ... as vital to US national interests' is extracted by Chomsky from Jules Kagian, *Middle East International*, Oct. 21, 1994.

22   Chomsky, ibid. 4–5. For more details Chomsky refers the reader to his *Deterring Democracy* (New York: Verso, 1991; expanded edition, New York: Hill & Wang, 1992, Chapter 11 and sources cited).

23   Mesqquita and Smith, *The Dictator's Handbook*, op. cit, 192.

While the plots and interventions cited by Chomsky and Mesquita and Smith are all wholly American the US has been generous or accommodating enough of *some* of the interests of the African people's 'former' colonial masters, as long as its 'vital interests' are not at stake or are respected when they are. The reasons, terms and conditions of the US accommodation of allied imperial interests in the 'post-war' dispensation, as Chomsky narrates them, do not promote greater respect for the will of subject peoples in Africa and elsewhere, however. As Chomsky quotes them:

> Southeast Asia was to provide resources and raw materials to the former imperial masters, crucially Britain but also Japan, which was to be granted 'some sort of empire towards the south', in the phrase of George Kennan, head of the State Department's Policy Planning Staff.'[24] *Some areas were of little interest to the planners, notably Africa, (and were to) be handed over to Europeans to 'exploit' for their reconstruction* ... [my emphasis]
> The Middle East, in contrast, was to be taken over by the United States.[25]

The first threat to the democratic wills of the peoples of Africa from the combination of this spoils-of-war arrangement and the Clinton-Albright-Obama doctrine quoted above is the obvious one: if the will of the formal owners of those resources stands in the way of any of America's 'vital interests', as unilaterally defined, it stands the risk of being crushed by hook or by crook. That is one measure of the limits of 'democracy' in the eyes of the principal Westocracy enforcer. But there is a second danger to the will and welfare of the African people from the American strain of neoliberalism which commands the globalization process, a strain which is hostile to 'social democratic' and welfare benefits, traditionally acceptable to the main imperial powers of Europe and tolerated in their 'dependencies' but rejected in America as 'creeping socialism' and obstacles to capital's 'pursuit of profit

24   Chomsky, 150 of *Hegemony or Survival*, quoting from Melvyn Leffler, *Preponderance of Power* (Stanford, 1992), 339.
25   Chomsky, *Hegemony or Survival*, 150.

wherever it wishes and on whatever terms it can impose'.[26] That danger would be familiar to victims and observers in Africa of the Washington Consensus and the virus of Structural Adjustment Programmes (SAPs) as barefaced attacks on Africa's already weak public health and education systems and utilities, among other assaults. Finally, demonstrations by the likes of Naomi Klein,[27] Noam Chomsky,[28] Luciano Canfora,[29] Charles H. Ferguson,[30] Dan Hind,[31] John W. Dean,[32] and Michelle Alexander,[33] among others, that 'government of the people, by the people and for the people' in the leading pusher of 'democracy' abroad is a charade at home provides further grounds to suspect that the neoliberals' 'democratization-of-Africa' project is yet another cynical manoeuvre.

Additionally, the African people can ill afford to ignore more direct indications that what is being pushed on them as 'democracy' cannot possibly be genuine. The following are but some of those indications:

- The repeated assaults on democracy in Haiti, sometimes in the name of democracy promotion;
- The mountains of further evidence in support of the observation by de Mesquita and Smith that 'US presidents have had no problem undermining democratic, or democratizing, regimes when the people of those nations elect leaders to implement policies US voters don't like';[34]

26 Colin Leys, *The Rise and Fall of Development Theory* (Bloomington, IN: Indiana University Press and Oxford: James Currey, 1996), vi.
27 Naomi Klein, 'Shock Therapy in the U.S.A: The Homeland Security Bubble', 283 and 'A Corporate State: Removing the Revolving Door, Putting in an Archway', 308 in *The Shock Therapy*.
28 Noam Chomsky, 'Democracy Promotion at Home', 205 in *Failed States*.
29 Luciano Canfora, *Democracy in Europe: A History of an Ideology*.
30 Charles H. Ferguson, *Predator Nation*.
31 David Hind, *The Return of the Public*.
32 John W. Dean, *Conservatives Without Conscience*.
33 Michelle Alexander, *The New Jim Crow: Mass Incarceration in the Age of Colorblindness*.
34 Mesquita and Smith, *The Dictator's Handbook*, op. cit, 191.

- The 1962 US National Security Council confession that 'it is U.S. policy, when it is in the U.S. interest, to make the local military and police advocates of democracy and agents for carrying forward the developmental process', which can only mean that US interests trump democracy;[35]
- The praises heaped by British Prime Minister, David Cameron, on the Westocracy-compliant 'democracy' in Ghana, against the judgement of disgusted and contemptuous independent Ghanaians and serious suggestions that Ghana may be more of a kleptocracy than a democracy;
- The West's economic war on Zimbabwe for implementing the land restitution its people had fought a fifteen-year national liberation war for;
- The effective takeover of state economic policymaking responsibilities, with the consent of their 'development partners' in Africa, by America's and the West's force multipliers;
- US and general Western complicity in some of the worst crimes against democratic forces and individual democrats in living memory;[36] and
- The arrogation to themselves by the US, Britain, France and NATO of the authority to make and unmake governments as they please, with or without United Nations Security Council cover.

---

35   National Security Council, 'U.S. Overseas Internal Defense Policy', 1 August 1962, op. cit.

36   Examples include the overthrow and murder of Chilean President Salvador Allende's government (on 9/11, 1973) and the massive human rights abuses which followed; Operation Condor (the attempt by 'the corporatist dictatorships of Latin America' in the 1970s to eliminate by all means necessary, including cross-border kidnappings and torture, opponents of the 'shock therapies' prescribed for their countries by the Chicago School economics at the time, 'aided by a state-of-the-art computer system provided by Washington', to quote Naomi Klein, op. cit, 91); General Suharto's massacre of 'communists' in Indonesia; and support for apartheid South Africa, the Mobutu regime in Zaire and some decidedly unsavoury 'democratic era' regimes in the Middle East and Africa.

Westocracy in Africa: A preliminary cost-benefit analysis – Pushers' benefits

Among the current and foreseeable benefits to the West of Westocracy in Africa are:

- Acceptance by too many Africans who should know better of 'the dual mandate' and its ideological counterpart – 'the white man's burden' – as, indeed, messianic undertakings by white race authority, especially when it adds the 'democratization' and 'democratic' policing of their countries to the 'civilizing mission';
- Reduced administrative, policing and moral costs of transforming target countries into 'market states' and 'market societies' for the benefit of Foreign Direct Investors and other Western constituencies;[37]
- Influence-peddling possibilities in local politics and governance as sponsors of constitution writing; open financiers of electoral processes; discrete campaign financiers; 'democracy promoters' in the manner observed in Haiti, for instance; election observers with the power to certify or refuse to certify elections as 'free and fair'; a new 'westernisation' device; sought-after 'development partners', etc.; and
- Acceptance by a critical mass of 'political Africans' of the West as generally welcome judges and guarantors of 'good governance' and development on their continent.

It should be easy to appreciate from the above how Westocracy and African submission to it perpetuate the dependency and dependency complexes of those of Africa's elites who are happy to transfer the development of their

---

37   See Michael Sandel (*What Money Can't Buy: The Moral Limits of Markets*) on how 'the market' is used in 'market economies' as 'a tool ... for organising productive activity' (10) in 'market societies' which are described in turn as societies 'in which market values seep into every aspect of human endeavour' (10–11). The obvious advantage of market economies and societies to the masters of 'the market' – and the universe – is that they can dispense with much of the costs of administering states, dispossessing individuals and communities which need to be dispossessed and policing the economic order through armies, police forces enforcement missions.

societies to their external patrons, as observed by Ake (op. cit.) – to the satisfaction and for the benefit of the latter.

Westocracy, the Bretton Woods system and the impoverishment of African and other peoples

The following reconstruction by Chomsky of how the neoliberal revolution has worsened the plight of the poor in the 'developing world', of which Africa is a part, is as instructive as it is damning:

> One basic principle of the Bretton Woods system was regulation of finance, motivated in large part by the understanding that liberalization could serve as a powerful weapon against democracy and the welfare state, allowing financial capital to become a 'virtual Senate' that can impose its own social policies and punish those who deviate by capital flight. The system was dismantled by the Nixon administration with the cooperation of Britain and other centres ...[38]
>
> For the 'developing world', the post-Bretton Woods era has been largely a disaster, though some escaped, temporarily, at least, by rejecting the 'religion' that markets know best ...[39]

Unfortunately for the African people, their 'leaders', 'governments' and mainstream 'elites' are among those in the 'developing world' who have embraced, not rejected, 'the "religion" that markets know best' – as the OAU/AU's comprehensive embrace of the New Partnership for Africa's Development (NEPAD), reflecting the neoliberalization of Africa at the country level, shows. Worse still, the following indictments by Demba Moussa Dembele of the International Monetary Fund and the World Bank in Africa, the continent's chief enforcers of Westocracy when military force is not deemed necessary, remain as valid as they were in 2004 when he published them:

> The IMF and World Bank have utterly failed in 'reducing poverty' and 'promoting development'. In fact, they are instruments of domination and control in

38 Chomsky, *Rogue States*, 113–14.
39 Chomsky, ibid. 115.

the hands of powerful states whose long-standing objective is to perpetuate the plunder of the resources of the Global South, especially Africa. In other words, the fundamental role of the Bank and Fund in Africa and in the rest of the developing world is to promote and protect the interests of global capitalism. This is why they have never been (interested) in 'reducing' poverty, much less in fostering 'development'. As institutions, their ultimate objective is to make themselves 'indispensable' in order to strengthen and expand their power and influence. They will never relinquish easily that power and influence. This explains why they have perfected the art of duplicity, deception and manipulation. In the face of accumulated failures and erosion of their credibility and legitimacy, they have often changed their rhetoric, but never their fundamental goals and policies.[40]

In other words, Westocracy (the economic and political system of which the World Bank and the IMF are chief enforcers) and its African administrators are yet more additions to the poor African's burdens!

The Westocrats' democracy as a system for mocking the African people

If, as the authors cited above and many others have pointed out, Western democracy at home is yet another opium of the people[41] it is no less obvious that Westocracy, the type of the opium processed and packaged for export, seems to assume the stupidity of the target audiences or is designed to stupefy them. It is difficult to believe otherwise when, for instance:

40   Demba Moussa Dembele, 'The International Monetary Fund and the World Bank in Africa: A "disastrous" record', *Pambazuka News*, 175, 23 September 2004, <http://pambazuka.org/en/category/features/24816>. It may be useful to point out that while Dembele is somewhat less restrained in his choice of words about the IMF and the World Bank than, for instance, Beckles (op. cit.), Murray (op. cit.) and Lopes (see Chapter 4) the essence of their critiques of the Bretton Woods institutions is the same. The quotation from Chomsky above is kinder to the 'Bretton Woods system' before the neoliberal revolution. But this in no way invalidates the critiques of it in what Chomsky calls the 'post-Bretton Woods era'.

41   The view attributed to Gerald F. Lieberman that 'elections are held to delude the populace into believing that they are participating in government' (<http://www.brainyquote.com/quotes/quotes/g/geraldfli153193.html>) makes the same point, essentially.

- 'Democratic' values, institutions and 'achievements' – such as the Magna Carta, 'free and fair elections', 'freedom of speech' and 'freedom of the press' (which are selectively observed),[42] respect for property rights and other accompaniments of idealized Western democracy – are proposed for unquestioning adoption by Africans who know their uses, abuses and limits in democracy's supposed homelands and how the West ignores and circumvents them abroad when its 'vital interests' are at stake;
- Some of those values and institutions have been employed, and seem designed, as cover for the dispossession of peoples, the destruction of traditional and only available welfare systems and the removal of traditional barriers to the commercialization of communal lands and other resources, for the benefit of Foreign Direct Investors and their local allies; and
- Non-governmental organizations in name only and civil society organizations (CSOs) are empowered to play in the region the same dubious roles they were caught playing in Haiti.

Trashing the people's concerns by ignoring them

The continuing division of too many African families and communities by the artificial borders created by colonial cartographers – and the burdens it places on many interpersonal, social and trading relationships among kins – are, undoubtedly, among the more irksome of Africa's colonial inheritances. Such, indeed, is the 'nuisance value' of the artificial divisions of African peoples and their negative social, political and economic consequences that, from different ideological perspectives and vantage points, Basil Davidson wrote book-length reflections about them[43] and Kwame

---

42   For more on this see, Finian Cunningham, 'The Farce of Western Free Speech', <http://www.informationclearinghouse.info/article40663.htm> (accessed 15 July 2015).

43   Davidson , *The Black Man's Burden: Africa and the Curse of the Nation-State*.

Nkrumah made them part of the centrepiece of his life's work.[44] But the 'black man's burden' described by Davidson is compounded by the pretence that attempting to 'transform colonial territories into national territories', as Davidson put it,[45] is other than a fool's errand. The first affront to the African people in such projects is that rather than recognize the attempted conversions as ridiculous – for very objective reasons – the 'nation builders' attempting to do so on the foundations of colonial cartography 'fall back into the colonial mentality of (treating) (Africa's wealth of ethnic cultures) as "tribalism" and, as such retrogressive'.[46] And, to add injury to insult, the poor are often denied the convenience, services and comforts of *independent* community and ethnicity-based mutual support associations by 'jealous' non-performing 'nation-states' and their rulers who oppose them as potential threats to 'national unity'. Unbowed, concrete evidence exists that some cross-border populations and communities do not recognize the 'nationalities' imposed on them either. On the Ghana-Togo border, for instance, there are eyewitness reports of houses with bedrooms, living rooms, kitchens and other facilities located on different sides of the border or border crossing, exposing the concerned households to neglect and harassment, consecutively and even simultaneously, according to the whims of border securocrats.

The feedback from interviewees in an FAO consultancy study on cross-border social and trading relationships and food security on the Ghana-Togo, Togo-Benin and Benin-Nigeria borders conducted in the mid-1990s is interesting in this regard. Asked whether the interviewees – who lived, studied or worked on both sides of their respective borders – considered themselves Ghanaians, Togolese, Beninois or Nigerian, respectively, the reported standard response was that they were Ewe or Yoruba and what 'national' labels 'others' chose to pin on them was the 'others' problem, not theirs.[47] At another level, descendants of the victims of '(the) chief in

---

44 See, for instance, Kwame Nkrumah, *Africa Must Unite*.
45 Davidson (1993), 99.
46 Davidson, ibid. 99.
47 Unpublished FAO consultancy report in the 1990s on Cross-Border Trade and Food Security in West Africa.

the Niger delta, who when exhorted to sell elephant tusks instead of men replied with more wit than humanity that it was far easier to catch a man than an elephant'[48] would presumably need more than colonial cartography to bind them to the descendants of that chief and his foot soldiers. Naana J. S. Opoku-Agyemang's retelling of how the slave-trading past of the Fon of present-day Benin lives in the memories and culture of the Yoruba people (of both Benin and Nigeria), their erstwhile victims, to the point where 'it is not uncommon for a Yoruba to respond to a knock in the night (with the security question): "Is it a human being or a Fon"'[49] is another salutary reminder that:

- The inmates of the 'colonial slave pens' (to borrow Ayi Kwei Armah's phrase) have historical memories which may translate into lingering antagonisms which do not necessarily disappear because colonial cartographers have enclosed them in the same 'pens';
- It is delusional to assume the convertibility of the 'colonial slave pens' into meaningful nation-states for all their peoples; and
- It is just as delusional to imagine that democracy is possible in situations where the populations concerned generally do not trust one another – for historical, structural, economic or cultural reasons; do not necessarily regard the 'nation states' which incorporate them as legitimate; and seem bound together by nothing more substantial, inspiring or unifying than the fact that they once served the same colonial master.[50]

---

48 W. E. Abraham, *The Mind of Africa*, 118.
49 Naana J. S. Opoku-Agyemang, *Where There is No Silence: Articulations of Resistance to Enslavement*, Inaugural Lecture 2006, Ghana Academy of Arts and Sciences, Accra, 2008, 5.
50 The well-known colonial tactic of 'divide and rule' by which differences and conflicts among peoples in the same territories were created or manipulated by colonial regimes for political, economic and administrative purposes and the tendency of many of their African successors to do the same add to the insanity of the pretence that colonial cartography is a basis for nation-building.

The pretence that democracy is possible in these circumstances is surely not backed by common sense, logic or the facts of African political life and instabilities which are blamed, wrongly, unjustly and foolishly, on virtually everything except the fact that the 'nation-states' of political fantasists and con men and women in Africa and abroad are fundamentally absurd products of the rape of the continent which have no right or serious reason to exist as political communities, emotional communities, economic unions or even commonwealths.[51]

Trivializing the people's central political and politically significant concerns

Playing Marie Antoinette by ordering Africans to metaphorically 'eat' 'neo-liberal democracy' may be ignorant, arrogant, cynical and insulting. But where the order is backed by threats and 'bribes', as the *US Strategy Towards Sub-Saharan Africa* clearly does, it can only be interpreted as designed to deprive the African people of their right to identify their political problems and solutions for themselves.

But besides also leaving deep-seated structural, identity and psycho-spiritual problems unattended to, the imposition of neoliberal 'democracy' on peoples who have good historical, economic, cultural, political and moral reasons to reject it cannot escape blame for deepening cynicism by turning politics into the industry, profession, business and arena for inter-mafia competition for the black empowered and cosmopolitan middle-class types in Africa who play it.[52] Other unwelcome consequences of this degradation of politics include:

---

51 As reminders of some of the underlying arguments see Basil Davidson, *The Black Man's Burden: Africa and the Curse of the Nation-State*; Kwame Nkrumah, *Africa Must Unite*; Ayi Kwei Armah, *Osiris Rising*; and Julius Nyerere, 'Without unity, there is no future for Africa', *New African*, 448, February 2006.

52 For a not untypical example of 'politics' as inter-mafia competition or kleptocratic rivalry see Michela Wrong, *It's Our Turn to Eat: The Story of a Kenyan Whistle-Blower* (London: Fourth Estate, 2009).

- The reduction of 'politics' to 'beauty contests' between or among 'leaders' and so-called political parties particularly in 'election years';[53]
- Imposition on the peoples of Africa of a one-size-fits-all governance straightjacket to suit the Westocrats' tastes and convenience, leaving aside African-interest concerns over and above the people's more commonly expressed ones: the continuing colonization of their politics and development; and
- The promotion of false messianism in African politics, as government of the people, by the people and for the people is disabled and replaced by 'government' by 'leaders' and 'political parties' with 'charisma' 'track records', 'magic wands', 'international approval' and other wonders as the new governance ideal!

In a not-unrelated sign of the degradation of democracy and the trashing of the people's political and related concerns, and indeed typical of it, President Obama was able to thrill his audience of parliamentarians in Ghana in 2009 with his declaration that their country enjoyed a healthy democracy because: 'leaders … accept defeat graciously'; 'peaceful transfers of power (take place) even in the wake of closely contested elections'; and 'President Mills' opponents were standing beside him … to greet (him, Obama) when (he) came off the plane' as he arrived in that country to begin a state visit![54]

---

53 Extreme but not insignificant examples of the trivialization are when an aspirant to the leadership of a political party before an impending presidential election somewhere in Africa campaigned on the basis, partly, that he was taller and more handsome than his rival and the case of the aspiring presidential candidate for a political party in Ghana which bore the name of Nkrumah's Convention People's Party expecting to boost his credentials by claiming that he had once attended a White House prayer breakfast.

54 The White House, Office of the Press Secretary, *Remarks by the President to the Ghanaian Parliament*, 11 July 2009, <https://www.whitehouse.gov/the-press-office/remarks-president-ghanaian-parliament>. In fairness to him, Mr Obama preceded the words quoted above with the following other magisterial pronouncement: 'In the 21st century, capable, reliable, and transparent institutions are the key to success – strong parliaments; honest police forces; independent judges; an independent press; a vibrant private sector; a civil society. Those are the things that give life to democracy, because that is what matters in people's everyday lives.' But by those

In so doing, however, he not only substituted his definition of politics and catalogue of political concerns for the Ghanaian people's – which include endemic poverty, corruption, unemployment, the poor quality and uneasy access to social services and the unresponsiveness of the political and governance systems in place to these concerns – but portrayed himself by the same token as a crusader for Westocracy, notwithstanding his protestation to the contrary before that same assembly.[55]

Unblocking the people's democratic options: Some essential tools recalled

The evidence that neoliberalism is fraudulent when it promises democracy and delivers and globalizes the market state,[56] instead, and *by design*,[57] is already so overwhelming that it would probably serve no useful purpose

---

words he erred grievously in presuming without the Ghanaian people's authority to list what mattered at the time they were spoken in their lives – and trivializing the daily struggles of the many Ghanaians who had to worry about how their daily physiological, social and ego needs would be met in an essentially anti-people and people-neglecting political environment exacerbated, no doubt, by the neoliberalism he supported as public policy in Ghana.

55   Note the contradictions between Obama's protestation that 'America will not seek to impose any system of government on any other nation' in the address to the Ghanaian parliament on one hand and his 'good governance' benchmarks in the same address, American practices in other Third World nations under his presidency (through 'force multipliers' and by direct US and proxy forces) and the breathtaking presumptuousness of the *US Strategy Towards Sub-Saharan Africa* on the other.

56   As Philip Bobbit, for one, describes it, with no hint of irony, the 'market state' is a 'constitutional order that promises to maximize the opportunity of its people, tending to privatize many state activities and making government more responsive to the market' (Philip Bobbit, *The Shield of Achilles*, London: Penguin, 2002, 912, quoted by Hind, 2010, op. cit.)

57   The off-the-record revelation to the historian, Bernard Porter, by an intelligence officer, reported in Bernard Porter, 'Other People's Mail', *London Review of Books*,

to pile on even more of it. In addition to the extensive literature already available on the subject the countless 'counter-insurgency operations' by the promoters and enforcers of neoliberal 'democracy' against the spectre of government of the people, by the people and for the people in Africa, in other 'poorer countries' and indeed all over the world since the first memorandum of the newly formed National Security Council (NSC1/3) cited above virtually speak for themselves. But proof that neoliberal 'democracy' is bogus and fraudulent when it poses as 'the real thing' is not necessarily a vote for any other system of government on offer or imaginable. Helping to limit 'sincere ignorance' as a viable excuse for collaboration with the globalizing neoliberal fraudsters and their African partners or for failure to join in combating it is, perhaps, the most that can be expected from a book or chapter.

But the following reminders and 'parting shots' may still be in order:

1. Westocracy cannot be other than a tool of continuing imperialist domination;
2. A people's right to determine its system of government is a human right and none may be allowed to take it away from the African people without a fight; and
3. The elevation of 'neoliberal democracy' to a religion or god in whose name weaker nations may be invaded, dubious 'civil wars' 'legitimately' provoked and fought on other people's lands, 'opposition' or 'pro-democracy' movements may be sponsored, etc., by 'world powers', 'the international community' and other pseudonyms for white race authority and its puppets must be seen and fought for what it is: another ruse by the same 'civilizing missionaries' who have turned Africa as a

---

19 November 2009, quoted by Dan Hind (op. cit, 91) that 'the Anglo-Saxon model of capitalism' which neoliberalism and the market state are designed to promote and defend are on 'MI5's list of potential targets to be safeguarded against subversion' should also dispel any illusion that neoliberalism, the market state and the 'democracy' they globalize do not have 'national security' implications for the 'democracy' exporting and importing countries!

whole into a 'scar on the conscience of the world', most African 'states' into declared and undeclared failed states 'on the dole' and the peace, security, dignity, concerns and very lives of 'black' and 'brown' people in countries marked for 'democratization' into trash.

CHAPTER 4

Reclaiming African Development for the African People

We cannot solve our problems with the same thinking we used when we created them.

— ALBERT EINSTEIN

The liberation of the minds of the African people will be a tougher battle than the eradication of settler regimes.

— PATRICE LUMUMBA

Development, freedom and the liberation-of-African-development imperative

A starting point of this book and chapter is that Africa deserves a better future than its present and past. But that better future cannot be envisaged, let alone constructed, unless the unsung 'Einstein's law' quoted above is acknowledged – and the acknowledgement leads to thinking about an alternative African development paradigm. To distinguish itself from the paradigm it has to displace it must, moreover, be people-owned and people-driven; must not be parachuted down from on high, even by 'radicals' and 'revolutionaries'; and, above all, must be equal and opposite to the paradigm which entrenches the mismatches between African production, African consumption and 'development' imposed by colonialism and continued by its 'idiotic neo-colonial states'. In other words, an alternative African development paradigm must free the African people *from* the consequences of the colonial development paradigm which continues to rule their lives

more than half a century after 'independence' and *for* the development of
Africa by Africans for Africans.

The deconstruction and reconstruction imperatives: The imperative
of mental rehabilitation

In the *Ghana Nsem* quotation with which the Introduction began, the
author does not say whether the 'rape' he complained of included the
rape of African minds as well as their bodies and resources. But as Fanon,
van Hein Sekyi, Ngugi wa Thiong'o and others have shown, the raping of
African minds began with the Atlantic slave trade itself, continued with
colonization and intensified under colonial rule with formal and informal
miseducation and plain propaganda.[1] The 'democracy' fraud – backed
by the same kinds of force, sanctions, threats and political and personal
inducements with which the slave 'trade' and colonization began – is proof,
moreover, that the imperialist forces are not about to give up the rape
of African minds as a weapon of domination. Nor – judging by Robert
Cooper's public proclamation of 'deception' as a valid instrument of his 'new
liberal imperialism', his career progression in the European foreign policy
establishment after the publication of his infamous treatise on the subject
and the audacity of their 'world radio' propaganda outputs – do the 'masters
of the universe' always consider discretion in their resort to this weapon a
virtue. But the fact that the imperialist establishment feels able to flaunt the
weapon in deeds as well as words should worry not only Africans but all
right-thinking members of humanity. There is, fortunately, an abundance
of intellectual material, practices and roadmaps which can be built upon
to give the African people the necessary protections against deception as
their enemies' command and control weapon.[2] Messay Kebede's demand

1   See, for instance, Fanon, *Black Skin, White Masks*, van Hein Sekyi, *Colour Prejudice,*
      Past, Present and Future and Ngugi wa Thiong'o, *Detained: A Writer's Prison Diary.*
2   See, for instance, Frantz Fanon, ibid., Julius K. Nyerere, *The Arusha Declaration: Ten*
      Years After, Amilcar Cabral, *Return to the Source: Selected Speeches of Amilcar Cabral,*
      Thomas Sankara, *Thomas Sankara Speaks: The Burkina Faso Revolution, 1983–1987,*

that 'the great task of freeing the African mind from Euro-centric constructions'[3] be prioritized is, in a sense, no more than a welcome echo, for the benefit of younger Africans, of the traditional calls for African minds to be liberated from the effects of colonial deceptions and indoctrination – as a prerequisite for the reclamation of African development as the development of Africa by Africans for the African people. But it is also particularly apt, given the new economic, social, moral and ideological environments created by the replacement of the immediate independence collaborator class of mere administrators and 'big men' often interested in power for its own sake by a new breed or generation of African leaders whom the empire and its corporations could do business with because they were, and are, more 'business oriented' and 'business friendly', proudly so and available to be used, and offer their own families and cronies to be used, as business as well as 'development' partners.

The following profile of imperialism's 'new breed' of junior partners in Africa gives them away, but only partly:

> The term 'new generation' or 'new breed' of African leaders was a *buzzword* widely used in the mid-late 1990s to express optimism in a new generation of African leadership. It has since fallen out of favour, along with several of the leaders.
>
> In the 1980s and 1990s, increasingly many *Sub-Saharan African* countries were holding *multiparty elections*. The *Cold War*, the *proxy wars* of the *US* and *Soviet Union* as well as *Apartheid* in *South Africa* had come to an end. A new generation of African leaders had been anointed who promised to transform their continent. That dream was dubbed the *African Renaissance*. This concept is often defined in

---

Ngugi wa Thiong'o, ibid, Claude Ake, *Democracy and Development in Africa* and Messay Kebede, 'African Development and the Primacy of Mental Decolonisation', *African Development*, Vol. XXIX, No. 1, 2004. Then fifteen year-old Lora Noreen S. Domingo, a Grade 9 student at the Philippine High School for the Arts, showed in a think piece on 'Colonial Mentality' (*Philippine Daily Inquirer*, 7 September 2014, <http://opinion.inquirer.net/78220/colonial-mentality>) that the assaults on colonized minds and the resulting colonial mentality have not been uniquely African.

3   Messay Kebede, 'African Development and the Primacy of Mental Decolonisation', *African Development*, Vol. XXIX, No. 1, 2004.

contrast to the *big man syndrome* – the autocratic rule by the so-called 'big men' of African politics during the first two decades after independence.

When US president *Bill Clinton* made his first African journey in March 1998 he helped popularise this notion when he said he placed hope in a *new generation of African leaders* devoted to *democracy* and *economic reforms*. [Italics in original][4]

The 'new generation' may have fallen out of favour as an expression and a class of people, as the writer alleged. But imperialism in Africa has never ceased manufacturing, looking for and finding new African leaders it can 'do business with' or employ, as evidenced by the following, among others:

- Obama's praises in 2009 for the Ghanaian political class to whom was owed their country's 'improved governance' and 'impressive' economic growth which will ultimately be more significant than the liberation struggles of the twentieth century, in his view;[5]
- His Young African Leaders Initiative (YALI) designed to 'provide outstanding young leaders with the opportunity to hone their skills at a US university, and support their professional development after their return home', clearly reminiscent of the US 'mentorship' programmes which served America during the Cold War years;[6]
- The 2014 US-Africa leaders' summit designed to reposition the United States as Africa's 'development partner' of choice;[7] and
- The manoeuvres which led to the adoption of *NEPAD* as Africa's economic policy framework document and its firm neoliberal orientation; a declaration like 'I also expressed to President Obama that without

---

4   'New Generation of African Leaders', <https://en.wikipedia.org/wiki/New_genera tion_of_African_leaders> (accessed 9 August 2014).

5   Obama, 'Remarks of the President to Ghanaian Parliament', op. cit. Full text available on the web.

6   For a historical overview of the older programmes see Ken Lawrence, 'Academics: an Overview' in *Dirty Work*.

7   In the words of the White House write-up on the summit its purposes were 'expanding trade and investment ties, engaging young African leaders, promoting inclusive sustainable development, expanding cooperation on peace and security, and gaining a better future for Africa's next generation'. See <https://www.whitehouse.gov/us-africa-leaders-summit> (accessed 25 January 2016).

building shared prosperity, our vision of a secure Africa and, indeed, a stable world will remain a fragile dream' coming out of Africa more than once;[8] and the dominance of the Washington Consensus in what passes for policymaking in Africa at the country level.

That dominance is a function of Africa's in-dependence, of course. But it is also, in part, a function of acceptance by the local governments concerned of the neoliberal ideology which underlies the Consensus, father of the Structural Adjustment Programmes (SAPs) which have tormented most of Africa since the 1980s. Carlos Lopes thus performs an essential intellectual, political and ideological function for the mental rehabilitation of the African perpetrators and passive victims of neoliberal thinking with the following demystification of the SAPs:

> Most assessments of the impact of SAPs on African countries and on development on the continent are to a large degree negative. The reduction of the role of the state resulted in the downsizing of the civil service, a decline in real wages and cuts in public expenditures.
>
> Along with the weakening of bureaucratic capacity and public institutions, these factors compromised the provision of basic services and investment in infrastructures, which eventually led to a reduction in private investment.
>
> Although the policy restored macroeconomic stability in some countries, economic growth stagnated and social conditions worsened considerably. For example, the decay in public health services in Nigeria made people to coin the phrase that government hospitals had become 'mere preliminary consulting rooms'.
>
> Many families were destroyed as their bread winners, who were rationalised out of employment or whose take-home pay could hardly take them home, were no longer able to cater for their dependants. One report said, thanks to the SAPs, some men in Zambia left home and abdicated their responsibility to their wives.
>
> Due to its one-size-fits-all nature, the adjustment programmes were unable to respond to specific country conditions and changing circumstances, leading to a lack of shared vision between the Bank and recipient governments concerning the aims of the programmes. No wonder they did not get the buy-in of many nations. In the end many opted out and, in the case of Nigeria, Ethiopia and others, developed their own home-grown equivalent.

---

8   Cf: <https://www.whitehouse.gov/the-press-office/2015/07/25/remarks-presi dent-obama-and-president-kenyatta-kenya-press-conference>.

The SAPs' devastating impact

In 2011, the Economic Commission for Africa (ECA) noted that the negative impact of SAPs was particularly visible in the African industrial sector. The Commission observed that growing dependence on imported goods driven by the SAPs' trade liberalisation eroded the weak industrial base of most African economies.

Effects on income and welfare were magnified by an increased debt burden, deteriorating terms of trade, declining flows of private capital and accelerating capital flight.

The lack of industrial development in Africa is, at least in part, a consequence, if not a result, of these interventions. In most of the cases, industries are yet to recover from the SAPs period.

More importantly, as many country examples in Africa demonstrate, the implementation of SAPs compromised government capability to design and put into action long term economic and social development strategies that are critical for enabling the private sector to develop and compete globally.

SAPs left behind, bright future ahead?

In their 2013 report, the ECA further highlights the failings of the SAPs: 'They did not raise productivity, boost manufacturing export performance or enhance value addition.' It also claims that the policy actually hurt technological capability and skills. 'Today, the weak African industrial structure still has to move out of the shadow of those interventions – a task made more onerous by the new international context', it said.

Now, thanks to a surge in the price of their natural resources and the development strategies and good economic management of more development-oriented governments, African nations are emerging from that period with some optimism.

The headlines in the international press these days usually proclaim 'Africa Rising'.

The trend has been helped by the emergence of China, Brazil and India that have ramped up demand for African raw materials for their burgeoning manufacturing industry. Chinese investment and aid has also helped to build roads, hospitals, railroads, and other infrastructure on the continent.

To keep the continent on the rise, the ECA is robustly arguing for governments to be involved in developing their countries rather than toe the IMF/World Bank line of promoting market fundamentalism with little or no state involvement.[9]

9   Carlos Lopes, 'How the World Bank's SAPs Impoverished Africa', *Development Diaries*, 11 September 2013 <http://developmentdiaries.com/how-the-world-banks-saps-impoverished-africa/>. Also in *African Agenda*, Vol. 16, No. 3, 2013.

Well before the piece by Lopes there had been enough evidence of the devastation caused in Africa by the neoliberal thinking (also known as the received neoclassical paradigm) reflected in the SAPs to cause Ake to complain as follows:

> One would have expected the poor performance of African economies to have undermined confidence in the received neoclassical paradigm. But far from being undermined, the validity of the paradigm was asserted so aggressively that the prospect of using another paradigm could no longer be seriously entertained. For, as African economies declined, they became more vulnerable and more dependent on the international development agencies, whose response to Africa's worsening crisis was to affirm the old paradigm in a more doctrinaire form.[10]

Ake need not have marvelled about this particular application by imperialism's junior partners in Africa of the logic of the absurd or rushed to ascribe their failure to detach themselves from the received neoclassical paradigm to more vulnerability and greater dependence on the international development agencies. A little less haste on this occasion would have reminded him of what he showed in other parts of *Democracy and Development in Africa* that he knew – namely that the attachment to the neoclassical paradigm in spite of its 'poor performance' has deep structural and psycho-pathological roots. When to that knowledge is added absorption of the full implications of the transformation of African states and societies into market economies and market societies it becomes that much easier to understand the complexities of the neoclassical-paradigm addiction and harder to miss the point that the mental rehabilitation required to resist neoliberalism, the neoclassical paradigm and their economic structural adjustments is impossible unless it is linked up with the moral, intellectual, political and cultural liberation of enslaved African minds.

It is remarkable in this connection that the one issue on which Africa is on record as having ignored or resisted Western pressure is 'gay rights'. The one solid explanation of the failure of US and British pressure on African states to get them to incorporate the American declaration that 'gay rights are human rights and human rights are gay rights' into their

10   Ake, op. cit. 12.

domestic legislation – with Kenya's President Uhuru Kenyatta able to
tell America's President Obama to his face at a joint press conference
in Nairobi Kenya on 25 July 2015 that 'gay rights' were a 'non-issue' in
his country – has to be that it ran into the hard rock of yet uneroded
African moral and cultural values which were shared by the West's junior
partners in Africa or which even they could not circumvent.[11] The contrast with Africa's deafening silence on issues of legitimate African concern – such as the 'new Jim Crow' and police violence against people
of African descent in his America, US occupation of Diego Garcia and
the trampling on the human rights of the Chagos Islanders, US involvement in the overthrow and murder of Libyan leader Muammar Kaddafi,
US sanctions against Zimbabwe and US crimes against the people of
Haiti from 1915 to date for which apologies and reparations are over-
due – even after Obama's sermons on domestic African matters in his
lecture tour of East Africa (which included an address at the headquarters of the African Union, chaired by the Commission's Chairperson,
where he delivered sermons on 'human rights' and governance failures in
Africa which are none of his business) – is just as remarkable.[12] Africa's
silence on those issues in the face of Obama's provocative sermons has to
mean either that his audiences did not find the sermons provocative or
did not feel strongly enough about the above-mentioned issues to raise
them with him even in the face of the 'frank discussions' he insisted on
having with his African hosts.

Either way the imperative of mental rehabilitation is further reinforced.

---

11   See <https://www.whitehouse.gov/the-press-office/2015/07/25/remarks-president-
      obama-and-president-kenyatta-kenya-press-conference>, op. cit. Recall also the rejec-
      tions by Uganda and Ghana of the Obama and (British Prime Minister) Cameron
      campaign to the same effect.

12   The deafening silence is inferred from the fact that the British Broadcasting
      Corporation (aka BBC) – which treated Obama's visit as a visitation – to the point
      of broadcasting his private dinner with his Kenyan family as 'news' – did not report
      his AU audience as having raised them with their august visitor.

Preparing for the alternative to dependent underdevelopment: Decolonizing minds and getting false alternatives out of the way

The pro-democracy bias of the only alternative to dependent underdevelopment recognized in this chapter is readily admitted. And, for the avoidance of doubt it is further submitted that the only logically possible alternative to Africa's dependent underdevelopment is one which advances the development of Africa by the African people for the African people. The contrast to the colonial, neo-colonial and neoliberal 'development' paradigm which has promoted 'development' in Africa as the movement of the people from one stage of development or underdevelopment to another for their ostensible benefit but delivered a continent which is 'a scar on the conscience' of the world, by the neo-imperialist Tony Blair's reckoning, should be, accordingly, obvious. It should also be obvious, from Africa's experience with virtually all the varieties of colonial development possible, that genuine democratic development requires freeing the people from the superstition that democracy, development, democratic development – and the people themselves – must fit into straightjackets tailored for them by some self-appointed 'democracy' and 'development' 'prophets', 'philosophers', philosopher-kings, 'experts', engineers and the Foreign Direct Investors and other 'force multipliers' who accompany them. By the same token the visionary and, in many ways inspiring, development experiments of the giants of the immediate post-colonial era – Kwame Nkrumah and Julius Nyerere included – need to be accepted as having fallen short of the imperatives of genuine alternatives to colonial development.

That may be a surprising thing to say about Nkrumah's development experiment which began with the unexceptionable pledge to his 'nation' in the year of its 'independence' that:

> ... we shall measure our progress by the improvement in the health of our people; by the number of children in school, and by the quality of their education; by the

availability of water and electricity in our towns and villages, and by the happiness which our people take in being able to manage their own affairs.[13]

That pledge implies, of course, a 'radical' departure from the colonial 'development' agenda which was more about the transformation and maintenance of colonial territories into 'looting machines' or garrison stations for the easy policing of the looting machines. Nkrumah's 'social-democratic' or 'welfare-state' ambitions were to be resourced, however, through the mining of his territory, where possible, for exportable minerals; the maintenance and development of the cocoa economy which was well within the place assigned to the Gold Coast within the imperial division of labour; and the super-exploitation of peasant farmers and agricultural and informal sector workers.[14] The contradiction between the 'radical' Nkrumah's laudable goal of transforming the colonial predator state he inherited into a welfare one and the colonial state-financing model he also inherited and relied on is accordingly undeniable. Nkrumah was no more successful in disengaging his country through his industrialization-by-imports-substitution strategy from the colonial development model. On the contrary the dependence of the local industries created under the strategy on imported technologies, imported raw materials, foreign experts, production licences and various 'invisibles' sucked his country even deeper into it. Nor was this outcome accidental: grounding industrialization on lifestyles and a consumption model derived from colonialism and so-called foreign trade – as Nkrumah's passion for 'catching up with the West' and his determination that 'what other countries have taken three hundred years or more to achieve, a once

13   Kwame Nkrumah, *Broadcast to the Nation*, 24 December 1957. Source: *Pan-African Perspective: Quotes from Kwame Nkrumah*, <http://www.panafricanperspective. com/nkrumahquotes.html> (accessed 4 August 2014).

14   As others have pointed out [see, for instance, Bernard Founou-Tchuigoua, 'Salariat de fait dans le Gésira Scheme (Soudan)' and J. Weber, 'La region cacaoyère du Centre Sud Cameroun (Essai d'analyse d'une forme locale de production dominée', in Samir Amin ed., *l'agriculture africaine et le capitalisme*, editions anthropos idep, 1975] the forms of super-exploitation include the informal submission of formally independent agricultural producers to labour exploitation through exploitative market mechanisms and institutions.

dependent territory must try to accomplish in a generation if it is to survive (and not) lag behind and ... risk everything for which it (had) fought'[15] led him to do – made the outcome inevitable and guaranteed the descent of his party and government into 'the pitfalls of national consciousness'.[16]

Not surprisingly in these circumstances the manipulation of cocoa prices on the 'international market' in the mid-1960s and the cancellation of $35 million of American 'aid' to Ghana in retaliation for Nkrumah's book on neo-colonialism in 1965[17] were almost sufficient to end the illusion of an Nkrumaist alternative to colonial development – and confirm the hollowness of Ghana's independence even under Nkrumah and the failure of his 'development alternative' as a resistance economy or nation-building project.

The 'alternative-development' project initiated by Tanzania's Julius Nyerere – with its socialistic but non-Marxist orientation, 'pragmatism', elevation of 'self reliance' to the status of a development principle where others took dependency (on the East or the West) for granted and unquestionable commitment to 'the toiling masses' – was, understandably, even more widely celebrated than Nkrumah's, especially in then 'socialist' Scandinavia. His reputation as a development innovator was, if anything, enhanced by the following criticism of his compatriots and cadres in *The Arusha Declaration: Ten Years After*:

> The fact is that we are still thinking in terms of 'international standards' instead of what we can afford and what we can do ourselves ...

---

15   Kwame Nkrumah, *Ghana: The Autobiography of Kwame Nkrumah* (Panaf Books, 2002), Preface. In choosing the more dependency-breeding industrialisation option, however flawed, Nkrumah could still claim, legitimately, in radio broadcasts to Ghanaians from Conakry, Guinea where he became an honoured guest after his overthrow that his was a better option than that of contemporary presidents who had preferred to spend their years in office comfortably enjoying the fruits of what has since come to be known as black empowerment.

16   On this see, Fanon, 'The Pitfalls of National Consciousness', in *The Wretched of the Earth*.

17   See June Milne, *Kwame Nkrumah: A Biography*, 113.

The same attitudes prevail about housing. Not very long ago it was estimated that to build an improved traditional house – that is one with a permanent roof, insect-proofed wood-work and a thin cement floor – cost about Shs.7,000/-; a smaller cement block house, costs at least Shs. 18,000/- to construct. Yet although we know that most of our people cannot afford the mortgage or rental costs of the cement house, we persist in promoting its construction ...

The present widespread addiction to cement and tin roofs is a kind of mental paralysis. A bati roof is nothing compared with one of tiles. But those afflicted with this mental attitude will not agree. Cement is basically earth; but it is called 'European soil'. Therefore people refuse to build a house of burnt bricks and tiles; they insist on waiting for a tin roof and 'European soil'. If we want to progress more rapidly in the future we must overcome at least some of these mental blocks![18]

Nyerere's virtue, as the above quotation shows, lay in his philosophy and practice of reaching into the traditions and achievements of his people, rather than 'what other countries have taken three hundred years or more to achieve' for responses to their physiological and social needs – giving greater hope, thereby, than Nkrumah did that the people, in his scheme of things, could look forward to the happiness which comes with being in a position to manage their own affairs, including their own development. But by Nyerere's own criteria – notably, his insistence that 'a poor nation does not develop on the basis of money (and) it cannot be independent if it depends upon external help'[19] – his self-reliant development project in Tanzania was shown to be, at best, short-lived when post-Nyerere Tanzania led post-Nkrumah Ghana in affording George W. Bush the opportunity to promote himself as a compassionate imperialist for whom the invasion of Iraq and the distribution of free insecticide-treated mosquito nets to deprived natives served the same humanitarian purpose!

Behind Tanzania's alternative-development fiasco is, as noted by Ake, the fact that political, economic and administrative practices even under Nyerere did not always match the rhetoric of a self-reliant and socialistic or communalistic African development alternative. As he further pointed out:

18   Julius K. Nyerere, *The Arusha Declaration: Ten Years After* (Dar es Salaam, Tanzania: The Government Printer, 1977), extracted from pages 29, 30 and 31.
19   Julius Nyerere, ibid. 31.

... while African leaders talked about the fragility of political independence and the need to buttress it by self-reliant development, they eagerly embraced economic dependence. In time, this frame of mind led to the conception of development as something to be achieved through changes in the vertical relations between Africa and the wealthy countries: a greater flow of technical assistance to Africa, more loans on better terms, more foreign investment in Africa, accelerated transfer of technology, better prices for primary commodities, greater access to Western markets, and so forth.

In this spirit African governments expected a large portion of their development budget to be financed externally. *That was true even for those countries such as Tanzania whose leaders seemed conscious of the need for self reliance. For instance, Tanzania's first post-independence plan of 1964, the first phase of an ambitious fifteen-year development plan, projected an expenditure of $285.7 million for the plan period, of which $222.7 million or 78 percent was to come from external sources.*[20] [My emphasis]

Nor was that the full extent of the gap between rhetoric and reality in Nyerere's Tanzania. His external image as 'moderate' and 'democratic' (based on his avoidance of the rhetoric of 'scientific socialism' and 'gradualist' approach to African unity) must be contrasted with the paternalistic and dictatorial sides of him which the following episode reveals:

On November 6, 1973, President Nyerere announced a new policy of compulsory villagization. In an uncharacteristically angry speech, the president reprimanded Tanzanians for not reciprocating all the effort and sacrifices the leadership had made to serve their needs and for frustrating the country's socialist development policies through indifference and idleness. The president said that, although he could not compel Tanzanians to be socialists, he would ensure that all Tanzanians lived in Ujamaa villages by 1976.[21]

The false development alternatives did not end with the end of the Ghanaian and Tanzanian illusions, however, as Patrick Bond has pointed out:

The death of Nelson Mandela, at age 95 on 5 December 2013, brings genuine sadness. As his health deteriorated over the past six months, many asked the more durable question: how did he change South Africa? Given how unsatisfactory life is for so many in society, the follow-up question is, how much room was there for Mandela to manoeuvre? South Africa now lurches from crisis to crisis, and so many of us are

20   Claude Ake, *Democracy and Development in Africa*, 7–8.
21   Ake, ibid. 59.

tempted to remember the Mandela years – especially the first democratic government – as fundamentally different from the crony-capitalist, corruption-riddled,
brutally-securitised, eco-destructive and anti-egalitarian regime we suffer now. But
were the seeds of our present political weeds sown earlier?

The critical decade was the 1990s, when Mandela was at the height of his power,
having been released from jail in February 1990, taken the South African presidency
in May 1994 and left office in June 1999. But it was in this period, alleges former
Intelligence Minister Ronnie Kasrils, that 'the battle for the soul of the African
National Congress was lost to corporate power and influence … We readily accepted
that devil's pact and are damned in the process. It has bequeathed to our country
an economy so tied in to the neoliberal global formula and market fundamentalism
that there is very little room to alleviate the dire plight of the masses of our people.'

Given much more extreme inequality, much lower life expectancy, much higher
unemployment, much worse vulnerability to world economic fluctuations, and
much more rapid ecological decay during his presidency, how much can Mandela
be blamed? Was he pushed, or did he jump?

South Africa won its democracy in 1994. But regardless of the elimination of
formal racism and the constitutional rhetoric of human rights, it has been a 'choiceless democracy' in socio-economic policy terms and more broadly a 'low-intensity
democracy', to borrow terms coined respectively by Thandika Mkandawire for Africa,
and by Barry Gills and Joel Rocamora for many ex-dictatorships. Nelson Mandela's
South Africa fit a pattern: a series of formerly anti-authoritarian critics of old dictatorships – whether from rightwing or left-wing backgrounds – who transformed
into 1980s/90s neoliberal rulers: Alfonsin (Argentina), Aquino (Philippines),
Arafat (Palestine), Aristide (Haiti), Bhutto (Pakistan), Chiluba (Zambia), Dae
Jung (South Korea), Havel (Czech Republic), Mandela (South Africa), Manley
(Jamaica), Megawati (Indonesia), Mugabe (Zimbabwe), Museveni (Uganda), Nujoma
(Namibia), Obasanjo (Nigeria), Ortega (Nicaragua), Perez (Venezuela), Rawlings
(Ghana), Walesa (Poland) and Yeltsin (Russia). The self-imposition of economic
and development policies – typically at the behest of financial markets and the
Washington/Geneva multilateral institutions – required an extraordinary insulation
from genuine national determinations: in short, an 'elite transition'.

This policy insulation from mass opinion could only be achieved through the
leadership of Mandela. It was justified by invoking the mantra of 'international
competitiveness', and it initially peaked with Mandela's 1996 Growth, Employment
and Redistribution policy. Obeisance to multinational corporations helped shape
the terrain on the platinum belt that inexorably generated the Marikana Massacre
in 2012, for example. In the South African case, it must be stressed, the decision to
reduce the room for maneuver was made as much by the local principals as it was by
the Bretton Woods Institutions, other financiers and investors.

South Africa's democratization was profoundly compromised by an intra-elite economic deal that, for most people, worsened poverty, unemployment, inequality and ecological degradation, while also exacerbating many racial, gender and geographical differences ... Ending the apartheid regime was one of the greatest human achievements of the past century. However, to promote a peaceful transition, the agreement negotiated between the racist regime and Mandela's African National Congress (ANC) allowed whites to keep the best land, the mines, manufacturing plants, and financial institutions, and to export vast quantities of capital.

For there had been only two basic paths that the ANC could have followed. One was to mobilize the people and all their enthusiasm, energy, and hard work, use a larger share of the economic surplus (through state-directed investments and higher taxes), and stop the flow of capital abroad, including the repayment of illegitimate apartheid-era debt. The other, which was ultimately the one chosen, was to trudge down the neoliberal capitalist path, with merely a small reform here or there to permit superficial claims to the sustaining of a 'National Democratic Revolution.'[22]

It would be observed that Bond's analysis complements, and is without prejudice to, the equally pertinent observations by Fanon on how 'revolutions' in Africa have been traditionally betrayed by those who rode on them to power. Indeed, Bond's reference to Mandela's leadership as a facilitator of 'the-day-after' insulation from mass opinion and 'genuine national determinations' recalls the following observations made by Fanon decades before Mandela:

The national bourgeoisie (read black empowered) turns its back more and more on the interior and on the real facts of its undeveloped country, and tends to look towards the former mother country (or the 'international community') and the foreign capitalists who count on its obliging compliance. As it does not share its profits with the people, and in no way allows them to enjoy any of the dues that are paid to it by the big foreign companies, it will discover the need for a popular leader to whom will fall the dual role of stabilising the regime and of perpetuating the domination of the bourgeoisie. The bourgeois dictatorship of under-developed countries draws its strength from the existence of a leader. We know that in the well-developed countries the bourgeois dictatorship is the result of the economic power of the bourgeoisie. In the under-developed countries on the contrary the leader stands

22   Patrick Bond, 'The Mandela Years in Power', *CounterPunch*, Weekend Edition, 6–8 December 2013, <http://www.counterpunch.org/2013/12/06/the-mandela-years-in-power/>.

for moral power, in whose shelter the thin and poverty-stricken bourgeoisie of the young nation decides to get rich.[23]

The scenarios described by Fanon, Bond and Mafeje (op. cit.) have persisted long enough and widely enough to be familiar to all but the wilfully blind. It should not be too difficult to agree that the only thing that would be worse than the fiascos described by Bond, and others, would be failure to convert the lessons from them into positive energies for positive action.

Some lessons and follow-up ideas

Behind the insistence that the *development of Africa by the African people for the African people* is the only hope for the African people's escape from white-race-authority-and-African-collaborator dictatorship, exploitation, marginalization and impoverishment are the following inconvenient but undeniable truths:

- As chattel or colonial, neo-colonial or globalized slaves the people have been on the losing end throughout the 500 years of the robbery and rape of their bodies, continent and natural resources; and
- It would be illogical, unnatural and against the lessons of African and world history to expect the current and future partners in the under-development of the continent to initiate, lead, control or not oppose a 'development paradigm' which takes away their power to dictate 'African development' for their sole or primary benefit.

One dimension of the people's folly when they think and behave in complete disregard of these lessons and put their faith in the power of 'business-as-usual' coping strategies to solve their problems is succinctly put by Zinn in the following reality check:

---

23   Frantz Fanon, *The Wretched of the Earth*, 133.

> Numbers of people all over the world have obeyed the dictates of the leaders of their government and have gone to war, and millions have been killed because of this obedience. (The) problem is that people are obedient all over the world in the face of poverty and starvation and stupidity, and war, and cruelty. (The) problem is that people are obedient while the jails are full of petty thieves, and all the while the grand thieves are running and robbing the country.[24]

The people are just as guilty of 'own goals' when, as argued or implied above, they allow the 'sincere ignorance and conscientious stupidity' denounced by Martin Luther King Jnr,[25] 'political' and purely criminal 'coping strategies' of the sorts denounced by Jan Breman,[26] queue-jumping for scarce public goods and services, using 'tribal', regional, 'party' affiliations and similar ascriptions and associations for preferential treatment, superstition, poor-on-poor violence and other such wrongs, searches for 'greener pastures' in Europe, the Middle East and elsewhere in place of productive work and political struggles at home, etc., to stand in the way of their just and necessary struggle against the oppression, exploitation, marginalization, dispossessions and underdevelopment which make and keep them poor. But by the same token relatively privileged Africans who believe in making 'poverty' in Africa in the midst of plenty history may well find the charges by Fanon, Sukarno and Sankara, respectively, quoted in the Preface relevant to their own missions on earth.

Below are some concluding principles and ideas drawn from the above considerations for possible follow up:

---

24 From Howard Zinn, *Failure to Quit: Reflections of an Optimistic Historian*, Google Books, quoted by *Information Clearing House*, 20 August 2015 edition, <https://uk-mg42.mail.yahoo.com/neo/launch?.rand=8796ijqu2f646#2737317679>.

25 Martin Luther King Jnr, 'Letter from Birmingham Jail', in *From Strength to Love*, Harper & Rowe, New York, 1963.

26 These include, 'at the lowest level', as Breman put it, thieving, snatching, trickery, pick pocketing, fencing of stolen goods, pornography, counterfeiting, all sorts of shady dealings', gambling, racketeering, trafficking in arms, drugs or hard drink and renting out of gang members as bodyguards to VIPs. (Jan Breman, 'The Undercities of Karachi', *New Left Review*, 76, July/August 2012).

1. The lessons from past 'alternative development' misadventures, as told by *free Africans*,[27] should be shared with the broad masses of the African people as widely as possible for the benefit of future alternative development strategists;

2. The African people should be encouraged and empowered by all means necessary and possible to take responsibility for their liberation from oppression, exploitation, dispossessions and impoverishment;

3. The superstition that dollars, euros, the British pound, rubles, the Japanese yen, the Chinese renminbi or yuan and other so-called hard currencies are what Africa needs for its development must yield to the recognition – articulated by Julius Nyerere, among others, confirmed by the grassroots Kamirĩĩthũ Community Education and Cultural Centre in Kenya, by the fact that 'the first developers' did not wait for these so-called hard currencies to develop and, indeed, by Africa's development history *before the slave trade and colonization* – that 'money (is) not the basis of development. Human hands and brains (are) ...';[28]

4. 'Development' in spite of the people, at their expense or without their informed consent must be recognized as the fool's errand which some two centuries of dependent development confirm it is;

5. In consonance with the above proposition the African peoples freedom to choose their forms of government and development paths should be respected, even if their choices seem weird to others – as long as they do not endanger other African communities, states or the Global African Community as a whole;

6. No African or person of African descent who matters or wishes to matter in the formulation and execution of African defence, diplomacy and development policies and projects should be allowed to forget that no single African or black majority state anywhere in the world can reclaim control over its political, economic and development

27 On 'free Africans' see the quotation and reference to Patrice Lumumba's 'Letter from Thysville Prison to Mrs Lumumba' in Chapter 5. But 'free Africans' in this usage refers to liberated Africans everywhere, not just those in the countries specified by him.
28 Julius Nyerere, *The Arusha Declaration: Ten Years After*, 31 and Ngugi, *Detained*, 75.

destiny *on its own* in the face of a hostile 'international' environment which has not changed or wavered in its opposition to such projects since the suppression of Palmares (or Quilombo dos Palmares) and the destruction of Haiti as a free and independent nation;

7. Without eternal vigilance it is all too easy for people's liberation and development movements at any level to be subverted, hijacked or neutralized;

8. Solidarity among Africans and peoples of African descent, not 'competitiveness', should be promoted as the key to the security, welfare and development of Africans everywhere; mutual and equitable benefit, where possible, should govern their relations with other peoples; and every effort should be made to create the longest possible distance between Africans and believers and practitioners of the laws of the jungle;

9. The welfare, happiness, security and dignity of the people, not just GDP growth (and certainly not the humours of the 'international community', foreign investors and their supporting casts), should be the drivers of public policies, programmes and projects in the African world;

10. In the relationship of African communities and states with their people the right to development must be recognized and incorporated as the right to *quality* 'food, clothing, shelter, education … work, rest, and reasonable payment' for all, as per the *Universal Declaration of Human Rights*; African states, communities and individuals in Africa and the Diaspora must accept it as their responsibility to contribute to the enjoyment of these rights by all Africans wherever they may be; and they must accept that it is not in the interest of the 'international community' to promote their enjoyment by the generality of Africans and cannot and ought not expect the 'international community' to consider these rights as binding on them in their relations with any Africans but their chosen 'cosmopolitan middle classes' or 'honorary whites';[29]

---

29 Note that these rights are largely dismissed by the core of the 'international community', the West – with one-time US Ambassador to the United Nations, Jeane Kirkpatrick, reportedly ridiculing them and the Economic, Social and Cultural Rights

11. Science and technology should be integrated into the people's culture as cultural and intellectual development and problem-solving resources and weapons against superstition and other mindsets which retard progress;

12. The absurdity by which the peoples of Africa and African descent are reduced to dependence on suspect 'world's radios' for 'news' and opinions about one another should be recognized as dangerous, degrading and unacceptable;

13. Africans and peoples of African descent across the globe should feel free to invent and reinvent themselves as a 'race', 'nation', people, community, etc., for their own purposes, as other peoples have done and continue to do – and certainly *not* as others define or label them;[30] and

14. Actions must be considered and taken at all levels by those 'who have nothing to lose but their chains'[31] to disable the 'looting machine' wherever it may be or rears its head in the African world.[32]

---

as a whole as a 'letter to Santa Claus' (Chomsky, *Rogue States*, 134). Likewise the right to food proposed by the developing countries at the World Food Conference of 1974 was watered down at the insistence of the major food power to 'the inalienable right (of every man, woman and child) to be free from hunger and malnutrition in order to develop fully and maintain their physical and mental faculties'.

30   See, for instance, Theodore W. Allen, *The Invention of the White Race*, Vols 1 & 2 and the more controversial *The Invention of the Jewish People* by Shlomo Sand (translated from the original Hebrew by Yael Lotan), Verso Books, 2009. See also Coates, *Between the World and Me*, op. cit. 'The West' also appears to have emerged from the 'Cold War' as a 'people', 'clan' or 'tribe' within the 'white race', with its own 'exceptionalist' characteristics and claims.

31   While the phrase, itself, is borrowed from the *Communist Manifesto* (Chapter IV, Section II) the reference here is not to the 'proletariat' of the African world only but to all in that world who are oppressed, exploited, marginalized, impoverished – and affronted – by the dictatorships of the 'black empowered' and their 'development partners'.

32   On the 'looting machines' see Tom Burgis, *The Looting Machine, Warlords, Tycoons, Smugglers and the Systematic Theft of Africa's Wealth* (New York: Public Affairs, 2015). It may be a measure of how 'revolutionary' the recommended action against looting machines is that while no less than three Articles of the *Constitutive Act of*

Endnote

When all is said and done it has to be conceded that while *some* men and women learn from history *not* all men and women do, and further that of those who do, not all act on the lessons they learn. In that sense the thesis by Frederick Douglass, the nineteenth-century African-American social reformer, abolitionist, orator, writer, and statesman, that 'knowledge makes a man unfit to be a slave' is not nearly as true as his other observation that 'If there is no struggle, there is no progress'. The fact that many Africans live undignified lives of poverty, hunger and other affronts and go without dignity to their graves – killed by genocidal economic and social policies orchestrated from abroad and implemented by governments and (mis) leaders they are fooled into calling their own – should be proof enough that knowledge does not always produce the struggles that may lead to progress for them or their loved ones. But while conscientization can produce the spark that ought to facilitate the conversion of the lessons of Africa's underdevelopment history into struggles and change, the conversion process requires inputs such as a fighting spirit and a willingness to overcome ones's own weaknesses which books cannot provide.

---

the African Union [Articles 4 ('Principles'); 23 ('Imposition of Sanctions); and 30 ('Suspension')] proclaim 'the right of the Union to intervene in a Member State pursuant to a decision of the Assembly in respect of grave circumstances, namely: war crimes, genocide and crimes against humanity', condemn and reject unconstitutional changes of government and warn that 'Governments which shall come to power through unconstitutional means shall not be allowed to participate in the activities of the Union', respectively, governments which turn their states into looting machines receive no threats or warnings!

CHAPTER 5

Plus Ça Change, Plus Ça Reste la Même Chose

The colonists usually say that it was they who brought us into history: today we show that this is not so. They made us leave history, our history, to follow them, right at the back, to follow the progress of their history.

— AMILCAR CABRAL

Why, man, he doth bestride the narrow world
Like a Colossus, and we petty men
Walk under his huge legs, and peep about
To find ourselves dishonourable graves

— WILLIAM SHAKESPEARE; Cassius on Julius Caesar,
in Julius Caesar

'Development' has been the password for imposing a new kind of dependency, for enriching the already rich world and for shaping other societies to meet its commercial and political needs.

— SUSAN GEORGE[1]

Getting the history and the lessons right

When Zinn's very pertinent observation that all history '(is loaded with and releases ideological distortions) into a world of contending interests, where any chosen emphasis supports ... some kind of interest, whether economic or political or racial or national or sexual'[2] is conjoined with Steve Biko's

---

1   Susan George, op. cit.
2   Zinn, op. cit, 8.

equally pertinent warning that 'the most potent weapon of the oppressor is the mind of the oppressed'[3] the importance of Patrice Lumumba's vision, in 1960, of an African history of the future which will be made, written and taught 'in the countries which have won freedom from colonialism and its puppets'[4] becomes all too obvious. Unfortunately for Lumumba's reputation as a seer and for Africa's dignity, then French President Nicolas Sarkozy was to insult Africans on African soil on 26 July 2007, a good forty seven years after Lumumba's optimistic declaration.[5]

Sarkozy had the temerity on that day to make the following scurrilous declarations about Africa and Africans at the Cheikh Anta Diop University, no less:[6]

> The tragedy of Africa is that the African has not fully entered into history. The African peasant, who for thousands of years has lived according to the seasons, whose life ideal was to be in harmony with nature, only knew the eternal renewal of time, rhythmed by the endless repetition of the same gestures and the same words.
>
> In this imaginary world where everything starts over and over again there is no place for human adventure or for the idea of progress.
>
> In this universe where nature commands all, man escapes from the anguish of history that torments modern man, but he rests immobile in the centre of a static order where everything seems to have been written beforehand.
>
> This man (the traditional African) never launched himself towards the future. The idea never came to him to get out of this repetition and to invent his own destiny.

3   <http://www.brainyquote.com/quotes/quotes/s/stevenbiko177008.html#jo D87bZHu44VqBbI.99>, op. cit.
4   Patrice Lumumba, 'Letter from Thysville Prison to Mrs Lumumba'.
5   See the first speech to Africa delivered by Nicolas Sarkozy, as the President of France, at the Cheikh Anta Diop, Dakar, Senegal, 26 July 2007, <http://kwani.org/edito rial/report_essay/37/Africa_le_pauvre.htm> (accessed 11 August 2014).
6   Cheikh Anta Diop (29 December 1923 – 7 February 1986), after whom the University of Dakar, Senegal was named, was the iconic historian, anthropologist, physicist, politician and authority on the human race's origins and pre-colonial African culture. His works, in the original French, include the very influential *L'Afrique Noire précoloniale* (Paris, Présence Africaine, 1960); *Antériorité des civilisations nègres : Mythe ou vérité historique ?* (Paris, Présence Africaine, 1967) and *Nations nègres et culture: De l'antiquité nègre égyptienne aux problèmes culturels de l'Afrique Noire aujourd'hui*, Vols I and II (Paris, Présence Africaine, 1979).

The problem of Africa, and allow a friend of Africa to say it, is to be found here. Africa's challenge is to enter to a greater extent into history. To take from it the energy, the force, the desire, the willingness to listen and to espouse its own history.

Africa's problem is to stop always repeating, always mulling over, to liberate itself from the myth of the eternal return. It is to realise that the golden age that Africa is forever recalling will not return because it has never existed.

Africa's problem is that it lives the present too much in nostalgia for a lost childhood paradise.[7]

Having thus rubbished Africans and their pre-colonial history, Sarkozy was 'generous' enough to propose an 'African renaissance' based on a Eurafrique project – 'this great common destiny that awaits Europe and Africa', in his words – which is, in reality, as old as colonization itself: the reconstruction of Africa as Europe's backyard rather than an independent entity! And in obviously feigned ignorance of the past five centuries of European, African and Euro-African history (comprising the first, relatively brief and only genuinely free trade between the two continents, the slave trade and imperial rule from the colonial through the neo-colonial era to the present US-led 'global order') and genuinely unrestrained contempt for the intelligence of his African audience he tried to advance his fatuous Eurafrique project on the claim that 'Africa has paid dearly for its disengagement from the world' and rendered itself 'vulnerable' as a result. Tony Blair, Sarkozy's ideological soul mate and the notorious Robert Cooper's one-time boss, approached his Eurafrique destination, which he preferred to call globalization,[8] via a different but no less nauseating mixture of cynicism, condescension and disrespect for African history. Showing or also feigning ignorance of the fact that Africa has, in effect, been 'globalized' for some five centuries the only room for debate about Tony Blair's version of the 'civilizing mission' – after his patronizing declaration that Africa was 'a scar on the conscience of the world'; claim that his prime ministerial experience in Britain gave him the mandate to initiate projects like the Blair Commission for Africa and his Africa Governance Institute and the authority to engineer a 'new'

---

7   Sarkozy, ibid.
8   See, for instance, his welcome message to the website of The Office of Tony Blair (<http://www.tonyblairoffice.org/> (accessed 5 September 2015)).

role for Africa in the world economic order; and his further declarations recalled below – is whether it is driven by classical imperialism of the type pioneered by the likes of Belgium's King Leopold II, the 'new liberal' variety promoted by Robert Cooper, his one-time adviser, or whether there is any real difference between the two:

> The evidence is clear: Africa needs better governance. None of the other issues it faces will be overcome without it. As Prime Minister, I learned that the gap between setting out a vision and seeing real change is hard to cross. But for African leaders, that gap can feel like a chasm. In the daily mechanisms of government, there is simply not the capability to make things happen. And when government doesn't work, it's the poor who suffer most.
>
> I believe that Africa can become in this century an engine of prosperity as powerful as Asia became in the last. That's the goal, but it will only become a reality if Africa's leaders are able to drive the reforms their countries need, and their governments have the capacity to deliver them.
>
> For a new generation of African leaders, this means that having a clear vision for their country is not enough. They also need to transform the capacity of their government to deliver it. I set up AGI to help them do that.[9]

Sarkozy's Eurafrique project is, in a sense, an evolution from the Françafrique reality which had boosted France as a 'world power' decades earlier. But, as with many of France's imperial projects in the 'post-war' and 'post-Charles de Gaulle' eras it also bears many of the hallmarks of US influence and inter-imperialist collaboration, making Western positions on non-Western events as a whole easier to understand and anticipate than ever before.[10] But by their *identical* distortions and deafening silences about the history of Africa – in, for instance, the words of Sarkozy and Blair quoted above,

---

9   The Tony Blair Africa Governance Institute, Message from Tony Blair, <http://www. tonyblairoffice.org/africa/pages/tony-blair-and-africa/>.

10 It is readily conceded that there are differences in emphasis and tone in some of the specific demands the three overlords make of their African subjects, reflecting the fact that the domestic constituencies and special lobbies they represent do compete as well as coalesce and do not all agree, for instance, that 'gay rights are human rights and human rights are gay rights' and it is incumbent on 'aid recipients' to incorporate this Obama-Hilary Clinton-David Cameron doctrine into their domestic laws.

Obama's principal Addresses to Africa[11] and his *US Strategy Towards Sub-Saharan Africa* – it is also all too obvious that the only purpose of their forays into 'African history' was the persuasion of Africans that it is in their interest to accept those who colonized and underdeveloped their continent (in the name of a 'civilizing mission' and 'white man's burden') and 'have a primary interest in its current condition' as their 'development partners'.

The West's past and current management of 'African news' leaves no doubt, moreover, about how Western historians are likely to twist current African events as African history in future to suit Western interests. It requires but little imagination to anticipate, for instance, how today's sanctions on Zimbabwe over its land restitution programme will be written and taught as a blow for democracy, the nineteenth-century-style recolonization of Libya will be portrayed as a humanitarian intervention, the neo-imperialist regime change in Côte d'Ivoire will be sold as democracy policing and France's *Operation Serval* in Mali and associated military operations by France and its allies in the rest of the Sahel will be narrated to unsuspecting future students of the history of the region as battles in the 'war on terror' or assistance to Mali and Niger, with hardly any mention of the French and allied interests in the mineral resources there behind the interventions.[12]

11 The reference is to Obama's 'remarks' to the parliament of Ghana, at Nelson Mandela's funeral, at the joint press conference with the president of Kenya and to the African Union (July 2015).

12 On the real reasons for the sanctions on Zimbabwe and for a future alternative history of the episode see, for instance, Baffour Ankomah, 'Zimbabwe: The land is back' and 'Zimbabwe; "The Conservatives would never have done that"' (Ankomah's interview with David Hasluck, a past director of Zimbabwe's white Commercial Farmers Union, CFU, who blamed Tony Blair's Labour government for messing up in Zimbabwe), both in *New African*, 415, February 2003. On the same for Libya, Côte d'Ivoire and *Operation Serval* and allied military activities see Majed Nehmé, 'Pourquoi veulent-ils l'abattre?' (referring to Muammar Gaddafi), in *Afrique Asie*, April 2011; Ekwe-Ekwe, 'France must now leave Côte d'Ivoire'; Traoré and Diop, 'African Impostures: Letters from a Proxy War'; and Keenan, 'How terror came to the Sahel', respectively.

Such, however, is the damage already inflicted on African knowledge systems and values by the propagation among Africans of the Sarkozy-Blair-Obama and associated views of Africa, African history and poverty in Africa that, based on that view and associated peddling of Euro-Africanism as a *sine qua non* for Africa's renaissance, Tony Blair was able to mobilize some very high-profile African personalities to join his Commission for Africa and, with rare exceptions inside Africa itself, Obama got away with his assertions and insinuations that US and African interests in African development are compatible and even identical.[13] Meanwhile, to follow up Mammo Muchie's plea for the promotion of 'Pan-African education' on the 'destruction of Africa' and other issues[14] and in the hope of repairing some of the damage caused by the high-pressure marketing of the Sarkozy-Blair-Obama distortions of African history and 'explanations' of poverty and 'bad governance' on the continent, the following uncensored bits and pieces of the 'alternative history of Africa' are offered for contemplation:[15]

I.   '... in the early centuries of trade (between Europe and Africa), Europeans relied heavily on Indian cloths for resale in Africa, and they also purchased cloths in several parts of the West African coast for resale elsewhere. Morocco, Mauretania, Senegambia, Ivory Coast, Benin, Yorubaland and Loango were all exporters to other parts of Africa – through European middlemen. Yet, by the time that Africa

13   Among the original membership of the Blair Commission for Africa were Meles Zenawi, Prime Minister of Ethiopia at the time of his appointment; Benjamin Mkapa, President of Tanzania from 1995 to 2005; the then governor of the Bank of Botswana; Trevor Manuel, South African Minister for Finance from 1996 to 2009 and Minister for Planning in the South African Presidency at the time of his appointment to the Commission; and a former Executive Secretary of the UN Economic Commission for Africa.

14   Mammo Muchie, 'Why Pan-African Education Should be Promoted', *New African*, 553, August/September 2015.

15   Obama can claim the merit of consistency at least on this point: he has earned similar rebuke for his treatment of the black or Afro-American condition in America. See Glen Ford, 'Obama's Anti-Black Rant', a Black Agenda Radio commentary, 4 September 2013, <http://www.blackagendareport.com/content/obama%E2%80%99s-anti-black-rant>.

entered the colonial era, it was concentrating almost entirely on the export of raw cotton and the import of manufactured cotton cloth. This remarkable reversal is tied to technological advance in Europe and to stagnation of technology in Africa owing to the very trade with Europe';[16]

2. 'Africans have made many discoveries in mathematics, astronomy, science and technology before; Africans established universities long before the contacts with Europe; carbon steel was made 2,000 years ago in Tanzania; important astronomical observations by the Dogons of Mali have been acknowledged internationally; in the fields of language, mathematical systems, architecture, agriculture, cattle-rearing, navigation of inland waterways and open seas, medicine and communication, writing systems Africans have been inventors; there was proto-maths in the form of Lebombo bone in South Africa and Swaziland, Ishango bone in the Congo, and in Ancient Egypt the Ahmose (Rhind) mathematical papyrus; there was in present-day Angola what is known as sona geometry, symmetrical and non-linear, which has become the basis for new mathematical ideas like mirror curves and various classes of matrices such as cycles, cylinder and helix; there were also African fractals (West and Central Africa), demonstrated by repeating geometric patterns on various scales that have been used in textiles, paintings, sculpture, cosmologies, architecture, town planning ... and are the basis of the worldwide web; In Ethiopia and Nigeria (among the Yoruba) the mathematics that applies binary logic has been used both for computation and metaphysics; and the ancient Ethiopian method of mathematical calculation is behind today's internet explorer and other computer-based systems.'[17]

---

16   Rodney, *How Europe Underdeveloped Africa*, 113. See also Toyin Falola and Tyler Fleming, 'African Civilizations: From the Pre-Colonial to the Modern Day' in Robert Holton and William R. Nasson, eds, *World Civilizations and History of Human Development (Encyclopedia of Life Support Systems)* (Paris: Eolss Publishers, 2010).

17   Mammo Muchie, 'Why Pan-African Education Should be Promoted', op. cit, 24–5. For other examples of deliberately forgotten African inventions and discoveries see 'Address Delivered to Mark the Opening of the First International Congress

3. 'In spite of the slave trade and of the import of European goods, most
    African handicraft industries still had vitality at the start of the colo-
    nial period. They had undergone no technological advance and they
    had not expanded, but they had survived. The mass-production of the
    more recent phase of capitalism virtually obliterated African industries
    such as cloth, salt, soap, iron and even pottery making.'[18]

4. African food systems (agriculture and support services) were able to
    produce the estimated 'few millions to over one hundred million' of
    preferred healthy young Africans (between the ages of fifteen and
    thirty-five) who were carted away to provide slave labour in 'the New
    World' for its development;[19]

5. The facts which support Brazilian scientist Josue de Castro's con-
    clusion about the absence of clinical signs of dietary deficiencies in
    tropical Africa before colonialism and direct scientific evidence that
    the famished, undernourished and malnourished children of NGO
    campaign posters are part of Africa's colonial heritage cannot but also
    show that those disasters are *not* the products of the black ineptitude,
    mismanagement and corruption but blameable, essentially, on the
    African people's imperialist burdens;[20]

6. Africa and the African world have paid a heavy price in inappropri-
    ate and sometimes harmful technological substitutions as a result of
    globalization;[21] and

---

of Africanists' by Osagyefo Dr Kwame Nkrumah, President of the Republic of
Ghana, *Proceedings of the First International Congress of Africanists*, Published for
the International Congress of Africanists by Longmans, 1964 and Cheikh Anta
Diop, *Nations nègres et culture*, op. cit. or Cheikh Anta Diop, *The African Origin
of Civilization*.

18 Rodney, *How Europe Underdeveloped Africa*, 252–3.

19 Rodney, ibid., Chapter 4, section 1 and, in particular, 104.

20 For more of de Castro's observations and the data on which they are based see Chapter
6, 'Colonialism as a System for Underdeveloping Africa' in Rodney, ibid. Recall also
his observations quoted in Chapter 2 above.

21 Recall in this connection Nyerere's criticism of his own people (op. cit.) and Nourbese
Philip's 'Letter to Haiti', *New Legon Observer*, Vol. 4, No. 1, 25 February 2010, op. cit,
13. Also to be factored into the equation is the unnecessary and expensive begging,

7. It is worth recalling, finally, that while imperialism has always relied on the Cooper trio of *force, pre-emptive attack* and *deception* for its conquest, command and control of Africa ignorance (including ignorance of their own history), dependency and dependency and inferiority complexes have been among its most powerful, if silent, weapons.

For the benefit, on the other hand, of those whose genius consists in part of their ability to 'engineer their own forgetfulness', as Coates put it,[22] as well as Africans whose responses to anti-black or anti-African 'racism' as an ideology, mental disease or piece of self-intoxicating buffoonery lack the necessary understanding of how it all began and its continuing uses today the following observations by Van Hien Sekyi on its past, present and possible future, are also offered for serious reflection:

> The earliest appearance in European literature of the African's denigration was in the context of slavery, and so it was to continue until the abolition of slavery, and even beyond, for by then the myth had acquired a life and momentum of its own, independent of its parent. All myths die hard.
>
> In the literature of England, denigration appeared in the Elizabethan era in the works of Sir John Hawkins, and so did the slave trade. Hawkins, the first English-man to engage in it, thus told his own story concerning his antics off the Guinea coast. He agreed to help the king of Mina in a local war, on condition that he be allowed to sell off all the prisoners of war as slaves across the Atlantic. Hawkins, however, was in the event not given the captives to sell, and in bitterness he wrote that the Negro 'in which nation is seldom or never found truth' meant nothing less than to keep his part of the bargain, for that night he removed his camp, prisoners and all.[23] And on such occasions Sir John was apt to vent his fury in accusations not merely of falsehood but of cannibalism as well. With Hawkins, England was committed officially as well as unofficially to the slave trade. The court encouraged or connived at it ... if we may trust his despatch to his sovereign, the shares in the venture were held not only by merchants, but secretly by members of the queen's council as well. The new

---

borrowing, adoption and importation of technologies (or, more accurately, systems and machines) to satisfy economically, socially and environmentally inappropriate or unsustainable lifestyles.

22   Coates, op. cit., 150.
23   Sekyi's source: Eldred Jones, *Othello's Countrymen* (Oxford: Oxford University Press, 1969), 13.

development seems duly reflected in Elizabethan and Jacobean drama, which, unlike preceding English literature, unlike Chaucer, Mandeville, and Dunbar, is full of quite nasty references to the black, in the true tradition of Sir John Hawkins.

Later, in answer to the challenges and queries raised by thinkers like Locke, Addison and Defoe, the apologists of the transatlantic slave trade, those who produced the most widely publicised and therefore the most influential rationalisations of the profitable but villainous system, were men who were themselves actively engaged in it. The Dutchman Bosman, long resident in Elmina and elsewhere as a factor or agent of the Dutch slaving company, dismissed the African character out of hand, and his view is reported to have become commonplace. Barbat was for many years the captain of a French slaving vessel, long accustomed to force-feed his human cargo by causing their front teeth to be broken where necessary. Such also were Phillips and Snelgrave, both slaving captains, both authors of the most lurid and circumstantial accounts of people and conditions in West Africa, the scene of their slaving activity. All these disseminated the view that Africans were, to use the actual words of Phillips, 'generally extremely sensual, knavish, revengeful, impudent, liars, impertinent, gluttonous, extravagant in their expressions, and giving ill language'.[24]

Such condemnations were common in the justification of slavery, especially where one particular race was the intended victim. Dr R. Gardiner produced an interesting example of this in his BBC Reith Lectures on the subject. Columbus's original description of the Amerindians was as a 'loving uncovetous people, so docile in all things that there is no better people or better country. They loved their neighbours as themselves and they had the sweetest and gentlest way of speaking in the world and always with a smile'.[25] Fifty or sixty years later, when Spanish slavery had actually exterminated them on some Caribbean islands, a different description was forthcoming from the tormentors. The Indians were then said to be 'lazy filthy pagans of bestial morals no better than dogs, fit only for slavery in which state alone there might be some hope of converting them to Christianity'.

In the argumentation of the pro-slavers, then, two main strands may be distinguished, both of which are now amongst the staple ingredients of the racist myth. The first strand aims at reducing the black man to subhuman status ... The Africans, in the opinion of Gibbon and of Hume, were little better than parrots, at the intellectual level.[26] As for their customs, 'they exactly resemble', according to one Dr Houston,

24   From Douglas Grant, *The Fortunate Slave*.
25   Sekyi's source: R. Gardiner quoted in *A World of Peoples*, BBC Reith Lecture (London: Longmans, 1966), 27 and note.
26   Sekyi's references are David Hume, 'Essay on National Characters', in *Essays and Treatises*, i.235 and Edward Gibbon, *Decline and Fall of the Roman Empire*, Vol. 5 (London: Dent, 1962).

'their fellow creatures and natives, the Monkeys.'[27] Even the liberal de Tocqueville admitted 'we are almost inclined to regard him (the African) as being intermediate between man and the brutes.'[28] [...]

The second strand in the pro-slaving propaganda was that of darkest Africa. For so indefensible was the enslavement of Africans in the New World that it could not be justified except by seeming or being made to seem preferable to freedom in a totally benighted continent; and to appear worse than a system so outrageous, Africa necessarily had to be represented in the worst possible colours. And so it was done. Inevitably there was the predictable allegation of cannibalism – an allegation liable to be levelled ... at all sorts of people, from Scotsmen to the inhabitants of the Sandwich Islands ...

The racist myth once established, it is not difficult to trace its progress and its consequences to our own day. Myths, it is well known, die hard. The institution of Negro slavery eventually perished and was superseded by a more industrialised method of profit. But the splendid victory over it, even if helped by the Industrial Revolution, was still that of those in Britain, the rest of Europe, and the Americas who so honourably championed the cause of the African. So slavery perished. *But the myth to which it gave birth marched on. It had penetrated into the humblest classes of Western society.* [My emphasis][29]

The target beneficiaries of van Hein Sekyi's observations cannot but include those 'who have been brought up to believe that they are white', to borrow Coates' phrase, and proceed from that mischaracterization and various psychopathologies to throw bananas at Africans and other dark-skinned footballers at stadia in Europe, Latin America and elsewhere, for instance – if they can read and understand Sekyi. But these may be the softer nuts to crack. Harder to crack are the mainstream, if sometimes unconscious, racist beneficiaries of the 'industrialised method of profit' in whom 'plunder has matured into habit and addiction', as Coates again put it.[30] The hope, however, is that after reading Sekyi on the racist origins of the following thoughts, practices and attitudes those of their number who participate in or encourage them will wake up to their own racism and do something

27   From James Houston, *Some New and Accurate Observations on the Coast of Guinea*, *1725*, 33–4.

28   Alexis de Tocqueville, *Democracy in America* (New York: Vintage Books, 1954), 372.

29   Van Hein Sekyi, *Colour Prejudice. Past, Present and Future* , 55–61.

30   Coates, 150.

about it – or feel forewarned that they are being watched by a reawakened African and black community worldwide:

1. Overt or covert advocacy or facilitation of imperialism in any shape or form or participation in imperialistic projects and practices;
2. Aiding and abetting the 'force multipliers' named by Obama and others unnamed, including the African Union, the European Union, so-called NGOs which serve as hidden arms of neoliberal imperialism, Foreign Direct Investors who do the same and advocacy groups, including 'international broadcasters', which serve as weapons of cultural and moral imperialism;
3. Imitations of the patronizing tone and substance of the *US Strategy Toward Sub-Saharan Africa*; Bill Clinton's casual presumption that it is permissible and even 'normal' for a president of the United States to make and unmake governments beyond his country's borders, as he avowed in his statement about restoring President Aristide of Haiti to power; and of the open attempts by the European Union and the United States 'to do a Haiti' in Zimbabwe through sanctions and open sponsorship of a 'Zimbabwean opposition party';
4. The continuing insistence by Western governments, NGOs, broadcasters, etc., on telling Africans what they should think; how they should behave; what they should believe; what they should do in what circumstances; how they should govern themselves; what sexual orientations to follow the West in decriminalizing, and presumably, which to keep on their crimes list until further Western notices;[31] which human rights, dear to 'the wretched of the earth', they should ignore and even trash, etc.;[32] and

31   An African wit once quipped that he did not wish to live to see the day when the West will decriminalize incest in their own countries and order Africans to follow suit or face the withdrawal of 'aid' or worse – unless Africa would be organized then to be able to tell the purveyors of the new morality, in the strongest possible terms, to keep what they can reasonably be expected to cloak in the language of 'human rights' to themselves.

32   See Chomsky, *Rogue State*, 'Economic, Social and Cultural Rights', 134–42 on the treatment by the US of the provisions of the *Universal Declaration of Human Rights* pertaining to these rights, including its veto of the Right to Development.

5. The use of 'market forces', foreign-direct-investor power, military and diplomatic muscle, 'force multipliers', bribery and corruption and other devices to dispossess indigenous people of their lands and other assets, turn formally independent producers into *de facto* cheap labourers and even slaves for employers and produce buyers – with weak local governments as collaborators.

But there is a third category of people who need correct African history as a warning, threat or simple cure for their miseducation: these are the Africans, past and present, who do not necessarily believe that they are '*white*' or even '*honorary white*' or '*Afropean*' and may or may not show obvious symptoms of *apism* but need to know that African history includes the history of African people who managed their own affairs, thought for themselves and reached the levels of reasoning and made the discoveries and calculations recalled by Muchie. Among these Africans are the moral descendants of those who were capable of emitting obscenities such as 'emotion is Negro and reason is Greek' ('*L'émotion est nègre, la raison est hellène*') and 'those who invented neither gunpowder nor compass; those who tamed neither steam nor electricity; (and) those who explored neither the sea nor the sky'.[33] The Senghors and the Césaires may or may not be extinct as a literary species. But at the political level they were very much alive and well when, in 2016, an African 'leader' and head of state, no less, virtually invited the European Union to take over the running of his country's economy (and the economies of other 'developing and troubled countries', for that matter) in the following words:

> One of the key issues for which Ghana will encourage Italy to rally and get the European Union to work hard at is the need to support countries like Libya to build

---

33   The words in the first of the negritude effusions quoted above are Léopold Sédar Senghor's. The second quotation is from Aimé Fernand David Césaire. For more on this see Think Piece by 'agabond' based on 'Birth of the Negro Myth', Cheikh Anta Diop, *The African Origin of Civilization* (Westport, CT: Lawrence Hill, 1974). For the agabond article, 16 July 2011, see 'Diop: Birth of the Negro Myth', <https://abagond.wordpress.com/2011/07/16/diop-birth-of-the-negro-myth> (accessed 22 June 2014).

a stable and functioning government. Developing and troubled countries must be supported by their development partners to build industry aimed at creating employment opportunities for young people in order to stem the regular migrant flows to Western Europe.[34]

There are, unfortunately for the African people, many more signs that the dependency and ignorance-fed African complexes are widespread and deep. Among them are:

• the African Union's adoption of the New Partnership for Africa's Development (NEPAD);
• the practice of knocking on the open doors of NATO, AFRICOM, French and other Western forces for the protection of African regions, states and governments from 'Islamo-fascist' 'terrorism', the crazed Joseph Kony's Lord's Resistance Army (an offshoot of the Holy Spirit Movement), other home-bred terrorist gangs, drugs traffickers, maritime pirates and other threats to national and international security and other objects of supposedly mutual interest to Africa and the West;[35]
• the stubborn and widespread superstition that the same powers which underdeveloped Africa and continue to do so as a matter of their strategic interest or acquired 'habit and addiction' hold the key(s) to the continent's development and, associated with that, the intellectual and political paralysis which renders too many African 'leaders' and 'intellectuals' incapable

34   'Create jobs for African youth to reduce migration – Mahama to EU', *Ghana Web* (Source: The Finder), <http://www.ghanaweb.com/GhanaHomePage/ NewsArchive/Create-jobs-for-African-youth-to-reduce-migration-Mahama-to-EU-412763> (accessed 4 February 2016).

35   For some written alerts on the problem in addition to those cited in previous pages see, for instance, Aminata Traoré and Boubacar Boris Diop, 'African Impostures: Letters from a Proxy War' and Abayomi Azikiwe, 'Imperialists host conference on Nigerian security in Paris', *Pambazuka News*, 679, 21 May 2014 <http://pambazuka. org/en/category/features/91841> (accessed 24 May 2014). As Traoré and Diop put it, commenting on 'the French military intervention against the Islamists' on 11 January 2013, '(the Malian people) (had) simply had (their) country stolen from them' (Traoré and Diop, ibid. 69).

of imagining African development without the inflow of 'foreign' (read Western) direct investors, Western aid, Western technology, 'foreign' tourists, etc.;

- the learned inability to imagine viable and sustainable African communities outside the nation-state model imposed by Europe;
- the insane pretence – against historical memories, logic and available and mounting evidence, including the differential impacts of globalization on the African rich and the African poor within the so-called nations – that the 'colonial slave pens' inherited from colonialism can ever constitute politically, economically, socially and culturally rational and sustainable bases for nation-building and meaningful and sustainable development;
- The *de facto* transformation of the OAU/AU *idea* from a body with a charter obligation to defend the sovereignty and independence of its Member States (Article 3, b of the Constitutive Act of the African Union and, before that, preambular paragraphs 1 and 6 of the OAU Charter) into a *living* 'force multiplier' within the meaning and intent of Obama's definition;
- Africa's continuing failure – after the deceptions of the First and Second 'World Wars' and the Cold War – to distinguish between African wars and proxy wars fought in Africa and at the African people's expense; and
- the importance which African and other 'black states' attach to their membership of colonial-relic 'communities' and organizations like the (British) Commonwealth, the Organisation internationale de la Francophonie (OIF) and the Community of Portuguese-Language Countries (*Comunidade dos Países de Língua Portuguesa*) at the expense of the development of a Pan-African community, commonwealth and African and black-consciousness networks for mutual economic assistance, disaster prevention and management, common defence, development co-operation and the advancement and protection of the human rights of Africans and people of African descent everywhere!

Which way forward for Africa and African development?

Getting the African history right is not a matter, simply, of empowering Africans to challenge their denigrators, giving mentally enslaved Africans the assurance that 'the black skin is not a badge of shame', celebrating past African achievements and heroes to encourage a culture of basking in past glories as a substitute for the pursuit of excellence in our age – or providing the African people with yet another opium. The more productive purpose of these pages is to arm potential activists for the decolonization of Africa and African development with the knowledge that their enterprise would not be about '*returning*' the continent to the jungle and barbarism but about returning to the continent and Africans the possibility denied them for centuries, to take their destiny into their own hands and write and teach their own history, as envisaged by Patrice Lumumba. It is worth adding, in this connection, the following riposte by Rodney to the myth, repeated by Sarkozy in Dakar, that colonialism modernized Africa – and offers the only realistic prospect for the modernization of the continent:

> The most convincing evidence as to the superficiality of the talk about colonialism having 'modernised' Africa is the fact that the vast majority of Africans went into colonialism with a hoe and came out with a hoe.[36]

More importantly, as the veneer of imported modernity which the likes of Sarkozy brag about continues to keep the continent underdeveloped by denying it the scope for self-sustaining intellectual and material growth and its people the space they need to develop African solutions to African problems, thus ensuring their permanent susceptibility to exploitation and blackmail, the above reminders that Africans were not the achievement-free anthropoids portrayed or imagined by Gibbon, Hume, Dr Houston,

---

36   Rodney, *How Europe Underdeveloped Africa*, 239. In Sarkozy's rendition of the 'modernisation-of-Africa' theory, he argues, in defence of colonialism, that 'the coloniser took, but ... he also gave. He built bridges, roads, hospitals, dispensaries and schools. He turned virgin soil fertile. He gave of his effort, his work, his know-how'.

Sarkozy and others – and their African disciples – will, hopefully, encourage some Africans to aim at following the examples of their distant ancestors in all fields of human endeavour and put behind them the defeatism and complexes of their mentally colonized kith and kin.

CHAPTER 6

Pan-Africanism in the Twenty-First Century: Old, New and Unearthed Challenges

History, despite its wrenching pain, cannot be unlived, but if faced with courage, need not be lived again.

— MAYA ANGELOU

Nothing in the world is more dangerous than sincere ignorance and conscientious stupidity.

— MARTIN LUTHER KING JNR

Unless territorial freedom was ultimately linked up with the Pan African movement for the liberation of the whole African continent there would be no hope of freedom and equality for the African and for people of African descent in any part of the world.

— KWAME NKRUMAH

African and black lives, in Africa and globally, as of 2015: A recap and more

Even without counting the activities of killer cops and other lunatics in and out of uniform in 'the land of the free and the home of the brave', the terrorism of anti-black and anti-African racists in various masquerades who operate under the protection of 'freedom of speech' and 'freedom of association' in 'free societies' and powerful nations treating African possessions as theirs for the grabbing, it seems obvious on the most casual of reflections that very few Africans and people of African descent in most corners of the world are protected from the hazards of being African or 'black'. The obvious exceptions are the 'black-empowered' and others who are 'good', 'clever', crooked or 'lucky' enough to be counted by the modern dispensers of fame and fortune among 'the great and the good'. But even these, as a rule, can only enjoy their privileges for as long as they remain useful or non-threatening to Anthony Eden's 'white race authority', known with a measure of disgust in some contemporary circles as 'masters of the universe' or owners of the world.[1] From Kobina Sekyi's 'Anglo-Fanti' and Fanon's 'black skin, white masks' through the more generally tagged 'Afropeans' to the contemporary cosmopolitan-middle-class types, therefore, 'successful' Africans and people of African descent on other continents (elects of white race authority or 'white civilization' in all but name) have tended to perceive themselves – and to be admired or derided by African and other black observers – as socially, economically and culturally apart from 'the people they have left behind'. Of greater Pan-Africanist interest, however, is the fact that in the global apartheid order the conditions of their empowerment and maintenance of their cosmopolitan-middle-class status also leave them *necessarily* indifferent to the conditions of the African people they leave behind or, worse still, complicit in their impoverishment, as they pursue their 'whitening' and class interests.[2]

In the Caribbean, the authoritative CARICOM Reparations Commission (CRC)[3] describes the descendants of the trans-Atlantic slave trade and associated genocide 'left behind' as a suffering people today on account of the persistent effects of their history. Among the 'heritage burdens' reported by CRC are development failure rooted in a century of racial apartheid after 'emancipation'; the massive psychological trauma resulting from slavery and the same 'post-emancipation' apartheid; and the

1   The phrase 'masters of the universe' is Osei Boateng's description in Osei Boateng, 'Masters of the Universe ... Still Meddling in Africa', *New African*, 490, December 2009.

2   For a discussion of 'globalization' as apartheid on a world scale see Samir Amin, 'Mondialisation ou apartheid à l'échelle mondiale', in *Actuel Marx*, 31, 2002.

3   The CARICOM Reparations Commission is an organ of the Caribbean Community established by the Conference of Heads of Government and is composed of the Chairs of the National Reparations Committees of CARICOM member states and a representative of the University of the West Indies (UWI).

unenviable status of black Caribbeans as the people with the highest incidence of hypertension and type two diabetes in the world, on account of the nutritional deficiencies and general stress levels they have acquired from their history. And to pile more insults and humiliation on the Caribbean people of African descent, European governments from whom the reparations are due – as the legal bodies that instituted the framework for developing and sustaining the crimes against the Caribbean people, served as the primary agencies through which slave-based enrichment took place and are the national custodians of criminally accumulated wealth – have refused to acknowledge the crimes or to compensate victims and their descendants.[4]

Outside the New World as a whole, the fate of Afro-Indians in general and the Jarawas of the Andaman Islands, in particular, would be regarded by many as worse than death.[5] The conditions of most Afro-Latinos, as they emerge from Dzidzienyo and Oboler (eds)[6] and other accounts, are, if anything, only marginally better. Credible verbal reports also abound with the continuing inhuman treatment of some old Arab slaves of African descent in the Middle East and in the Arabic-speaking African Union and Arab League member state of Mauritania. In some other parts of the Arab World African domestic workers recruited under false pretences are also treated as slaves or turned into sex slaves.

In Africa itself, the 'dirty work' exposed in Ray, Ellen, William Schaap, Karl van Meter and Louis Wolf (eds),[7] the dictatorships run by the 'force multipliers' and their auxiliaries in their fields of competence, and the antics of indirect-rule presidents, ministers and their cronies in the neo-colonial

---

4 See the Caricom Reparations Commission, *Caribbean Reparatory Justice Program: Ten Point Action Plan*, accessed via *Pambazuka News*, 674, 16 April 2014, <http://pambazuka.org/en/category/features/91378>.

5 The author personally watched an *Al Jazeera* documentary in 2012 showing a 'human-safaris' episode in which naked Jarawa women and children were made to parade and otherwise perform for tourists – under tour-operator control! See <https://www.google.com.gh/?gfe_rd=cr&ei=aIO1VqynK-2r8wfxo7jgAg&gws_rd=ssl#q=Al+Jazera+documentary+on+the+Jawaras>.

6 Dzidzienyo and Oboler, eds, *Neither Enemies nor Friends: Latinos, Blacks, Afro-Latinos*, op. cit.

7 Ellen Ray, William Schaap, Karl van Meter and Louis Wolf, eds, *Dirty Work 2: The CIA in Africa*, op. cit.

and globalization era, provide ample confirmation that the 'transformation of colonization into cooperation' proclaimed by De Gaulle was a ruse.
The result is that the development of Africa's underdevelopment was not
reversed or arrested by 'decolonization' but remains active, and is reinforced in some cases, by the blend of neo-colonialism and Pax Americana
dubbed 'globalization'.

The imperial propaganda machine – with its combination of truth
disappearances, misinformation and plain lies about Africa's development
achievements, failures and responsibilities for them – has also been as active
as ever. Tony Blair's 'scar-on-the-conscience' posturing on the basis of half-
truths to justify *his* civilizing-development mission, Sarkozy's mistreatment
of Africa's history as a launch pad for his new Eurafrican project and Bill
Clinton's call on the Haitian people to shake off their history (as if their
minds, not imperialist exploitation is the problem) are all too familiar to
students of the practice of misrepresenting Africans even to themselves for
the purpose of continuing and justifying their treatment as circus animals.
And, to cap it all, open and closet imperialists and racists continue to seize
every opportunity in words spoken and unspoken to cast the poverty of
the Africans they have underdeveloped and impoverished as proof of their
'racial inferiority'.

Not surprisingly, and in line with the racist tradition of ascribing
all African achievements to non-African origins, a new myth of 'Africa
Rising' which followed the 'hopeless Africa' and 'scar-on-the-conscience'
noises from Britain also gave full credit to America and two of its 'force
multipliers' or proxies for the alleged development (and no mention of
any African contribution) thus:

> The UN Security Council, at America's behest, started this year with a 'month of
> Africa'. It went well. AIDS, refugees and wars were all on the agenda, and there were
> signs that the new concern was not just a 31-day wonder. The Clinton administra-
> tion, for instance, has since pressed ahead with plans to combat AIDS, doubling
> its budgetary requests to Congress. Congress, for its part, is backing a bill that will
> ease or abolish trade restrictions for 48 African countries. The World Bank and
> other donors showed last month that they were ready to intensify the fight against
> malaria, a disease that causes misery in Africa. And the UN has gone ahead with
> its peacekeeping plans, sending 8,000 troops to Sierra Leone and pledging another
> 5,500, all being well, for Congo.

> *All, however, is not well. Since January, Mozambique and Madagascar have been del-uged by floods, famine has started to reappear in Ethiopia, Zimbabwe has succumbed to government-sponsored thuggery, and poverty and pestilence continue unabated. Most seriously, wars still rage from north to south and east to west. No one can blame Africans for the weather, but most of the continent's shortcomings owe less to acts of God than to acts of man. These acts are not exclusively African – brutality, despotism and corrup-tion exist everywhere – but African societies, for reasons buried in their cultures, seem especially susceptible to them.*[8] [My emphasis]

The 'white saviour' theme apart, *The Economist* sinned by disappearing the African people entirely from society when it turned its attention to Africa's economic health, as the following report shows:

> A booming economy has made a big difference. Over the past ten years real income per person has increased by more than 30%, whereas in the previous 20 years it shrank by nearly 10%. Africa is the world's fastest-growing continent just now. Over the next decade its GDP is expected to rise by an average of 6% a year, not least thanks to foreign direct investment.[9]

The credit given to foreign direct investors for the so-called economic growth performance of Africa which *The Economist* and its ideological soul mates find impressive and the sheer arbitrariness of their measure are not the only grounds for faulting Africa's self-appointed performance overse-ers, however, as Rick Rowden points out in the following critique of their pontifications on economic Africa:

> Recent high growth rates and increased foreign investment in Africa have given rise to the popular idea that the continent may well be on track to become the next global economic powerhouse. This 'Africa Rising' narrative has been most prominently presented in recent cover stories by *Time Magazine* and *The Economist*. Yet both publications are wrong in their analysis of Africa's developmental prospects – and the

8   *The Economist* magazine op-ed, 'Hopeless Africa', from the print edition, May 11th 2000, also online at <http://www.economist.com/node/333429> (accessed December 2013).

9   *The Economist*, 'Africa rising, A hopeful continent', Special Report, print edition, 2 March 2013, <http://www.economist.com/news/special-report/21572377-african-lives-have-already-greatly-improved-over-past-decade-says-oliver-august> (accessed 20 April 2013).

reasons they're wrong speak volumes about the problematic way national economic development has come to be understood in the age of globalization.

Both articles use unhelpful indicators to gauge Africa's development. They looked to Africa's recent high GDP growth rates, rising per capita incomes, and the explosive growth of mobile phones and mobile phone banking as evidence that Africa is 'developing'. *Time* referred to the growth in sectors such as tourism, retail, and banking, and also cited countries with new discoveries of oil and gas reserves. *The Economist* pointed to the growth in the number of African billionaires and the increase in Africa's trade with the rest of the world.

But these indicators only give a partial picture of how well development is going – at least as the term has been understood over the last few centuries. From late 15th century England all the way up to the East Asian Tigers of recent renown, development has generally been taken as a synonym for 'industrialization'. Rich countries figured out long ago, if economies are not moving out of dead-end activities that only provide diminishing returns over time (primary agriculture and extractive activities such as mining, logging, and fisheries), and into activities that provide increasing returns over time (manufacturing and services), then you can't really say they are developing.

What's striking about the two articles cited above is that they don't mention manufacturing, or its disturbing absence, in Africa. And that, in turn, confirms once again the extent to which the idea of development as industrialization has been completely abandoned in the last few decades. Free market economics has come to advise poor countries to stick with their current primary agriculture and extractives industries and 'integrate' into the global economy as they are. Today, for many champions of free markets, the mere presence of GDP growth and an increase in trade volumes are euphemisms for successful economic development. But increased growth and trade are not development.[10]

But worse than perhaps even Rowden realized the two pompous monitors of Africa's economic performance omitted to note, as is the custom of mainstream Western historiographers and commentators, that the increased growth rates and trade have been and continue to be 'achieved' on the backs of the dispossessed, exploited, marginalized, impoverished and dehumanized African workers, 'independent producers' and individual and communal assets owners. That, and the fact that the growth rates on which the

10 Rick Rowden, 'The Myth of Africa's Rise: why the rumours of Africa's explosive growth have been greatly exaggerated', *Democracy Lab*, 4 January 2013 (Tracking a World of Change, A Special Report of the Legatum Institute), <www.foreignpolicy. com/articles/2013/01/04/the_myth_of_africa_s_rise> (accessed 15 May 2014).

myth-makers rely to peddle their 'Africa Rising' message are often directly associated with environmental degradation (and turn negative when environmental accounting is factored in), should be sufficient to condemn it as yet another piece of Bad Samaritanism from Africa's self-appointed judges and friends.[11] But Xan Rice adds the following devastating critique of an 'Africa Rising' narrative based on growths in the purchasing power, lifestyles and number of the continent's 'cosmopolitan middle classes' and billionaires:

> On a recent sweaty night at Murtala Muhammed international airport in Lagos, a Nigerian man strutted towards the boarding gates like somebody who knows – or rather hopes – that he is being watched. He was pulling a carry-on Louis Vuitton suitcase, with a smaller Louis Vuitton bag on top. His shoes were from Louis Vuitton and so were his trousers, belt, shirt and sunglasses. It was over-the-top, even by the standards of Nigeria, where some of the elite love to flaunt the luxury brands purchases in the boutiques in European capitals.
>
> Until very recently, flying abroad was the only way for them to buy luxury goods. Now, things may be changing. In April, Ermenegildo Zegna opened a store in Lagos, the first luxury clothing brand to do so. Its setting – on Akin Adesola Street, a busy road that links the lagoon and ocean on either side of Victoria Island, the city's financial district – is not glamorous. But Zegna, which had never had a store in sub-Saharan Africa, is betting that customers more accustomed to shopping on Bond Street or the Champs-Élysées will not mind.
>
> Zegna is considering opening a store in Angola, which, like Nigeria, has a small but extremely wealthy elite thanks to its oil industry, and in Mozambique, the site of large new gas finds. Africa 'is going to be a territory that's very important for luxury', even if the market is still at an early stage, according to Gildo Zegna, chief executive. Describing the company's strategy in emerging markets, including Africa, Mr Zegna told the FT last year that it was targeting 'the top 1 per cent of the population, or perhaps even less'.
>
> Zegna's African expansion may initially seem startling – both Angola and Mozambique experienced devastating wars not long ago – but the company is not

11   To go back to some of the basics see Rodney, *How Europe Underdeveloped Africa*, George, *How the Other Half Dies* and Comité d'Information Sahel, *Qui se nourrit de la famine en Afrique?*. See also IRIN, 'The downside of foreign land acquisitions', 19 January 2012, <http://www.irinnews.org/report/94680/west-africa-the-downside-of-foreign-land-acquisitions> (accessed 21 August 2014) and Emira Woods, 'Africa: burdened with too much oil', *African Agenda*, Vol. 9, No. 4, 2006, 5–6.

alone. Breitling now distributes its watches through wholesalers in at least a dozen African countries, including Ghana. The trend is less surprising when you look at Africa's place in the global economy. Sub-Saharan African economies are expanding faster than any other region, bar developing Asia, with the IMF forecasting growth of 5.4 per cent in 2013 and 5.7 per cent in 2014. Though many African countries are growing from a very low base – and income distribution is often very unequal – the number of wealthy, status-conscious people is rising and will continue to do so while commodity prices stay high.

For now, the only entrenched market for luxury goods in sub-Saharan Africa is South Africa, which has the continent's second largest economy and a largely urban population. A recent report by the consultancy Bain noted that South Africa has 71,000 dollar millionaires, 60 per cent of the total number in sub-Saharan Africa. That is more than Saudi Arabia or the United Arab Emirates and not that far off the 95,000 millionaires in Russia. Bain estimated that by 2020, 420,000 households in South Africa would have disposable income of more than $100,000 and forecasts that the luxury goods market, worth about $1bn a year, will grow by 20–30 per cent for the next five years.

In South Africa's favour is its large number of high-end shopping malls that offer the sort of retail space attractive to international brands such as Louis Vuitton, Burberry, Gucci and Fendi, all present in the country. South Africa has its own luxury brands working mainly with leather and jewellery.

In Lagos, the continent's most populous city, with more than 12m people, there (are) only two small malls of international standard – compared with 74 in Johannesburg – and even these may not be of a high enough standard for the likes of Louis Vuitton.

Francesco Trapani, head of LVMH's jewellery and watches division, said last year that Africa remained 'a very, very small market for us'. Hermès said that despite looking at South Africa, it had not yet found any suitable opportunities to do business or open a shop on the continent. Yet as Zegna's foray into Lagos shows, the amount of money sloshing around – and the appetite for conspicuous consumption – means that some luxury goods companies no longer feel content simply to wait for change.

According to Euromonitor, Nigeria was the second fastest growing market in the world for champagne between 2006 and 2011, by which time it had become the 17th biggest consumer of bubbly in the world, with 752,879 bottles drunk. Over the five years to 2016 the trend will continue, with only France experiencing a larger rise in champagne consumption, by volume. And it's not the cheap stuff – Moet, Veuve Clicquot and Dom Pérignon are all popular among Nigeria's elite.

Carmakers have taken note. Porsche opened a dealership in Lagos last year, a short walk away from the Zegna store. For luxury to take full flight will require the emergence of a middle-class. That said, for some luxury bosses, a narrow band of super-rich people will do for now.[12]

Accompanying the article was a picture with the caption, 'A good night: empty bottles of champagne at a Lagos nightclub frequented by wealthy Nigerians'. None of this makes Africa's '1 per cent' necessarily more vulgar or parasitic than their (mostly 'white') Western role models.[13] Nor does it necessarily make it a Pan-Africanist issue: asceticism has never really been built into Pan-Africanism per se. But if being 'cosmopolitan middle class' means that the super affluent of Africa mimic and keep the company of the 'corporate criminals'[14] in Ferguson's book who '(become) wealthy by being well connected and crooked',[15] '(use) their wealth to acquire and manipulate political power to their own advantage',[16] enjoy 'pay levels that disorient moral compasses', live debauched lives,[17] and promote 'obscene (and) morally indefensible decline in the fairness of (their societies)',[18] among other offences, then Pan-Africanists have cause to worry about their presence among Africans, on the grounds that it is logically, politically and morally impossible to be one of the African hares and the globalizing hounds simultaneously. Worse still, their very emergence and sustenance cannot but promote the parasitism and inclination of those concerned 'to destroy (their lands) for their unthinking profit'. By the same token the 'rise' of this category of 'black skin, white masks', 'apes' and quislings (in the sense of Cabral) cannot be a boon to African development, by any stretch of the imagination.

12   Xan Rice, 'Sub-Saharan Africa: Where some purveyors of luxury goods are happy to tread'.
13   For an explanation of why the 'colour separation' is necessary see 'How Segregation Destroys Black Wealth', *New York Times*, 15 September 2015, <http://www.nytimes.com/2015/09/15/opinion/how-segregation-destroys-black-wealth.html?_r=0> (accessed 15 September 2015).
14   'Corporate criminals' is, of course, part of the subtitle of Ferguson's *Predator Nation*.
15   Ferguson, *Predator Nations*, 5.
16   Ferguson, ibid. 20.
17   Ibid. 19.
18   Ibid. 9.

Pan-Africanism today: A movement abused and defanged in the face of its twenty-first-century challenges

The abuse of the name, symbols and spirit of Pan-Africanism, in the face of the above challenges, is among the more disturbing signs of the condition of the movement in the twenty-first century. Chapter 1 ended with examples in the globalization era of the shameless appropriation, for self-aggrandizement and other dubious purposes, of the name and symbols of Pan-Africanism by persons and cliques whose personal and official records show their profound misunderstanding of the movement or their outright repudiation of what it stands for. But the movement has also been consciously or unconsciously defanged by persons and other bodies which do not fit too readily into either of the above categories. One such example was provided in the second decade of the twenty-first century by the fifteen-member Southern African Development Community (SADC) – a body which counts resource-rich countries like Angola, Botswana, Democratic Republic of the Congo, Mozambique, South Africa and Zambia as well as Zimbabwe among its members. Ostensibly acting in the spirit of African solidarity SADC, a product of Pan-Africanism and 'building block' of the African Union, cast itself as a pleading lapdog on the issue of Western sanctions against Zimbabwe, rather than the African people's principal guard dog in Southern Africa which its roots in the 'Frontline States' against apartheid South Africa had led many to expect it to be. The following newspaper report on a SADC leaders' meeting at which the sanctions featured shows how far they could go to humiliate themselves, their (sub) region, Africa and the African world by *pleading* where they should have *demanded*:

> Southern African leaders have called for the West to lift all sanctions imposed on Zimbabwe after endorsing President Robert Mugabe's victory in disputed elections last month.
> Zimbabweans have 'suffered enough', Malawian President Banda said …
> Ending a meeting of the Southern African Development Community (SADC) in the Malawian capital, Lilongwe … regional leaders said in a statement that 'all

forms of sanctions' imposed on Zimbabwe should be lifted following the holding of 'free and peaceful' elections.[19]

But worse than the kowtowing itself was the underlying form and substance of the plea, with its thrust that Zimbabwe be pardoned because it had met the West's demand for the 'free and peaceful' elections! That was, of course, as laughable then as it is now: all but the 'sincerely ignorant and conscientiously stupid' knew that an election in Zimbabwe would be acceptable to the sanctions-wielding West if and only if it was won by a 'party' which was willing and able to reverse the Zimbabwean land reforms. It requires no wizardry, moreover, to be able to count the number of countries in Africa, the Middle East and elsewhere which have never tasted or needed to fear Western sanctions – and enjoy the status of allies of the US or the West as a whole – without passing any of the 'free-fair-and-peaceful-elections' tests imposed on Zimbabwe. But by the substance and tone of the mercy plea to the sanctioning powers the SADC leaders did worse than humiliate themselves and damage Zimbabwe's cause: they emboldened the bullies, implicitly accepted their right to decide how target states and societies are to be governed and, thereby, legitimized their interference in the internal affairs of a SADC member state and beyond!

The contrast between the SADC leaders' performance on Zimbabwe sanctions, on one hand, and Marcus Garvey's defiant response to the colonial atrocity in Kenya in 1922 cited in Chapter 1; progressive Africa's confrontations with Britain over its 'kith-and-kin politics' following Ian Smith's 1965 Unilateral Declaration of Independence (UDI); Algerian, Egyptian, Ethiopian, Ghanaian, Guinean, Nigerian, Tunisian, Zambian and other frontline states' support to the national liberation struggles in Southern Africa as they became relatively free themselves; Nkrumah's provision of ten million pounds sterling (£10 million) in bailout money to Guinea-Conakry to enable it to survive France's scorched-earth attack on it for choosing independence over a France-Afrique alternative offered by then President Charles De Gaulle in a 1958 referendum ruse; pre-independence

---

19   *Daily Graphic*, 20 August 2013, quoting an AFP report carried by the BBC.

Jamaica's courage in leading the world's trade boycott of apartheid in July
1959, to cite but these, is one measure of the difference between the Pan-
Africanism of old and the Pan-Africanism of the 'new generation' of African
leaders and arm-chair Pan-Africanists.

In addition, many acts and omissions by the African Union and
its member states – such as the hosting by the AU of a NATO liaison
office at its headquarters; facilitation by the African members on the
UN Security Council of the overthrow by NATO and its proxies of
the AU and internationally recognized government of Libya in 2011;
acceptance by Nigeria, 'the giant of Africa', of compromising 'security
assistance' from France, Britain and the United States to overcome
Boko Haram, a local terrorist group; ready acceptance by other African
'states' of security cover from NATO, AFRICOM, the French military
and other imperial forces when confronted with imported or locally
brewed security challenges, etc. – suggest that as of 2015 it was the
'Brzezinski doctrine', rather than the spirit of vintage Pan-Africanism,
which drove 'African defence policy'.[20]

---

20   At page 52 of *Imperial Ambitions* Chomsky quotes Zbigniew Brzezinski as writing in
     The Grand Chessboard (New York: Basic Books, 1998, 40) that 'the three grand imper-
     atives of (US) imperial geostrategy' are: 'to prevent collusion and maintain security
     dependence among the vassals, to keep tributaries pliant and protected, and to keep
     the barbarians from coming together'. On 'the giant of Africa' and the US and Western
     security umbrella see, for instance, Abayomi Azikiwe, 'Imperialists host conference on
     Nigerian security in Paris', *Pambazuka News*, 679, 21 May 2014, <http://pambazuka.
     org/en/category/features/91841>; Daniel Flynn, 'U.S. army to provide equipment,
     intelligence to fight Boko Haram', *Reuters*, 17 February 2015, <http://www.reuters.
     com/article/2015/02/18/us-nigeria-violence-usa-idUSKBN0LL0W320150218>
     (accessed 20 February 2015); and the BBC, 'Boko Haram crisis: UK boosts Nigeria
     military aid', <http://www.bbc.com/news/world-africa-27812766> (accessed 14 June
     2014). Zbigniew Brzezinski, originator of the doctrine, was US President Jimmy
     Carter's National Security Adviser.

A liberation movement in need of salvation from its friends – as well as opportunists

One of the many remarkable fallouts from the recasting of Pan-Africanism by 'the new generation of African (and Pan-African) leaders' as another globalization tool has been an understandable misperception of African unity, or integration, in some circles as yet another means of aping the West and Western-inspired 'market integration' and 'community' and union-building movements. In an embarrassing fallout from this fallout a life-long Pan-Africanist and writer of no mean repute was misled by the misperception into 'confessing' on one of 'the world's radios' in 2012 that her faith in Pan-Africanism had been shaken by 'what was happening to the European Union and the Euro' – two totally different kettles of fish! But that is not necessarily the worst of the movement's misrepresentation and misperception troubles. Nor was her misperception totally misguided when the transition from the Organization of African Unity to the African Union itself involved study trips by OAU staff and consultants to the EU headquarters in Brussels for lessons on its transformation processes.

But the crass commercial exploitation of the movement's name is, by any standard, a more unpardonable twenty-first-century abuse. The government of Ghana, for one, made itself guilty of that practice in 2007 in the shape of a so-called Joseph Project: a gimmick to promote Ghana as a tourist destination whose crude commercialism and political cynicism could not be concealed by its false advertising as a Pan-Africanist initiative to bring the people of Ghana and their brothers and sisters in the Diaspora together and establish Ghana as the true gateway to the homeland for Africans in the Diaspora. The choice of that country's then Ministry of Tourism and Diaspora Affairs (a suspicious and undignified amalgamation of portfolios in its own right) as the project's base was not the only sign that packaging Ghana as a heritage-tourism destination for commercial purposes, not Garvey-style Pan-Africanism, was its driving force. The fact that the supervising minister and prime mover of the project was more qualified and better known as a businessman and products advertisement practitioner than as a Pan-Africanist was another telltale sign. As will be seen from the quotation below the project's credibility was to suffer equally from perceptions in the Diaspora about the Pan-Africanist credentials of the sponsoring government as a whole. And in Africa itself the sponsoring government's self promotion as an offspring of a so-called 'Danquah-Busia tradition' which was discredited, possibly forever, when one of its founders, Kofi Abrefa Busia, used his brief reign as Prime Minister of Ghana (1969–1972) to attempt to undermine Africa's diplomatic struggle against apartheid South Africa with his advocacy of 'dialogue' with the odious regime – on the grounds that tea with the 'white man' was all it took to resolve conflicts with him – doomed all efforts to sell the Joseph Project to the general public as a Pan-Africanist initiative.

From the Diaspora Sharon Minor King dismissed the Joseph Project in the following words:

> Ironically, the primary supporter of this fresh approach to an old [Pan-Africanist] vision (the 'back to Africa' vision) was none other than the current President of Ghana, John Agyekum Kufuor. At the end of his presidency, he has become very visible in promoting the late Kwame Nkrumah's vision of Ghana as a place Diaspora Africans can call 'home' again. Throughout the cities and countryside, billboards of Kufuor and Nkrumah give the impression that these relatively distinctively different statesmen would actually have something collective to say to one another about the fifty-year celebration of Ghana's independence. I would love to have been a mosquito in their office during those conversations![21]

In the same sceptical vein King continued:

> While I applaud the courage of the Ghana government to take on such a visible effort towards reconciliation, I am also critical of The Joseph Project for many reasons. Twenty million cedis were controversially spent on Ghana's 50th anniversary, and a relatively significant portion of that sum was allocated for The Joseph Project.

---

21   For an abridged version of Sharon Minor King's reflections on the Joseph Project, see 'The Joseph Project' in Sharon Minor King, 'WE HEAR YOU ALL ... But We Don't Understand What You Are Saying: Personal Reflections on the Joseph Project of Ghana, West Africa, Summer, 2007', <www.ghanaiandiaspora.com/wp/wp-content/uploads/2013/06/Sharon-Minor-King-Ph.D.pdf>. For the entire article, email <prof.k.2013@cyberchurchinternationalacademy.com> or <sharonk@umbc.edu>.

Where did the money go ... and who benefited from all the pomp? Did Diaspora Africans gain anything from the millions of dollars that flooded Ghana's tourist market besides a good 'feeling of healing'? Did they really 'come home' or were they merely a line item within Ghana's tourist revenue of the economy? How were we 'marketed' to the diverse members of Ghana's class-conscious society? What were school children learning about any of this? What were the actual experiences of those who travelled so far to find what they could not find at home in America? And was it worth it or could it possibly do additional harm to what is already a very sensitive relationship between us?[22]

The Global African Diaspora Summit – an assembly of heads of state and government of the African Union, the Caribbean and South America[23] – convened under the auspices of a so-called African Diaspora Marketplace[24] and the African Union which co-hosted it with the South African government and the Pan-African Parliament, according to its communiqué – was even more blatant in demonstrating by its design and output that its 'Pan-Africanism' was for business promotion, not the liberation of oppressed Africans in Africa or the Diaspora. That much is evident from the priority projects and ideas of the Summit which were listed as:

- promotion of African and Diaspora business partnerships;
- governmental actions to foster increased economic partnerships;
- mobilization of capital from within Pan-African space;

22   Sharon Minor King, ibid. She, mercifully, omitted to add that the 'Pan-Africanism' of the Joseph Project vendors was for people of African descent in the Diaspora who could afford commercial travel by air or sea to Ghana!

23   See *Declaration of the Global African Diaspora Summit*, <http://www.dfa.gov.za/docs/2012/diaspora_declaration0525.pdf> (accessed 24 September 2015).

24   The African Diaspora Marketplace (ADM) was launched in 2009 by the eminently non-Pan-Africanist US Agency for International Development (USAID), Western Union and the Western Union Foundation. Its official aim, according to its website, is 'to identify and support entrepreneurs seeking to launch business ventures in Africa that could contribute to long-term economic growth'. See the ADM Website: <diasporaalliance.org/what-is-the-african-diaspora-marketplace/> (accessed 19 May 2014).

- the creation by the AU and CARICOM of a conducive environment for the African Diaspora to invest, work, and travel on the African continent and the Caribbean;
- the adoption and promotion of the Development Market Place for the African Diaspora Model as a framework for innovation and entrepreneurship that would facilitate development;[25]
- enhanced utilization of African and Diaspora expertise on economic development issues at regional and continental levels, and exploration of the possibility of creating Diaspora Advisory Board(s);
- enhancement of South-South co-operation through closer collaboration between the African Union (AU) and all inter-governmental entities in regions of which African Diaspora populations are a part;
- leveraging the collective efforts of the African Union and all inter-governmental entities in regions where there are African Diaspora populations to promote and advance issues of critical importance to Africa and its Diaspora;
- encouragement of AU member states to establish more formal relations with the Caribbean and Latin American nations and vice versa and, where practicable, open more missions in the respective regions;
- close collaboration to advance the international agenda on climate change in international fora, given its devastating effects particularly on Africa and the Caribbean; and
- support for efforts by the AU to accelerate the process of issuing the African Union passport, in order to facilitate the development of a transnational and transcontinental identity.[26]

Many of the above project titles cover what they should reveal about their business versus people friendliness. More revealing is how closely

---

25   The reference is obviously to the multi-donor-funded World Bank African Diaspora Programme, allied to the ADM (see above note), whose purpose is the mobilization of the African Diaspora for development – as the donors see it.

26   African Union, *Declaration of the Global African Diaspora Summit*, Sandton, Johannesburg, South Africa, 25 May 2012, <http://summits.au.int/en/sites/default/files/FINAL%20Diaspora%20Declaration-E-25%20May%20(1).pdf>.

the agenda of the African Diaspora Marketplace (ADM) which sponsored the Summit – '(identifying) and (supporting) entrepreneurs seeking to launch business ventures in Africa' – resembles that of the US government's US-Africa Business Forum and Young African Leaders Initiative.[27] But if the quiet transformation of Pan-Africanism from a liberation movement whose mission is far from accomplished into a business tool is obscene the accompanying AU definition of the African Diaspora as 'peoples of African origin living outside the continent, irrespective of their citizenship and nationality and who are willing to contribute to the development of the continent and the building of the African Union' is downright scandalous.[28] For, what the definition does is deny their humanity or Africanity to people of African descent living outside the 'mother continent' who lack the means, and therefore the *effective will*, to 'contribute to the development of the continent and the building of the African Union'. Fascist may or may not be too harsh a characterization of the minds which produced that definition of Diaspora Africans. The fact that those who led the transformation of the OAU into the African Union had a problem even recognizing the African Diaspora as an African constituency, and only developed an interest in this category of Africans when it dawned on them that the Diaspora was a potential source of 'development support' for the continent or the Union, exposes them purely and simply as unworthy of the Pan-Africanism of Nkrumah and others whose mantle they sometimes claimed, however. Belinda Otas' recollection of the following episode should leave no doubt about the frame of mind of the AU's founding chairperson at least:

---

27 For US President Barack Obama's ambition for the Young African Leaders Initiative in his own words, see 'Remarks by President Obama to the People of Africa, Mandela Hall, African Union Headquarters, Addis Ababa, Ethiopia', <http://www.shal lownation.com/2015/07/28/video-president-obama-speech-in-addis-ababa-ethi opia-african-union-july-28-2015/> (accessed 22 August 2015). On the US-Africa Business Forum, see, for instance, <https://en.wikipedia.org/wiki/United_ States%E2%80%93Africa_Leaders_Summit#US.E2.80.93Africa_Business_Forum>.

28 Quoted by Belinda Otas in 'Why the AU is Courting the Diaspora', *New African*, 519, July 2012, 20. Otas, the versatile journalist, writer, cultural critic and independent blogger attended the Summit.

When the AU chairperson at the time (of the AU's launch on 9 July, 2002), President Thabo Mbeki of South Africa, was asked where the Diaspora fit in, he first laughed, then became pensive, and finally dismissed the question by saying the AU's inaugural summit in Durban was reserved for 'heads of state'. He then suggested that those Diasporan Africans wishing to participate in the Union should contact 'our ambassadors in Washington DC; and even easier the black media in the USA should 'look it up on the Internet'.[29]

The Global Summit's so-called Legacy Projects and Programme of Action suggest that the Summiteers were just as cynical, but in their own way. But the list below of 'priority projects' it adopted to 'give practical meaning to the Diaspora programme and in order to facilitate the post-Summit implementation programme' can only confirm the impression:

1. The production of a Skills Database of African Professionals in the Diaspora;
2. Establishment of the African Diaspora Volunteers Corps;
3. Establishment of the African Diaspora Investment Fund;
4. (Development and implementation of) a programme on the Development Marketplace for the Diaspora, as a framework for facilitating innovation and entrepreneurship ...; and
5. Establishment of an African Remittances Institute (aka the African Institute for Remittances (AIR).[30]

Not surprisingly, Diaspora African entrepreneurs seeking to launch business ventures in Africa were thrilled by the Summit's outputs. Otas quotes the chairperson of the Nigeria Diaspora Committee, for example, as observing that: 'the current global environment ... provided an opportune time for African leaders to attract Diasporans to come back home

---

29 Belinda Otas, 20, ibid. The omission of the Diaspora in South America, the Caribbean and elsewhere in that gut response cannot be dismissed as insignificant either.

30 *Declaration of the Global African Diaspora Summit*, op. cit. The AIR was, *not incidentally*, launched by the African Union with the support of the World Bank and the European Commission, and in co-operation with the African Development Bank and the International Organization for Migration. See <http://pages.au.int/remittance/about> (accessed 8 October 2015).

and invest.'[31] Another investment-opportunities-and-profits hunter, the African-American founder and head of the Ghana-based Diaspora African Mission, is reported to have waxed enthusiastically that:

> the kind of returns you can make on investments in Africa, you cannot make it anywhere else in the world. Everybody is here in Africa investing except us, the Diaspora, and that's one of the things I'm really working on, and helping our Diaspora to see the potentials in Africa. There are vast opportunities here. The Chinese, Lebanese and Indians are all here doing business in Africa – everyone but us; and that is one thing I think we need to wake up to.[32]

The foregoing confirms, once again, the transformation by some of Pan-Africanism from a liberation movement to a Trojan horse for profit seekers of African descent. But this only accentuates the need to separate the wheat of vintage Pan-Africanism from the chaff of the cynical, the fatuous and the downright treacherous 'Pan-Africanisms' currently on the market.

The ABC of authentic Pan-Africanism, in some of the militants' own words

The task of separating vintage Pan-Africanism from the cynical, the fatuous and the treacherous varieties is simplified, fortunately, by the living words and declarations of the movement's founders and their unquestionable heirs, a sample of which follows:

---

31 Otas, ibid. 22.
32 Otas, ibid. 22. No indications were given of the enthusiast's thinking about how the anticipated high profit yields for Diaspora investors would translate into prosperity for the host communities and how the *modus operandi* of Diaspora investors are expected to differ from or resemble those of their Chinese, Lebanese and Indian counterparts.

From the Fifth Pan-African Congress

The delegates of the Fifth Pan-African Congress believe in the right of all peoples to govern themselves. We affirm the right of all Colonial peoples to control their own destiny. All Colonies must be free from foreign imperialist control, whether political or economic. The peoples of the Colonies must have the right to elect their own governments, without restrictions from foreign powers. We say to the peoples of the Colonies that they must fight for these ends by all the means at their disposal. The object of imperialist powers is to exploit. By granting the right to Colonial peoples to govern themselves that object is defeated. Therefore, the struggle for political power by Colonial and subject peoples is the first step towards, and the necessary prerequisite to, complete social, economic and political emancipation.[33]

Marcus Garvey

There shall be no solution to this race problem until (Africans) (themselves) strike the blow for liberty.[34]

No race, no people, no nation has ever been freed through cowardice, through cringing, through bowing and scraping, but all that has been achieved to the glory of mankind, to the glory and honour of races and nations was through the manly determination and effort of those who lead and those who are led.[35]

W. E. B. Du Bois

The cost of liberty is less than the price of repression.[36]

---

33   From 'DECLARATION TO THE COLONIAL WORKERS, FARMERS AND INTELLECTUALS', in George Padmore, ed., *History of the Pan-African Congress* (London: The Hammersmith Bookshop Ltd, undated). Accessible at <http://www. prisoncensorship.info/archive/etext/countries/panafrican/padmorefifthpac1947. html#p6> (accessed 25 March 2014).

34   'Marcus Garvey Quote', <http://www.brainyquote.com/quotes/quotes/m/marcus garv365161.html#v4d4mCDJKxc4PW6P.99> (accessed 25 January 2015)

35   Quoted by *Solidarity Equals Victory*, <https://www.facebook.com/ SolidarityEqualsVictory/posts/421472951311026> (accessed 25 September 2015).

36   <http://www.goodreads.com/author/quotes/10710.W_E_B_Du_Bois>.

Patrice Lumumba

Without dignity there is no freedom, without justice there is no dignity and without independence there are no free men.[37]

Malcolm X

You can't understand what is going on in Mississippi if you don't understand what is going on in the Congo. And you can't really be interested in what's going on in Mississippi if you're not also interested in what's going on in the Congo. They're both the same. The same interests are at stake. The same sides are drawn up, the same schemes are at work in the Congo that are at work in Mississippi. The same stake—no difference whatsoever.[38]

Kwame Nkrumah

Imperialism [has] grown stronger, more ruthless and experienced, and more dangerous in its international associations. Our economic advancement demands the end of colonialist and neo-colonialist domination in Africa[39]

Thomas Sankara

Let there be an end to the arrogance of the big powers who miss no opportunity to put the rights of the people in question.[40]

Just as instructive as the above and other immortal words of the icons of pristine Pan-Africanism are their lives and deeds which are immortalized

37 'Letter from Thysville Prison to Mrs Lumumba'.
38 Malcolm X, 1964, speaking on the importance of the Pan-African political framework. Malcolm X at the Audubon Ballroom in Harlem, 20 December 1964, <https://www.facebook.com/kambalemusavuli/posts/10151367123169379>.
39 Address to the Conference of African Heads of State and Government.
40 <http://www.brainyquote.com/quotes/quotes/t/thomassank582045.html>.

in books and other memorabilia. While it would certainly be foolhardy of anyone to attempt a comprehensive 'who is who' of Pan-Africanism's departed and living legends the lives and deeds of the likes of Marcus Garvey, W. E. B. and Shirley Du Bois, Amilcar Cabral, Ahmed Ben Bella, Kwame Nkrumah, Frantz Fanon, George Padmore, Stokely Carmichael (Kwame Turé), Walter Rodney, Thomas Sankara, Steve Biko, Mohammed Ali and Angela Davis, among others, can hardly fail to lead contemporary and future Pan-Africanists in the right direction.

Some parting thoughts and aides memoires

For the benefit of the likes of Nicolas ('No one can ask of the sons to repent for the mistakes of their fathers')[41] Sarkozy, 'development partners' who reject African and Afro-Diasporan demands for reparations for slavery and colonization with barely concealed contempt and Africans whose response to Pan-Africanism and continuing demands and struggles for the decolonization of Africa has hardly changed from the position on liberation articulated by Archie Mafeje's Treason Trialist it is worth recalling some of the many reasons why imperialism and anti-African and anti-black racism cannot be said to be dead and, for freedom-loving and self-respecting Africans, *a luta continua*:

- the need, as of 2015, for a 'black lives matter' movement and other movements for racial justice in the 'land of the free';[42] racial injustices against peoples of African descent in much of Latinized America;

---

41   From his Cheikh Anta Diop University Speech, op. cit.
42   Those who use that appellation for America also fail to point out, understandably, that Francis Scott Key, the composer of those words, also spoke publicly of African-Americans as 'a distinct and inferior race of people, which all experience proves to be the greatest evil that afflicts a community.' See Jefferson Morley, 'The Land of the Free and the Home of the Brave', *GLOBALIST*, 4 July 2013, <http://www.theglob

and the constant reminders by the sons and daughters of those who invented 'the white man's burden' and the 'civilizing mission' that the business of shaping and re-shaping African societies to further empower and enrich the West at the expense of the African people remains 'the black man's burden' it has been since the nineteenth century;

• the reported gathering by some 'powerful white folks' 'to celebrate the deaths and displacement of millions of black people as an act of God to cleanse their premises of miscreants' 'at the height of the hurricane Katrina disaster in New Orleans';[43]

• 'Man of God' Pat Robertson's celebration of the 2010 earthquake in Haiti as God's 'punishment for making a pact with the devil' because of the recognition the Haitians give to voodooism, an African religion;

• Robert Cooper's open advocacy of 'a new kind of imperialism' which has been shown to target Africans among others;

• The display by Dylann Roof, the Charleston shooter, of the apartheid South African and Rhodesian flags as well as the Confederate Flag on his Facebook wall;[44] and

• The routine and almost unconscious nonverbal repetition of General Émile Janssens' notorious 'Before independence = After

---

alist.com/the-land-of-the-free-and-the-home-of-the-brave/> (accessed 9 February 2016).

43 Sodzi Sodzi-Tettey, 'Dying to Live – Undoing Racism in America', *Daily Graphic*, 19 September 2015, 10.

44 This is how Wikipedia described the incident which brought the said Dylann Roof to global attention and exposed the connection, mostly hidden in 'modern times', between imperialism and racism: 'On the evening of June 17, 2015, a mass shooting took place at Emanuel African Methodist Episcopal Church in down town Charleston, South Carolina, United States. During a prayer service, nine people were killed by a gunman, including the senior pastor, state senator Clementa C. Pinckney; a tenth victim survived. The morning after the attack, police arrested a suspect, later identified as 21-year-old Dylann Roof. One image from his Facebook page depicts the shooter as wearing a jacket decorated with two emblems that are popular among American white supremacists: the flags of the former Rhodesia (now known as Zimbabwe) and apartheid-era South Africa.' See <https://en.wikipedia.org/wiki/Charleston_church_shooting> (accessed 27 September 2015).

independence' equation by representatives of white race authority
like British Prime Minister David Cameron and US President Barack
Obama, with the presumption of their right to use the power of 'aid'
to dictate sexual-morality laws to Africans; their standing instructions
to Africans on how they should govern themselves more generally;
and the West's decades-long attempt to change the government in
Zimbabwe and success in changing governments in Côte d'Ivoire and
Libya as vivid post-Cold War examples.[45]

If Cabral is right, furthermore, that the pests of the African people have
always needed African collaborators to do their blood sucking[46] – and it
is difficult to see how he could have been wrong, although his proposition is yet to be seriously tested – then the response of freedom, justice
and development-loving Africans to continuing imperialist exploitation
should be to oppose the imperialists and their African 'development' and
security 'partners' equally. They would have the benefit of some five centuries of relevant history to learn from as they marshal their forces to liberate
themselves and their people from both anti-people forces.

*Towards an experience-informed search for 'the political
kingdom': Failures as intellectual capital*

With the benefit of hindsight, and greater analytical clarity, it is possible to
fault Nkrumah's 'seek ye first the political kingdom' mantra as partly responsible for entrenching the false equation of 'flag and anthem independence'
with the real thing which has caused untold suffering in the African world

---

45   The 'before independence = after independence' provocation by General Émile
     Janssens, the Belgian commander of Congo-Kinshasa's Force Publique (or Armed
     Forces) is, of course, what triggered the first of a series of army mutinies in the new
     republic in July 1960 whose effects continue to be felt in the Democratic Republic of
     the Congo (DRC) some five decades later. For more on this see Joe Trapido, 'Africa's
     Leaky Giant' in *New Left Review*, 92, Mar/Apr 2015.
46   Cabral (1974), op. cit.

since the Haitian liberation fiasco. Taken in conjunction with Nkrumah's Independence Day declaration that 'At long last, the battle has ended (and) Ghana (was) free forever' – and his general readiness to work within the neo-colonial system until it was too late – it is hard to entertain the charitable view that he was not, himself, fooled by the magic of 'the political kingdom' (narrowly defined) at the times he repeated such declarations but was simply biding his time. The constructive use of the 'mistake' which Nkrumah was not alone in making but was certainly guilty of, obviously, is not to use it to vilify him but to learn from it. The same goes, *mutatis mutandis*, for other past liberation mistakes and failures.

For such purposes – and to ensure that the learning is deep, systematic, institutionalized and sustained – contemporary Pan-Africanists may wish to consider the establishment of centres, networks and projects for African and Pan-African Liberation and Development Studies and permanent and *ad hoc* arrangements for follow-up of relevant study conclusions and recommendations.

Avoiding 'the pitfalls of national consciousness' and messianism

Fanon's strictures on the pitfalls of national consciousness in his treatise on the subject,[47] and developments on the same theme by Cabral, Mafeje, Prashad, Patrick Bond and others,[48] have probably said all that can be said about the root causes of the African world's countless liberation fiascos. But the following lessons from the fact that even the modest 'revolutionary' achievements of the 'messianic' or 'charismatic' Ben Bella, Nasser,

47 Frantz Fanon, 'The Pitfalls of National Consciousness' (Chapter 3) in *The Wretched of the Earth*.

48 See, for instance, 'Brief Analysis of the Social Structure in Guinea' (Chapter 5) of *Revolution in Guinea*, Mafeje, 'South Africa at Crossroads: Liberation or Betrayal?' in, *In Search of an Alternative* and Prashad, 'Pitfalls' ('Algiers: the perils of an authoritarian state', 'Arusha: socialism in a hurry') in *The Darker Nations* and Patrick Bond, 'The Mandela Years in Power'.

Nkrumah and Nyerere, for instance, died with their overthrow or physical death may be highlighted:

1. None may substitute themselves for the people;
2. Only the people themselves can guarantee the success and irreversibility of their liberation and development; and
3. The people, who are permanent, must own revolutions carried out in their name in fact and not just in theory if they are to outlast leaders who can only 'come and go'.

Outside Africa the fate of Maoism after Mao is perhaps the best confirmation of these truths.

Rethinking the organization of African and Pan-African unity

Behind the African Union's failure to promote the effective decolonization of Africa and African development – and its collaboration with imperialism on many fronts, instead – is the original sin of the 'radical' and 'nationalistic' 'Casablanca Group' of African states in dropping their 'nationalism' and 'radicalism' and accommodating the rival, and Western-sponsored, Monrovia and Brazzaville Groups to form the Organization of African Unity which then proceeded to hijack the African Unity movement. The AU's implication in the Global African Diaspora Summit process and other acts unworthy of the people of Africa; the snub by the AU of Haiti's bicentennial celebrations; the absence of any Pan-African structure(s) the African peoples of the continent and Diaspora can identify with; and, following the African Union's lead, the generalized indifference of black governments to the oppression of black people in their neighbourhoods and across the globe are examples of the price the peoples of Africa and the Diaspora continue to pay for an African Union which is more inclined to echo the voices of its 'development partners' and serve their interests than lead the African people out of the physical, spiritual and intellectual bonds which have long oppressed them.

Attempting to lift the OAU/AU curse through management and staff changes or 'institutional reforms' would be a fool's errand, of course, as long as it, or any Pan-African body of its kind, remains an association of Ayi Kwei Armah's 'idiotic neo-colonial states' under the leadership of the black empowered and cosmopolitan-middle-class elite types. The African people's only possible, imaginable and practical alternative to an African Union which embraces and is embraced by the United States, the European Union, NATO, the World Bank and other 'force multipliers' of the rebranded white race authority has to be the replacement of the dubious body by Africanist and Pan-Africanist bodies and networks dedicated to their liberation, security, development and welfare. It is further suggested that while the liberation, security, development and welfare of Africans in the Diaspora who suffer on account of their 'Africanness' or 'blackness' need not depend on free, independent and liberation-promoting institutions and networks in the motherland such bodies may be legitimately judged by their implication or otherwise in the liberation and human and civil rights struggles of African peoples and individuals everywhere. For the Afro-Latinos, Afro-Indians, Afro-Arabs and other 'lost' or neglected 'tribes' of Africa support bases on the African continent are probably essential.

More reasons to treat the United Nations as part of the problem, not part of the solution

For Africans in Africa and the Diaspora whose taste of US power include the rape and destruction of Haiti, the assisted or orchestrated overthrow and murders of Patrice Lumumba and Muammar Gaddafi, the overthrow of Kwame Nkrumah, support for apartheid South Africa and Portuguese colonialism and the many other crimes against the African people in Africa reported in *Dirty Work 2: The CIA in Africa* up to 1980 alone; the boast in President Obama's 2014 West Point Commencement Address that the United Nations is a 'force multiplier … reducing the need for unilateral American action and (for increasing) restraint among other nations' should put Africans and the African world, in general, on notice that the organization was not designed as an African-people-friendly body. But there are more direct reasons why the African people should see the United Nations as part of their problem, not a solution to their woes.

For a start direct overt and covert UN collusion with the US in the pursuit of US objectives in Africa, for instance, was an open secret even before Obama's boast. On the overthrow and murder of the Congo's Patrice Lumumba and his replacement by Mobutu, for instance, this is what an informed observer wrote nearly forty years before Obama's West Point Address:

> The U.N. controlled potentially decisive military and financial resources in Leopoldville (present-day Kinshasa). But its dependence upon American economic, political, logistical and administrative support ensured that these trumps would be used either directly in behalf of American objectives or indirectly in the manner of benign neutrality. Thus U.N. Representative Andrew Cordier did not discourage Kasavubu from his CIA-supported coup and gave it a probably decisive boost by closing the airports and radio station, preventing Lumumba from mobilising his supporters. Having invoked the shibboleth of 'law and order' this time, the UN fell silent and remained impassive when its military protégé, Mobutu, pulled off another CIA coup several days later.[49]

Similarly, the US- and Western-sponsored regime changes in Côte d'Ivoire and Libya in 2011 were executed by kind courtesy of UN Security Council resolutions. Parts of the United Nations Development System, as opposed to the Security Council but including the United Nations Development Programme and the UN Secretariat (an organ in its own right) have strived to resist the 'force multiplier' role, of course.[50] But the taming of UNESCO, the US'

---

49 Stephen Weissman, 'The CIA and U.S. Policy in Zaire and Angola' in *Dirty Work 2: The CIA in Africa*, op. cit., 188.

50 The UNICEF campaign of the 1990s for debt reduction, and debt cancellation under certain conditions, for Africa; establishment in 1974 of the defunct United Nations Commission and Centre on Transnational Corporations (UNCTC); the United Nations Conference on Trade and Development (UNCTAD) when it was allowed to support the Third World Demands in the 1970s for a New International Economic Order (NIEO); and UNESCO's even shorter-lived attempt to do the same in the fields of culture and information, provoking the US's 1984 withdrawal from membership of the Agency on the grounds that it had exhibited a hostility towards what it called 'the basic institutions of a free society, especially a free market and a

refusal to allow Boutros Boutros Ghali (the Egyptian Secretary General who was appointed to that position as a reward for his contribution to the management of the Camp David Agreement between Israel and Anouar Sadat's Egypt and became too independent as Secretary General for America's liking) a second term (as convention demanded), and the treatments given to the UNCTC, UNCTAD and other 'errant' UN bodies and organs (see note below), should be proof enough that the 'leader of the free world' and its followers would rather not have a United Nations Organization, UN Secretaries General and UN bodies with minds of their own.[51]

But the United Nations is also problematic for what it symbolizes: 'world government' (when it pleases the Security Council) according to the will of the principal victor in the 'war for empire, of which the struggle between Germany and the Allies over Africa was both symbol and reality'. African trust and obedience to it thus amounts to yet another rite of submission to white race authority or specific members of the authority with a special place in the hearts, minds or stomachs of given groups of the African faithful. The symbolism and underlying superstition were very much in evidence in the call by the General Secretary of a 'political party' in Commonwealth, Anglophone and Anglophile Ghana on its 'former' colonial master and permanent member of the UN Security Council 'to support (its) electoral reforms ... and (calls by various 'opposition' and pressure groups) for a new voters register as the current register's credibility (had) been called into question.'[52] But more to the present point, a worshipful desire to please a 'higher force' (in the shape of the embodiment of 'white power' and the outed force multiplier that the UN is)

---

free press' (See US Statement on UNESCO, *New York Times*, 30 December 1983 at A4, also available at <http://www.nytimes.com/1983/12/30/world/us-statement-on-unesco.html> (accessed 11 October 2015)), are among the notable temporary exceptions to the 'force multiplier' rule.

51   On this particular point see also, Chomsky, *Rogue States*, 3–4, where he quotes one-time US Secretary of State, George Shultz' derision of those who advocate 'utopian, legalistic means like outside mediation, the United Nations and the World Court while ignoring the power element of the equation'. There is nothing in the US and Western conduct of war and peace to suggest that the US position on the United Nations and the World Court articulated by Shultz has changed.

52   *Daily Graphic*, 8 October 2015, 18.

was just as evident in the trouble taken by the president of independent Ghana to persuade the United Nations, through the General Assembly, in October 2015, that '(his country had) begun a process to review its rules of engagement in order to strike a balance between the maintenance of law and order and the basic rights of the people to free speech and free expression'; that his country 'would further promote Ghana's enviable democracy'; that Ghana 'was making strides in economic growth'; and that '(its) current agenda for transformation was aimed at diversifying the economy and accelerating growth.'[53]

It is difficult, otherwise, to understand the Ghanaian president's accounting to the United Nations on purely domestic affairs of the people of Ghana. By the same token it is difficult to exclude the de-idolization of the United Nations from the African people's mental decolonization agenda. The spectacles of an African 'political party' calling on Britain to intervene in its country's domestic affairs in its favour and the president of the same African 'nation' (noted for both hosting a 'Pan-African Congress' and embracing NATO and AFRICOM) opening the door to UN meddling in its internal affairs do, however, have at least one merit: they demonstrate once again the fact that different kinds of Africans and 'Pan-Africanists' draw different conclusions from the UN-US military alliance for the underdevelopment and military occupation of Haiti and similar white-race-authority projects in Africa itself.

---

53   *Daily Graphic*, 1 October 2015, 3. As if on cue the United Nations, in the person of the Special Representative of the United Nations Secretary-General for West Africa, was to assert its authority over 'democracy' in Ghana barely nine months later. Commenting on that country's police chief's indication that he would be prepared to impose a 'social media' ban on its election day, for security reasons, the Special Representative is reported to have declared, *inter alia*, that the UN was against the idea. In his own words, he is quoted to have declared 'without hesitation that from a UN point of view, we would be obviously averse to any steps that will amount to restricting the democratic space particularly any steps that will be taken to restrict the freedom of expression.', 'UN against social media ban on Election Day – Ibn Chambas', *GhanaWeb*, 18 June 2016, <https://www.google.com. gh/?gfe_rd=cr&ei=K1tlV9SvKvGr8wey_YCADQ&gws_rd=ssl#q=UN+against+ social+media+ban+on+Election+Day+%E2%80%93+Ibn+Chambas> (Source: <citifmonline.com>).

The imperative of political, economic, intelligence and general information sharing among Africans in Africa and the Diaspora

Embarrassing episodes like the chairperson of the AU Commission lauding 'the plan of death' imposed on the Haitian people and the call by Barbados Underground on October 19 2014 for a ban on travellers from all of Africa – on account of an Ebola outbreak in three (3) West African countries (see Chapter 2) – can only be avoided with functioning systems of information and intelligence gathering and distribution on events and developments of Pan-African interest in all the above departments of life. It is, in any case, a scandalous failure of African leadership and common sense that Africans in Africa and the Diaspora should continue to rely on the imperialist media for news and views about themselves, their kith and kin across the globe and the rest of the world. And this long after the struggles of Africa and the Third World in the 1970s exposed the absurdities and inequities of the World Information Order – and the spirited defence of that order (by all means necessary) by those who hold the power under it to tell the rest of the world what to think and what to think about. For, while the spirited fight by 'the masters of the universe' against a New World Information Order when the idea was canvassed by the Third World in the 1970s and 1980s is a measure of the power they derive from the current world information order Africa's failure to establish solid news and other information gathering and dissemination alternatives suggests passive or active complicity in the non-stop rape of African minds by 'the world's radios' and the interests they serve.

Another reason for the discomfort with African reliance on 'the world's radios' for information and opinions about Africans and black people in general is summed up by the following confession by a former editor of Britain's *Sunday Telegraph* (1986–1991), published by Britain's *Daily Mail* in April 1998:

> Race is still a problem for some of my generation. No longer because we regard blacks as inferior but because, having done so in the past, traces of that prejudice remain in the blood despite being banished from the brain ... Looking back, I am amazed about the depth of racist indoctrination which I received at school and in the home, not explicitly but implicitly. At the best, blacks were regarded as delinquent children

and the worst cannibals and savages. For years, those assumptions lingered, seriously affecting my reporting on the decolonising process in Africa.[54]

Education and re-education to re-energize African self-esteem for the liberation of the African people

The only worthy African response to imperialism's continuing use of force, pre-emptive attack and deception to rape the African people's bodies, minds and resources is to detoxify African minds and develop, implement and sustain programmes designed to, in Surkano's immortal words, suitably adapted, liberate every African everywhere from the bonds of fear, the bonds of poverty and the physical, spiritual and intellectual bonds which have for long stunted the development of the bulk of the African people across the globe.

Concluding thoughts

Making Pan-Africanism a mass movement rather than a movement for the masses

For reasons partially covered by Cabral's explanation of why the Guinean liberation struggle had to be launched by petty bourgeois elements like himself and not by the masses,[55] Pan-Africanism was led from inception by Western-educated petty bourgeois or bourgeois African, North American and Caribbean born Africans who were good enough to use

---

54   Quoted by Baffour Ankomah in 'What exactly is their problem?', *New African*, 562, June 2016. Ankomah provides examples of traces of the attitudes revealed in the above confession in British and Western reporting of Africa-related events – in 2016.
55   Cabral, 'Brief Analysis of the Social Structure in Guinea' in *Revolution in Guinea*, 51–2.

their relative political awakening not to lord it over their less fortunate kith and kin or ally '(themselves) with imperialism and the reactionary strata in its own country to try and preserve (their petty bourgeois status)'[56] but as a call on them to take on the burden of the people's liberation. Several eyewitness accounts of how Cabral's own movement organized and conducted itself suggest that some of the petty bourgeois initiators of people's liberation from colonialism and neo-colonialism were also keenly aware of the need for the democratic engagement of the people in their own liberation if the process was to be successful. As Cabral himself put it, 'the workers and peasants ... must themselves take power or control to make the revolution'.[57]

But examples of successful popular uprisings against oppression and exploitation leading to government and development of the people by the people and for the people are rare, indeed, for the reasons outlined by Fanon, Cabral, Patrick Bond and others. The unfortunate common practice is for 'the pitfalls of national consciousness' to take over. Having, unfortunately, allowed Pan-Africanism to be hijacked in the post-black-empowerment environment by characters who seem structurally and intellectually incapable of distinguishing between confronting the imperialist enemy and collaboration with it, on one hand, and conference-hopping 'paper Pan-Africanists', on the other, the movement itself appears to have 'taken refuge in an attitude of passivity, of mute indifference, and sometimes of cold complicity'. A clear example of how tarnished Pan-Africanism has become is the red carpet treatment extended in February 2016 to the President of India for his country's 'support'[58] by the same African President

---

56 Cabral, ibid. 57.
57 Cabral, ibid.
58 *Daily Graphic*, 14 June 2016, which did not report a single manifestation of opposition to the visit, the 'red carpet' or apparent official failure to raise the issue of black and African lives in India before, during or after it – despite an extensive of the event which included an over-the-top build-up, a special supplement on it during the visit itself and some three more pages on it two days after it ended.

who had hosted the second '8th Pan-African Congress' two years earlier –
and this, barely a month after African attention had been drawn to racism
in India by the killing of a Congolese student by racist thugs, prompting
African Heads of Diplomatic Missions in New Delhi to issue a statement
asking the government of India to address 'racism and Afro-phobia' there.[59]

But these all add to the mountains of evidence that making Pan-
Africanism a mass movement rather than a movement for the masses – to
ensure its credibility and efficacy as an African people's liberation tool – is
a task for the masses themselves and no one else.

*Between allowing and not allowing historical animosities among Africans
to work for the African people's 'enemies of yesterday and today'*

It is a virtual law of what one might call 'political physics' – as well as
many religious and secular beliefs – that, to quote the Christian bible, 'if
a house be divided against itself, that house cannot stand'.[60] None has seriously argued that the Global African Family is exempt from this law. For
Africans who seriously believe that the lives and dignity of Africans and
peoples of African descent everywhere matter, and that the unity of the
Family is a necessary condition for the success of the struggle to get the
African people's enemies of yesterday and today to take note, the removal
of identifiable obstacles to that unity is thus an obvious Pan-Africanist
imperative. And none of these obstacles can be more damaging to the unity
of the African Family as a whole than:

---

59 "'We are scared", Africans in India say racism is constant', Yahoo.com and <https://
    www.google.com.gh/?gfe_rd=cr&ei=4d9gV-fEGuir8weAgKqoBg&gws_rd=ssl#
    q=%E2%80%98We+are+scared%E2%80%99+-+Africans+in+India+say+racism
    +is+constant>.
60 *The Gospel of Mark*, Chapter 3, verse 25.

1. Historical hostilities and antagonisms carried into the Bantustans which most Africans living in Africa must call their countries – many of them against their will, as the persistence, use and in some cases increasing and increasingly open use of 'tribalism' at all levels demonstrates;
2. Class and ethnic antagonisms created by black empowerment and other social and political aspects of the servicing of the 'looting machine' in neo-colonial and globalized Africa; and
3. The misguided tendency among some in the New World Diaspora to blame *all* Africans who remained in Africa during the slave trade and their descendants (who suffered the ignominy and worse of colonial slavery and are stuck with neo-colonialism and neoliberal globalization for the privilege) for that inhuman 'trade'.

Naana Opoku-Agyemang's reference to how the slave-trading past of the Fon still lives with them and in the memories of the Yoruba they used to raid for slaves so many centuries ago (see Chapter 3) and other 'articulations of resistance to enslavement' she shared[61] are salutary reminders of both the general truth she expressly sought to convey – namely, that 'all creatures with brains have memory of their past that informs their present'[62] – and a warning that it is burying one's head in the sand to pretend that memories of who did what to whom during the slave trade, and resulting mistrusts and animosities, can be swept away with the same cheek with which Nicolas Sarkozy (for France) and David Cameron (for Britain), for instance, have rubbished Caribbean and other African demands for reparations for their respective countries' roles in both the commodification and the enslavement of their ancestors.[63] But what is true at the local levels described by Opoku-Agyemang has to apply, naturally and with at least equal force, at

---

61 Naana Opoku-Agyemang, *Where There is no Silence: Articulations of Resistance to Enslavement.*
62 Naana Opoku-Agyemang, ibid. 1–2.
63 See, for instance, Nicolas Sarkozy's First Speech to Africa as President of France, Cheikh Anta Diop University, Dakar, Senegal, 26 July 2007 and 'Cameron says no reparations for slave trade', BBC, 1 October 2015, <http://uk.reuters.com/article/2015/10/01/uk-britain-slavery-idUKKCN0RV36420151001>.

the Global African level. It is, accordingly, idle to pretend that toxic historical memories from the same 'trading' activities in the same period cannot and do not have the same effects on the feelings of at least some people of African descent in the New World towards Africans in Africa which the Yoruba have towards the Fon, for instance. The following quotation from an article in the Friday, 2 October 2015 edition of the *Jamaica Observer* should end all illusions in that regard:

> I once asked my class what was the main lesson of slavery. One student said, 'You can't trust black people.' Why so? 'They sold us for guns, beads and mirrors and never said sorry.'[64]

The student or pupil who allegedly expressed those feelings cannot possibly be alone in harbouring them, if Opoku-Agyemang is right about creatures, brains, memory and their effects on present beliefs. Indeed, the author of the *Jamaica Observer* article, described in the accompanying biographical note as an advisor to Jamaica's minister of education, confirmed both Opoku-Agyemang's thesis and the student's beef with his follow-up comment that the student's outburst was 'unexpected, unwelcome, but logical'. But neither Opoku-Agyemang nor anyone else has ever claimed, to my knowledge, that all creatures with brains are right in the lessons they draw from their past. The Yoruba in the Yoruba-Fon story and the sweeping condemnation of 'black people' by the Jamaican student and his teacher do indeed suffer at least three glaring intellectual and political defects: failure to acknowledge that the black accomplices of the European slave traders generally operated societies stratified by class in which black people other than those who were processed for export suffered treatments often as bad as the treatments suffered by their counterparts overseas; that there are black people on the continent who were nowhere near the 'slave-trading markets'; and that there were at the material times other black people in Africa who may have escaped commodification but were, like

---

64   Franklin JOHNSTON, 'Reparation, Caricom and Jamaican hospitality', *Jamaica Observer*, 2 October 2015, <http://www.jamaicaobserver.com/columns/Reparation--Caricom-and-Jamaican-hospitality-_19231636> (accessed 4 October 2015).

the Yoruba in the Yoruba-Fon encounters of old, hunted, not hunters. To condemn all black people who were left on the continent as people who sold other black people 'for guns, beads and mirrors and never said sorry' is thus downright silly. But the greater devils are in the practical consequences of the folly. To stick to the *Jamaica Observer* story, the poor student and his/her tutor seem almost doomed to a mind-and-soul-destroying double agony – the agony of total estrangement from the important segments of humanity which are labelled black and white: from those who are tagged 'black' for untrustworthiness by virtue of skin colour and those tagged 'white' just as collectively for partnering untrustworthy 'black' people in the abominable trade and refusing to say sorry as well; and the agony of self-hate, if student and teacher also see themselves as black. A third agony awaits them if they consider themselves whitened enough but encounter the occasional rejection from 'born whites'. But the damage of their form of 'negrophobia' extends beyond the self-inflicted wounds of black negro-phobes: it gifts black disunity to those who invented the 'black race' and have always created and used its divisions 'to prevent the barbarians from coming together', as Brzezinski (op. cit.) put it. *That is a gift that no self-respecting black person will knowingly offer the African people's 'enemies of yesterday and today'.*

But even better than refusing to play into their enemies' hands is the option of using the 'accident' of the Global African Family's significant presence in many parts of the world to build a formidable force for collective self-defence, development and promotion of the welfare and dignity of all people of African descent where other 'races' and peoples have used similar dispersals for world dominance. This is not to deny one crucial lesson from the difficult Yoruba-Fon relationship and the *Jamaica Observer* story – namely that a great Global-African-Family future in which every African and man, woman and child of African descent can look forward to full and unconditional enjoyment of their human rights, including their right to think for themselves and craft their own modernities, cannot be realized on the sole foundations of common black skin colour, common (ancient) ancestry and common 'modern' history as chattel or colonial slaves. The obvious flipside of that lesson is that wishful thinking is not and cannot be a substitute for apologies and reparations by Africans to 'other' Africans where due and popular mobilization, conscientization and follow-up political, economic and social programmes to ensure that never again will miscreants be allowed to sacrifice the African people 'for their unthinking profit' or stand in the way of their independent development.

If the past cannot be unlived it can surely be better employed than as a source of self-destructive recriminations which can only benefit those with a vested interest in the division of the African people in accordance with the Brzezinski doctrine of 'keeping the barbarians from coming together'.

Total black liberation, the wisdom and virtue to say 'No' to selective incorporation, and inclusiveness as a Pan-African development principle

In the interest of Pan-African unity among individual Africans, families ('royal' and otherwise), interest groups and communities whose ancestors once enslaved, dispossessed or otherwise exploited and humiliated, other Africans may wish to consider summoning the wisdom and courage to render due apologies and reparations to descendants of erstwhile victims, where due – and they should be obliged to qualify for the forgiveness and friendship of those whom their ancestors treated inhumanely or unjustly by not treating the fruits of the 'mistakes' (in Sarkozy's terminology) or sins of 'their fathers' as acquired rights and interests to be defended at all costs. But while voluntary African family reconciliation moves of this kind should be welcomed and encouraged where memory-based animosities otherwise stand in the way of Pan-African unity for liberation third-party Africans ought to feel free to demand them from those concerned if they are not volunteered. To encourage and regulate authentic intra-African 'truth and reconciliation' for African peace-building-for-unity-and-development purposes African minds should volunteer or be tasked to explore the development of fair and effective mechanisms at the community, 'national', regional and Global African Family levels for public education as well as truth and reconciliation.

Considering, also, how deeply and disastrously the Global African Family has been divided along class lines – fuelled by co-optation via 'black empowerment' and promotion to 'cosmopolitan middle-class' status and exhibited by, for instance, the mindset of the Global African Summiteers, the condescending lectures to Africa by the first 'black' President of the United States and the murder of Gaddafi, destruction of Libya and effective US military occupation of Africa under his presidency[65] all with continental African connivance – the decency to 'say no' to selective incorporation by white race authority at the expense of the material and security interests and dignity of other black people and people of African descent 'left behind' should be promoted as a Pan-African virtue.

It must be pointed out upfront – and in anticipation of the familiar objections of those who argue or imply that social and economic justice is utopian, tantamount to 'creeping socialism', the stifling of initiatives and excellence and inimical to 'growth' – that the sorts of quislings identified by Cabral have done more harm to the African people than the pursuit of justice for Africans and peoples of African descent at home and abroad.

---

65   On some military aspects of Obama in Africa see, for instance, John Glaser, 'The US's Invasion of Africa That Nobody Knows About', 15 April 2014, <antiwar.com/ blog/2014/04/15/the-uss-invasion-of-africa-that-nobody-knows-about/>.

Epilogue

We must dare to invent the future. All that comes from man's imagination is realisable for man.

— THOMAS SANKARA

Injustice anywhere is a threat to justice everywhere.

— MARTIN LUTHER KING JNR

The final wrap-up

The various substantive chapters have each sought to wear their purposes on their sleeves. Hopefully, that does not make a final parade of actionable ideas redundant. The following is a selection of some of them.

Global concerns and actionable ideas: Imperial languages, globalization and imperialism

As Rao and many others have shown[1] the globalization of some imperial languages has been a fully functioning imperialist vehicle. In his words:

> As the Kenyan novelist in the study of linguistic oppression says: 'A new world order that is no more than a global dominance of neo-colonial relations policed by a handful of Western nations ... is a disaster for the people of the world and their cultures' (Thiong'o 1993:35). What he says of Africa is also true of India. 'In my view language was the most important vehicle through which that power (the power of the

---

1   See, for instance, 'Globalisation Unleashes the English Tsunami' (Chapter 9, 114–26) in Rao, *Expansion of Cultural Imperialism through Globalisation*.

colonisers) fascinated and held the soul prisoner. The bullet was the means of physical subjugation. Language was the means of spiritual subjugation'. (Thiong'o, 1986)[2]

Examples of the spiritual subjugation and its deleterious effects of include:

- General use of literacy in the imperial languages as a condition for election or appointment to high offices of state in all but a tiny minority of 'independent' African states;
- Effective continuation in most of 'post-colonial' Africa of the colonial practice of treating indigenous African languages as the inferior languages of backward people;[3]
- Voluntary orbiting by most African states around the languages of their 'former' colonial masters, with labels like Anglophone, Francophone and Lusophone worn by their governments and elites as badges of honour and membership of the Commonwealth, the Organisation internationale de la Francophonie and the Community of Portuguese Language Countries taken almost as a matter of course;
- Infiltration of Western newspeak into the language of private and public conversations in Africa – with words and phrases like 'terrorist' and 'terrorism', 'international community', 'democracy', 'freedom', 'free markets', 'government', 'regime', First and Second World Wars, 'gay', 'black' and 'white' (for people who are, in reality, pink or brown in skin colour), 'liberal', 'moderate', 'conservative', 'extremist', 'sex worker' and 'sex industry' carelessly deployed with whatever political, cultural and ideological meanings and intents the West's wordsmiths choose to assign them;
- Inappropriate references by too many 'educated' Africans to indigenous African political entities and nations, no matter how sophisticated, as

2   Rao, ibid. 123.
3   Regrettably, the colonial and settler practice of showing contempt for peasant languages by dismissing them as 'vernaculars', 'meaning the languages of slaves', according to Ngugi (*Detained*, 59), had not been totally discarded by some 'educated' Africans as of 2015.

'tribes' – a European construct usually attached, or intended to refer, to collections of savage creatures;[4]

- The OAU/AU/ECOWAS practice of using the Anglophone, Francophone and Lusophone brand names for African states in the making of high-level executive appointments;

- The resounding failure of too many supposedly independent African states to consider the preservation and development of indigenous languages as national, official and working languages at the higher levels of executive, legislative and judicial power; and

- The deference accorded to the British Broadcasting Corporation (BBC) and Radio France Internationale (RFI) by African dignitaries, as exemplified by the state honour given to a dead BBC broadcaster by the Republic of Ghana on account of his '*rise to the lofty heights of being one of the lead presenters of BBC TV and Radio in the UK*' (first quoted in Chapter 1) and the liberties given by some African Heads to BBC interviewers to pose to them demeaning questions they dare not and have not been known to pose to sitting British and other Western heads of state and government.[5]

Whether the dogged attachment to the languages of Africa's colonizers exposed by the above and similar catastrophes – and the accompanying devaluation of indigenous languages – are excused as pragmatic responses to need or condemned as more evidence of the dependency and inferiority

---

4   On this see Archie Mafeje, 'The Ideology of Tribalism', *Journal of Modern African Studies*, Vol. 9, No. 2, August 1971. Some have also argued, persuasively, that it is yet another sign of the colonized mind that Africans who accept the demeaning reference to their original nations as 'tribes' are generally unwilling or unable to apply the same descriptions to their European counterparts.

5   E.g. Ghanaian President Mahama's interview with a BBC reporter in May 2016 in which he allowed him to ask whether he takes bribes himself and answered the journalist politely (<https://kasapafmonline.com/2016/05/12/havent-taken-bribe-prez-mahama-tells-bbc-reporter/>) and a similar incident (also in May 2016) in which Nigeria's President Buhari confirmed in a BBC interview that his country was 'fantastically corrupt' as charged by British Prime Minister David Cameron (<http://www.bbc.com/news/world-africa-36265998>).

complexes of the black-empowered and cosmopolitan-middle-class types responsible for the situation the impression remains of an indecent tendency to leave native or 'ethnic' identities behind in favour of 'white masks'. By the same token the impression of a predisposition to trash the people's heritage and cultural resources and turn them into 'apes' to please their 'development partners' is that much harder to dismiss.

It also seems to follow that the burden of cultural decolonization, including the rehabilitation and development of African languages, should not remain confined to the margins of nationalist and Pan-Africanist concerns but mainstreamed – in recognition of the fact that the struggle for the political, economic, social, cultural and spiritual liberation of the peoples of Africa is indivisible. But that leaves the very real challenge of ensuring that the rehabilitation and development of the many local nations and languages of the African world support the rehabilitation and development of the Global African Family and vice versa, for obvious reasons: members of the very culturally and linguistically diverse Family will need to communicate with one another more, not less, as the Pan-African community becomes a fact not just an aspiration. Pan-Africanists may wish, therefore, to consider designing and implementing strategies, institutions, policies, projects and competences for stimulating the harmonious and interlinkable development of the African world's diverse communities and cultures and languages for intra Global Community communications. One idea which may be considered in this connection is the development of a Pan-African *lingua franca* – to be promoted alongside local national languages for local purposes.

Two basic objections can be anticipated to the above proposals. The first – to the rehabilitation and development of indigenous African languages – would be that such a process is unnecessary and backward-looking because the English language, in particular, already catapults all into the modern world at no cost to Africans, and with tangible benefits. Africans who object to the indigenous African languages rehabilitation-and-development proposal on this ground would, in effect, be falling into the trap set by the patronizing Sarkozy by which Africans are to define themselves as 'heir(s) to all that the West has placed in the heart and soul of Africa'[6] with no need for an independent African renaissance or modernity. By the same token, it implies acceptance by Africans of their place in the English language-dominated world which the notorious Samuel P. Huntington (see Chapter 2) has bragged about.[7]

The contradiction between the Sarkozy and Huntington visions for Africa and the Pan-Africanist dream of Africans making and teaching their own history, as opposed to the history taught in Brussels, Paris, Washington or the United Nations articulated by Lumumba,[8] is also, thus clearly, the choice between the *status quo* and an Africa in which Africans work to liberate themselves from the bonds enumerated by Sukarno, including in particular the continuing colonization of African minds via the imperial languages. It is just as obvious, in any case, that it is a choice which Africans must make for themselves and not allow the likes of Sarkozy and Huntington to make for them.

But the anticipated objection to the development of a Pan-African *lingua franca* would also be flawed on other political grounds, and ahistorical or ignorant to boot. For it flies in the face of Rao's short history of Huntington's English language quoted below:

Two thousand years ago, the English language was confined to a handful of savages, now forgotten tribes on the shores of Northwest Europe; there was no English in England. Today, it is used, spoken or written in some form or the other, by about

6　Nicolas Sarkozy, Cheikh Anta Diop University Address.

7　Huntington is quoted by Rao (op. cit, 115) as 'observing' (in his *The Clash of Civilisations and the Remaking of World Order*) that 'English is the world's way of communicating internationally and inter-culturally just as the Christian calendar is the world's way of tracing time, just as the Arab numbers are the world's way of counting, and first as the metric system is, for the most part, the world's way of measuring'. The costs to the African people of Sarkozyism and Huntingtonism should be obvious to all who have waded through this book and, more importantly, observed how the European languages have served as yet another tool of cultural imperialism and imperial arrogance and sustained the inferiority complex and 'ape syndrome' among susceptible Africans.

8　Patrice Lumumba, 'Letter from Thysville Prison to Mrs Lumumba', op. cit.

1.5 billion people around the world; of the English users, three hundred and fifty million use it as the mother tongue, and the rest as a foreign or second language.[9]

With currently available intellectual and technical skills at the African people's disposal a *lingua franca* for the Global African Family should take considerably shorter to develop; need not and ought not be another case of 'catching up', and should be a worthy community-building project for the same reasons that Africa and Africans need their liberation from imperialist and racial oppression. But above all, it is another project idea which Africans and other peoples of African descent may wish to evaluate, accept or reject for themselves.

Other specific problem areas of Pan-African interest and corresponding project ideas

The unknown, forgotten and neglected Diaspora

Given its parentage and the historical epochs in which it was born and has been nurtured it is understandable that Pan-Africanism's preoccupation has traditionally been with the living effects of the trans-Atlantic slave trade, the institution of slavery in North America and colonial slavery in Africa and the Caribbean Islands and the ravages of follow-up neo-colonialism and neoliberal globalization, to the exclusion of Africa's enslaved children in Latin America, parts of the Arab world, Asia and other 'tribes of Africa', 'known' and 'unknown'. Publications like *Neither Enemies nor Friends* and the many other titles cited in it[10] as well as the *Al Jazeera* exposés on the plight of the Jarawa people of India's Andaman Islands[11] take away the excuse of sincere ignorance about the conditions of these Diaspora Africans, however. The plight of many of the descendants of African slaves

---

9   Rao, op. cit., 115.
10   Dzidzienyo and Oboler eds, *Neither Enemies nor Friends: Latinos, Blacks, Afro-Latinos*.
11   See <https://www.google.com.gh/?gfe_rd=cr&ei=4XAeVvuKKeKr8weJl77ICA &gws_rd=ssl#q=Al+Jaeera+on+the+Andaman+people> (accessed 14 October 2015) for a selection of the exposés.

subsisting in the Arab world is also a secret in the twenty-first century only to the wilfully ignorant.

Based on now widely available information current and future Pan-Africanists may wish to correct past 'sins of omission' by *inter alia*:

- Shaming and pressurizing through campaigns, boycotts and other legitimate means states and territories where the exploitation, inhumanities, oppression and humiliation of Diaspora Africans are known or found to occur – wherever they may be, and especially but not exclusively where the oppressed Africans are 'voiceless' – until the unacceptable practices are effectively and irreversibly eliminated; and
- Mobilizing all the instruments of people's power to ensure that governments and other civil and political actors in Africa and the Diaspora which claim to be Pan-Africanist 'put their monies where their mouths are' by entrenching the defence and advancement of Diaspora African people's rights and interests wherever they may be in their policies and activities.

Pan-Africanists may also may also consider it their calling to set up mechanisms for seeking out 'lost tribes' of Africa – so that their discovery and place on the Pan-Africanist agenda do not remain a matter of chance.

Promotion of social and economic justice at home

The great Pan-Africanists were always sensitive to issues of social and economic injustice but not necessarily unanimous on where the fault lines lay even among people of the same colour. Most importantly, while some of their number professed Marxism, socialism, communism consistently or at different points in their political careers, it is obvious that as a movement Pan-Africanism was, in essence, a movement for the liberation of the African or black person from colonial and imperialist exploitation – and certainly not against any people *as a class*. The founding fathers went out of their way, on the contrary, to promote inter-class co-operation in the liberation struggle. The following extract from the *Declaration* of the Fifth

Pan-African Congress is worth noting as evidence of the Congress' refusal to equate class differences with class antagonism:

> The Fifth Pan African Congress ... calls on the workers and farmers of the colonies to organise effectively. Colonial workers must be in the front lines of the battle against imperialism.
>
> The Fifth Pan African Congress calls on the intellectual and professional classes of the colonies to awaken to their responsibilities. The long, long night is over. By fighting for trade union rights, the right to form cooperatives, freedom of the press, assembly, demonstration and strike; freedom to print and read the literature which is necessary for the education of the masses, you will be using the only means by which your liberties will be won and maintained. Today, there is only one road to effective action – the organisation of the masses.[12]

It has to be added, however, that Nkrumah, who wrote this portion of the *Declaration*, according to June Milne,[13] did not have, in 1945, the advantage Cabral and others did much later of seeing the same erstwhile intellectual and professional classes of the colonies, and their descendants, transformed by black-empowerment and opportunities to join the 'cosmopolitan middle class' into imperialism's African collaborators. The post-independence experience of virtually all existing African states, including those which emerged from national liberation struggles, exposes the Fifth Pan-African Congress' assumption of the essential harmony of the interests of the 'workers and farmers of the colonies' and those of the 'intellectual and professional classes' (not to mention the professional 'politicians' and administrators created by black empowerment and the so-called business men and women created by neoliberal globalization) as somewhat naive – and suggests, as indicated by Cabral and others, that the only guarantee against the short-changing of 'the masses' in a renewed Pan-Africanist struggle is for them to take matters in their own hands. In philosophical, economic, social and public and development administration terms this can only mean the promotion of social and economic justice, the replacement of greed and charity by social

---

12   June Milne, *Kwame Nkrumah: A Biography*, 24, among other sources.
13   June Milne, ibid. 23.

solidarity, and recognition that all human beings are equal and all human needs are legitimate and deserving of policy concern.

Gender and African nationalism

The African people have not always treated their 'girl children' and womenfolk with the dignity and fairness due them as human beings, mothers, spouses, sisters, daughters, nieces and companions. But this does not put the African people as a whole in need of lessons from the West or the 'international community' about gender and justice. To cite but two reasons why from a tiny part of Africa:

- The War of the Golden Stool, also known as the Yaa Asantewaa war fought by the Ashanti Kingdom against British imperialism which the British won in 1901, was led by a Queen, Yaa Asantewaa – a phenomenon which was foreign to British colonial troops in the nineteenth century, according to Wikipedia;[14] and
- In civil life Ghana had its first female High Court Judge, in the person of Justice Annie Ruth Baeta Jiagge – in 1961, i.e. four years before Britain.

This is not to say that Africa cannot do better for its girls and women. There are, indeed, pockets of Africa where 'traditional' attitudes and treatments of women compare with the norms and practices towards them in Homeric Greece, the Hebrew Bible, medieval Europe and early modern Europe recalled by Pinker.[15] But Pan-Africanism has nothing to apologize for in that regard. On the contrary, Kwame Nkrumah President of the first Ghanaian Republic who made the historic female High Court Judge appointment is, by general acclamation, the preeminent Pan-Africanist of all time. And not far behind him is the author of these words, 'the revolution and women's

---

14 <https://en.wikipedia.org/wiki/Yaa_Asantewaa>. See, also, Kwame Arhin, 'The Political and Military Roles of Akan Women', in Christine Oppong, ed., *Female and Male in West Africa* (London: Allen and Unwin, 1983).
15 Pinker, *The Better Angels of our Nature*.

liberation go together. We do not talk of women's emancipation as an act of charity or out of a surge of human compassion. It is a basic necessity for the revolution to triumph. Women hold up the other half of the sky'.[16] There is no excuse, accordingly, for allowing the legitimate struggles for the human rights of African girls and women, however labelled, to be used as a cover for what Rao called the 'expansion of cultural imperialism through globalisation' or a Trojan horse in imperialism's 'war on … other cultures', as he also put it, with the 'globalisation of defeminisation', 'the (pan-sexualisation) of society' and equal opportunities for women in war machines as indicators of human progress in Africa.[17] Nor, for that matter, should genuine feminists allow a noble movement to be hijacked by cosmopolitan middle-class ladies for their own purposes or the way profit-seeking Africans have sought to use Pan-Africanism as a vulgar investments and business promotion vehicle.

Pan-Africanism in the twenty-first century: Actions, not words or phoney wars

Undeniably Pan-Africanists have had their phoney wars before – the most infamous of them being the personal and personality conflict between W. E. B. Du Bois and Marcus Garvey.[18] But even that 'phoney

16   Thomas Sankara, <http://www.azquotes.com/quote/877691>.
17   See Rao, *Expansion of Cultural Imperialism through Globalisation* (op. cit.) for his insights on the 'globalisation of defeminisation'. For not-dissimilar perspectives see Nancy Frazer, 'Feminism Co-opted'.
18   For a brief history of the conflict see Joseph E. Holloway, 'The Collision in Liberia of Marcus Garvey's and W. E. B. Du Bois's Version of Pan Africanism', in *The Slave Rebellion*, <http://slaverebellion.org/index.php?page=the-collision-in-liberia-of-marcus-garvey-s-and-w-e-b-du-bois-s-version-of-pan-africanisms> (date, place of publication and page numbers not given). See also <https://www.google.com.gh/?gfe_rd=cr&ei=zOgeVr76LeSr8weSmoaIBg&gws_rd=ssl#q=The+Du+Bois+vs+Marcus+Garvey+conflicts+> for other articles on the subject.

war' was no case of vulgar personality clashes or grandstanding: as others have pointed out the ostensible inter-personal conflict between the two was, in fact, an ideological one between the Jamaican-born and 'dark skinned' Garvey with memories of the exploitation of black workers by 'white and mulatto overseers' and articulate mass organizer and the different-looking and differently formed Du Bois, the mulatto 'intellectual father' 'who could articulate the movement and its philosophy academically'.[19] But more importantly and indisputably each of these two 'feuding brothers' went beyond the trading of personal insults to serve the Pan-Africanist cause as they saw it through concrete follow-up projects. The Black Star Steamship Line which Garvey established 'to serve as a commercial and spiritual tie among Black People everywhere' and Du Bois' life's works before and after the 5th Pan-African Congress will forever remain testimonies to their commitments to the changing of African lives. That is more than can be said for the organizers of the two rival 8th Pan-African Congresses, for instance – or indeed any of the so-called Pan-African Conferences and Congresses since the fifth instalment.

Parting shot

All the evidence suggests that, for structural, ideological and evident dependency and inferiority complex reasons, African governments and their conscious and unconscious enablers have effectively passed on the responsibility for the governance, security and development of their countries to

---

19   For more on the personal, philosophical and political conflicts between the two see, 'Marcus Garvey: Conflicts with Du Bois and others', <https://en.wikipedia.org/wiki/Marcus_Garvey#Conflicts_with_Du_Bois_and_others> (accessed 1 August 2015).

foreign patrons, as charged by Ake and others.[20] The following are remind-ers of some of the evidence of the surrender:

- The OAU's decision to abandon the rhetoric of collective self-reliance as a cornerstone of African development in favour of an open and not-so-new international development paradigm and open support for the submission of the continent and its parts to the Washington Consensus;
- The tendency of some power elite groups in both 'government' and 'opposition' to hold themselves accountable to the 'international com-munity' for the governance of their countries through the United Nations, Western Chancelleries, 'aid' administrators, the Western press, etc.;[21]
- General acceptance by governments and Bantustani (those who regard themselves as 'citizens' of the West's Bantustans across Africa) alike

20   Ake, op. cit. See also Yao Graham, 'From Liberation into NEPAD', 4–7; Adebayo Olukoshi, 'Africa from Lagos Plan of Action to NEPAD', 8–9; Jimi O. Adesina, 'NEPAD, the post-Washington Consensus, 16–17 (all in *African Agenda*, Vol. 5, Nos 2 & 3, 2002); 'Buhari to meet Obama over Boko Haram', Reuters, World News of Thursday, 25 June 2015; and Abayomi Azikiwe, 'Imperialists host conference on Nigerian security in Paris', *Pambazuka News*, 679, 21 May 2014, <http://pambazuka.org/en/category/features/91841>.

21   The growth of 'election-monitoring tourism' and election-observer 'postcards' con-firming elections in Africa as 'free and fair' or otherwise is one symptom of the dis-ease. Others are the pledge by the President of Ghana to the UN General Assembly in 2015 'to enhance democracy' ('Prez renews pledge to enhance democracy', *Daily Graphic*, 1 October 2015, 3); the petition reportedly filed by a local pressure group in Ghana (the Let My Vote Count Alliance or LMVCA) at the Human Rights Council of the United Nations General Assembly against the government of Ghana and the head of the Ghana police service for 'human rights violations' ('LMVCA files peti-tion at UN against govt, *police*', *Daily Graphic*, 8 October 2015, 17); the spectacle of some Ghanaians in the United Kingdom picketing No. 10 Downing Street, the official residence of the British Prime Minister, as part of a global campaign to get the Electoral Commission of Ghana to replace a Voters' Register deemed by Ghana's official opposition to have been bloated to the ruling 'party's' advantage; and the virtual takeover of economic and fiscal policymaking by the Washington Consensus and its IMF, World Bank and other 'donor' enforcers.

that the economic health, growth and development of their 'countries' depend not on their hands, brains and natural resources – and trade and co-operation with their *natural partners* – but on the 'aid' of 'development partners' and the 'kind consideration' and 'favours' of Foreign Direct Investors, 'development NGOs', foreign tourists and other sources of foreign exchange, technology and 'development ideas';

- The farce by which the African Union and some of its member states allowed NATO to play arsonist in Libya in and around 2011 (by arming and backstopping jihadists to overthrow its government) and firefighter in neighbouring Mali when the selfsame jihadists – and others empowered by the regime change in Libya – proceeded to spread their brand of 'civilization' or barbarism in the hapless country;[22]

- The apparent readiness to lend African armies and the African Union flag for the Bush-Obama 'war on terror' in return for 'international security assistance' and various other regime benefits, including assistance to the regimes concerned for the containment of domestic opposition; and

- The humiliating Africa-EU Summit of November 2015 whose preannounced purpose and outcome was the establishment of an EU Trust Fund to address 'the root causes' of unwanted African migration to Europe and facilitate the return and reintegration into their countries

---

22   Other signs that neoliberalized Africa is happy to entrust its security to 'the international community' include its tendency to run to the UN Security Council and even AFRICOM, the French Armed Forces and NATO for military solutions to its major security crises; the NATO-AU Agreement of 8 May 2014, designed to facilitate greater co-operation between the two organizations 'in areas of mutual interest' such as logistics, interoperability of alliance forces, training, exercise planning and lessons from respective operational experiences (see 'NATO and the African Union boost their cooperation', <http://www.nato.int/cps/en/natolive/news_109824.htm>); and US military involvement in more than 90 per cent of Africa's fifty-four nations as of November 2015, according to Nick Turse. See Nick Turse, '"Tomorrow's Battlefield": As U.S. Special Ops Enter Syria, Growing Presence in Africa Goes Unnoticed', *Democracy Now!*, <http://www.democracynow.org/2015/11/13/tomorrows_battlefield_as_us_special_ops>.

of origin of rejected economic migrants: an obvious invitation to the EU and its member states to tighten their neo-colonial screws on Africa.[23]

It is hard to distinguish between the 'traitors: traditional chiefs and bandits in the times of slavery and of the wars of colonial conquest, gendarmes, various agents and mercenary soldiers during the golden age of colonization, self-styled heads of state and ministers in ... the time of neo-colonialism' in Cabral's demonology and the 'black-empowered' and 'metropolitan-middle-class' types who have provided and continue to provide comparable services to state and corporate imperialism in the age of 'globalization'. Perhaps only the future can also tell whether 'the future will have (more) pity for those men [and women] who, possessing the exceptional privilege of being able to speak words of truth to their oppressors, (take) refuge in an attitude of passivity, of mute indifference, and sometimes of cold complicity' than Fanon anticipated. Above all, whether the tools of *force, pre-emptive attack and deception* will continue to prevent the people 'taking matters into their own hands' forever may or may not be a matter of legitimate conjecture.

23   See, for instance, *Valletta Summit, 11–12 November 2015 Action Plan*. When read in conjunction with calls by 'Africa', in the person of some of its leaders, for Marshall Plan-like programmes by 'donors' for Guinea-Conakry, Liberia and Sierra Leone to manage the effects of the Ebola epidemic which devastated those countries between 2013 and 2015 and *NEPAD* itself the slave-who-will-not-be-free syndrome becomes unmistakable.

Bibliography

Books

Abraham, W. E. *The Mind of Africa.* London: Weidenfeld and Nicolson, 1962.

Ake, Claude. *Democracy and Development in Africa.* Washington, DC: The Brookings Institution, 1996.

Alexander, Michelle. *The New Jim Crow: Mass Incarceration in the Age of Colorblindness.* New York: The New Press, 2011.

Allen, Theodore, W. *The Invention of the White Race Vol. 1: Racial Oppression and Social Control.* New York: Verso, 1994 and 2012.

—— *The Invention of the White Race Vol. 2: The Origin of Racial Oppression in Anglo-America.* New York: Verso, 1997.

Amin, Samir. *Accumulation on a World Scale: A Critique of the Theory of Development Vol. 1.* New York: Monthly Review Press, 1974.

—— *Permanent War and the Americanisation of the World: The Liberal Virus.* New York: Monthly Review Press, 1974.

—— *L'agriculture africaine et le capitalisme.* Paris: Anthropos, 1975.

—— *Delinking: Towards a Polycentric World.* London: Zed Press, 1990.

—— *Obsolescent Capitalism: Contemporary Politics and Global Disorder.* New York: Zed Books, 2003.

—— *The World We Wish to See: Revolutionary Objectives in the Twenty-First Century.* New York: Monthly Review Press, 2008.

—— *Eurocentrism: Modernity, Religion and Democracy: A Critique of Eurocentrism and Culturalism.* 2nd edn. New York: Monthly Review Press, 2009.

Appiah, K. A. *The Honour Code: How Moral Revolutions Happen.* London: Norton, 2010.

Armah, Ayi Kwei. *Osiris Rising: A novel of Africa, past, present and future.* Popenguine: Per Ankh, 1995.

—— *Two Thousand Seasons: A Novel.* Popenguine: Per Ankh, 2000.

—— *Peace Without Power: Ghana's Foreign Policy 1957–1966.* Accra: Ghana Universities Press, 2004.

Bacevich, Andrew J. *The Limits of Power: The End of American Exceptionalism.* New York: Metropolitan Books, 2008.

Baptist, Edward E. *The Half Has Never Been Told: Slavery and the Making of American Capitalism*. New York: Basic Books, 2014.

Biney, Ama. *The Political and Social Thought of Kwame Nkrumah*. Basingstoke: Palgrave Macmillan, 2011.

Blair, Tony. *A Journey*. London: Hutchinson, 2010.

Bobbit, Philip. *The Shield of Achilles*. New York: Knopf, 2002.

Bond, Patrick. *Looting of Africa*. London and Pietermaritzburg: Zed Books, 2006.

Brett, E. A. *Colonialism and Underdevelopment in East Africa: The Politics of Economic Change, 1919–39*. Nairobi: Heinemann, 1973.

Brzezinski, Zbigniew. *The Grand Chessboard*. New York: Basic Books, 1998.

Cabral, Amilcar. *Return to the Source: Selected Speeches of Amilcar Cabral*. New York: Monthly Review Press, 1973.

—— *Revolution in Guinea: An African People's Struggle. Selected Texts*. New York: Monthly Review Press, 1974.

Canfora, Luciano. *Democracy in Europe: A History of an Ideology*. Oxford: Wiley-Blackwell, 2006.

Caufield, Catherine. *Masters of Illusion: The World Bank and the Poverty of Nations*. London: Pan Books, 1996.

Chang, Ha-Joon. *Bad Samaritans: The Myth of Free Trade and the Secret History of Capitalism*. New York: Bloomsbury Press, 2008.

Chomsky, Noam. *Powers and Prospects: Reflections on Human Nature and the Social Order*. London: Pluto Press, 1996.

—— *Rogue States*. London: Pluto Press, 2000.

—— *Hegemony or Survival: America's Quest for Global Dominance*. New York: Owl Books, 2004.

—— *Failed States: The Abuse of Power and the Assault on Democracy*. New York: Metropolitan Books, 2006.

—— and David Barsamian. *Noam Chomsky: Imperial Ambitions – Conversations on the Post-9/11 World*. London: Penguin Books, 2006.

——, David Barsamian and Arthur Naiman. *How the World Works*. London: Hamish Hamilton, 2012.

Chossudovsky, Michel. *The Globalisation of Poverty and the New World Order*. 2nd edn. Pincourt: Global Research, 2003.

Coates, Ta-Nehisi, *Between the World and Me*. New York: Spiegel & Grau, 2015.

Comité d'Information Sahel. *Qui se nourrit de la famine en Afrique?* Paris: François Maspero, 1975.

Davidson, Basil. *The Black Man's Burden: Africa and the Curse of the Nation-State*. Ibadan: Spectrum Books, 1993.

Davis, Mike. *Planet of Slums: Urban Involution and the Informal Working Class.* London: Verso, 2006.

Depelchin, Jacques. *Silences in African History: Between the Syndromes of Discovery and Abolition.* Dar Es Salaam: Mkuki na Nyota Publishers, 2005.

Diop, Chiekh Anta. *The African Origin of Civilization.* Westport, CT: Lawrence Hill, 1974.

Dzidzienyo, Anani and Suzanne Oboler, eds, *Neither Enemies nor Friends: Latinos, Blacks, Afro-Latinos.* New York: Palgrave Macmillan, 2005.

Fanon, Frantz. *The Wretched of the Earth.* Harmondsworth: Penguin Books, 1967.

—— *Towards the African Revolution: Political Essays.* New York: Grove Press, 1969.

—— *Black Skin, White Masks.* London: Paladin, 1970.

Farmer, Paul. *The Uses of Haiti.* Monroe, ME: Common Courage, 2003.

—— et al. *Getting Haiti Right This Time.* Monroe, ME: Common Courage, 2004.

Ferguson, Charles H. *Predator Nation: Corporate Criminals, Political Corruption, and the Hijacking of America.* New York: Crown Business, 2012.

Frank, André Gunder. *Capitalism and Underdevelopment in Latin America.* New York: Monthly Review Press, 1967.

Freeh, Louis J. *My FBI: Bringing Down the Mafia, Investigating Bill Clinton, and Fighting the War on Terror.* New York: St Martin's Press, 2005.

George, Susan. *How the Other Half Dies: The Real Reasons for World Hunger.* Harmondsworth: Penguin Books, 1977.

Gibbon, Edward. *Decline and Fall of the Roman Empire Vol. 5.* London: Dent, 1962.

Gott, Richard. *Britain's Empire: Resistance, Repression and Revolt.* London: Verso, 2011.

Grant, D. *The Fortunate Slave.* Oxford: Oxford University Press, 1968.

Gray, John. *Al Qaeda and what it means to be modern.* London: Faber and Faber, 2003.

Hallward, Peter. *Damming the Flood: Haiti, and the Politics of Containment.* New York and London: Verso Books, 2010.

Hancock, Graham. *Lords of Poverty.* London: Mandarin, 1989.

Harvey, David. *A Brief History of Neo-Liberalism.* Oxford: Oxford University Press, 2007.

Hayter, Teresa. *Aid as Imperialism.* Harmondsworth: Penguin Books, 1971.

Hein Sekyi, Henry van. *Colour Prejudice. Past, Present and Future.* New York: Vantage Press, 1994.

Hind, Dan. *The Return of the Public.* London: Verso, 2010.

Howard, Rhoda. *Colonialism and Underdevelopment in Ghana.* London: Croom Helm, 1978.

Huntington, Samuel P. *Political Order in Changing Societies.* New Haven, CT: Yale University Press, 1968.

Kagan, Robert. *Dangerous Nation: America and the World 1600–1900*. Berkeley, CA: Atlantic Books, 2006.

Kenyatta, Jomo. *Suffering Without Bitterness: The Founding of the Kenyan Nation*. Nairobi: East African Publishing House, 1968.

Kiernan, Victor. *America: The New Imperialism: From White Settlement to World Hegemony*. London: Zed Press, 1978.

—— *European Empires from Conquest to Collapse, 1815–1960*. Leicester: Leicester University Press/Fontana Paperbacks, 1982.

Klein, Naomi. *The Shock Doctrine. The Rise of Disaster Capitalism*. New York: Picador, 2008.

Klitgaard, Robert. *Tropical Gangsters: One Man's Experience with Development and Decadence in Deepest Africa*. New York: Basic Books, 1990.

Kodjo, Edem. *Et demain l'Afrique*. Paris: Stock, 1985.

Kolko, Gabriel. *Confronting the Third World*. New York: Pantheon Books, 1988.

Kwarteng, Kwasi. *Ghosts of Empire: Britain's Legacy in the Modern World*. London: Bloomsbury, 2012.

Lappé, F. M., Joseph Collins and Cary Fowler. *Food First: Beyond the Myth of Scarcity*. Boston, MA: Houghton Mifflin, 1977.

Leys, Colin. *The Rise and Fall of Development Theory*. Indianapolis, IN: Indiana University Press, 1996.

Mafeje, Archie. *In Search of an Alternative: A Collection of Essays on Revolutionary Theory*. Harare: SAPES Books, 1992.

Mesquita, Bruce Bueno de and Alastair Smith. *The Dictator's Handbook: Why Bad Behaviour is Almost Always Good Politics*. New York: BBS Public Affairs, 2011.

Milne, June. *Kwame Nkrumah: A Biography*. London: Panaf, 1996.

Nabudere, Dan. *The Political Economy of Imperialism: Its theoretical and polemical treatment from Mercantilist to Multilateral Imperialism*: London: Zed Press and Dar es Salaam: Tanzania Publishing House, 1977.

Ngugi wa Thiong'o. *Detained: A Writer's Prison Diary*. London: Heinemann, 1981.

Nixon, Ron. *Operation Blackwash*. Mampoer Books, e-books publisher, 2013, <http://www.amazon.co.uk/Operation-Blackwash-Ron-Nixon-ebook/dp/B00EJN6QV6>, accessed 14 August 2014.

Nkrumah, Kwame. *Africa Must Unite*. London: Panaf, 1963.

—— *Ghana: The Autobiography of Kwame Nkrumah*. London: Nelson, 1965.

—— *Neo-Colonialism: The Last Stage of Imperialism*. New York: International Publishers, 1965.

—— *Challenge of the Congo: A Case Study of Foreign Pressures in an Independent State*. New York: International Publishers, 1967.

—— *Revolutionary Path* (published posthumously). London: Panaf, 1973.

Nyerere, Julius K. *The Arusha Declaration: Ten Years After*. Dar es Salaam: The Government Printer, 1977.

Opoku-Agyemang, Naana J. S. *Where There is no Silence: Articulations of Resistance to Enslavement*. Accra: Ghana Academy of Arts and Sciences, Inaugural Lecture 2006, 2008.

Owen, David. *The Hubris Syndrome: Bush, Blair and the Intoxication of Power*. York: Methuen, 2012.

Panitch, Leo and Sam Gindin. *The Making of Global Capitalism: The Political Economy of American Empire*. London: Verso, 2013.

Pilger, John. *Freedom Next Time*. Ealing: Bantam Press, 2006.

Pinker, Steven, *The Better Angels of our Nature: Why Violence Has Declined*. New York: Penguin Books, 2011.

Prashad, Vijay. *The Darker Nations: A People's History of the Third World*. New York: The New Press, 2007.

Rao, Krishna V. *Expansion of Cultural Imperialism through Globalisation*. New Delhi: MANAK Publications PVT, 2008.

Ray, Ellen, William Schaap, Karl van Meter and Louis Wolf, eds, *Dirty Work 2: The CIA in Africa*. London: Zed Press, 1980.

Reinert, Erik S. *How Rich Countries Got Rich and Why Poor Countries Stay Poor*. London: Constable, 2008.

Rodney, Walter. *How Europe Underdeveloped Africa*. London: Bogle L'Ouverture Publications, 1972.

Sandel, Michael J. *What Money Can't Buy: The Moral Limits of Markets*. New York. Farrar, Straus and Giroux. 2012.

Sankara, Thomas. *Thomas Sankara Speaks: The Burkina Faso Revolution, 1983–1987*. New York: Pathfinder Press, 2007.

Schwartz, Timothy. *Travesty in Haiti: A true account of Christian missions, orphanages, fraud, food aid and drug trafficking*. Charleston, SC: BookSurge Publishing, 2008.

Sekyi, Kobina. *The Blinkards, a Comedy: And The Anglo-Fanti, a Short Story*. Portsmouth: Heinemann, 1997.

Sen, Amartya. *Development as Freedom*. Oxford: Oxford University Press, 1999.

Spykman, Nicholas. *America's Strategy in World Politics: The United States and the Balance of Power*. New York: Sempa Books, 1942.

Stockwell, John. *In Search of Enemies: A CIA Story*. New York: W. W. Norton, 1984.

Williams, Eric. *Capitalism and Slavery*. Chapel Hill, NC: University of North Carolina Press, 1994.

Williams, William Appleman. *Empire as a Way of Life*. Oxford: Oxford University Press, 1982.

World Bank. *Accelerated Development in Sub-Saharan Africa: An Agenda for Action.* Washington, DC: World Bank, 1981.

Wrong, Michela. *It's Our Turn to Eat: The Story of a Kenyan Whistle-Blower.* London: Fourth Estate, 2009.

Zoellick, Robert et al. *Project for the New American Century.* Letter to President Bill Clinton. Washington, DC, 1998.

Zinn, Howard. *A People's History of the United States: 1492-Present.* New York: Harper, 2005.

Articles in hard-copy and online journals, and chapters in books (named author)

Addai-Sebo, Akyaaba. 'Never again! ... Why Africa can no longer believe in UN neutrality', *New African*, 509, August 2011.

AFP, 'Resettle Haitians in Africa: Senegal President', 17 January 2010, <http://www.thefreelibrary.com/Resettle+Haitians+in+Africa%3A+Senegal+president-a01612121133>, accessed 18 August 2014.

African Diaspora Marketplace. <diasporaalliance.org/what-is-the-african-diaspora-marketplace/>, accessed 19 May 2014.

African Union Commission. 'Haiti earthquake', 14 January 2010, <http://appablog.wordpress.com/2010/01/14/Haiti-earthquake-chairperson-of-the-african-union-commission-auc-condolence-letter/>, accessed 18 August 2014.

Ajamu Baraka, Ajamu. 'Iraq, Libya, Syria: Three reasons African Americans should oppose U.S. intervention in Africa', *Pambazuka News*, 685, 2 July 2014, <http://pambazuka.org/en/category/features/92338>, accessed 21 August 2014.

Amin, Samir. 'Underdevelopment and Dependence in Black Africa – Origins and Contemporary Forms', *Journal of Modern African Studies*, Vol. 10, No. 4, 1972.

—— '"Le Sud, quelles alternatives?": une utopie créatrice nécessaire'. *Afrique Asie*, November 2013.

Anderson, Perry. 'On the Concatenation in the Arab World', *New Left Review*, 68, March/April 2011.

—— 'American Foreign Policy and Its Thinkers', *New Left Review*, 83, September/October 2013.

Ankomah, Baffour. 'The Republic of Corruption: Shady deals threaten Ghana's future', *Africawatch*, Ghana Edition, February 2014.

Anyang Nyong'o, Peter. 'Lecture in Memory of Dr Abdul Raheem Tajudeen and Prof. Chinua Achebe', *Pambazuka News*, 637, 3 July 2013, <http://pambazuka.org/en/category/features/88087>, accessed 8 May 2014.

Austin, Hal. 'Notes from a Native Son: Nelson Mandela and the Politics of Forgiveness', *Barbados Underground*, 13 December 2013, <bajan.wordpress.com/2013/12/13/notes-from-a-native-son-nelson-mandela-and-the-politics-of-forgiveness>, accessed 16 December 2013.

Azikiwe, Aboyomi. 'Imperialists host conference on Nigerian security in Paris, Reports of mutinies within the army mount while tensions escalate', *Pambazuka News*, 679, 21 May 2014, <http://pambazuka.org/en/category/features/91841>, accessed 25 May 2014.

Baxter, Joan. 'The New African Land Grab', *Al Jazeera*, 30 June 2011, <www.aljazeera.com/indepth/opinion/2011/06/20116288424012951\5.htlm>, accessed 12 June 2014.

Beckles, Hilary. 'The Hate and the Quake', *The Barbados Advocate*, 19 January 2010, <http://www.barbadosadvocate.com/newsitem.asp?more=letters&NewsID=8490>, accessed 20 April 2014.

Bentsi-Enchill, Nii K. 'Silence means consent – A note on 55 years of in-dependence', *Ghana Nsem*, <http://ghanansem.org/index.php?option=com_content&task=view&id=251&itemid=345>, accessed 12 June 2013.

Boateng, Osei. 'Masters of the Universe ... Still Meddling in Africa', *New African*, 490, December 2009.

Bond, Patrick. 'The Mandela Years in Power', *CounterPunch*, Weekend Edition, 6–8 December 2013, <www.counterpunch.org/2013/12/06/the-mandela-years-in-power/>, accessed 24 May 2014.

Brath, Elcombe. 'Aristide's Ouster, African Lessons', *New African*, 428, April 2004.

Breman, Jan. 'The Undercities of Karachi', *New Left Review*, 76, July/August 2012.

Busch, Gary K. 'What is Boko Haram and whence did it arise?', *Pambazuka News*, 678, 15 May 2014, <http://pambazuka.org/en/category/features/91745>, accessed 25 May 2014.

Carrie, Giunta. 'Blood Coltan, Remote-controlled warfare and the demand for strategic minerals', *Pampazuka News*, 655, 21 November 2011, <http://pambazuka.org/en/category/features/89735>, accessed 12 May 2014.

Chamley, Santori. 'Brazil: It's Not Fun to be Black', *New African*, 511, November 2011.

Cooper, Robert. 'The new liberal imperialism', *The Guardian*, 7 April 2002, <http://www.theguardian.com/world/2002/apr/07/1>.

—— 'Reordering the World: The Long-Term Implications of September 11'. In Mark Leonard, ed., *The Post-Modern State*. London: Foreign Policy Centre, 2002.

Dalal, Meera. 'Cholera in Haiti: From Control to Elimination', *Al Jazeera*, 14 January 2012, <http://www.aljazeera.com/indepth/features/2012/01/2012111193155842439. html>, accessed 18 August 2014.

Darimani, Abdulai. 'Renewal of scramble for Africa', *African Agenda*, Vol. 14, No. 3, 2011.

Debray, Regis. 'Decline of the West', *New Left Review*, 80, March/April 2013.

Democracy Now! '"We made a Devil's Bargain": Fmr President Clinton Apologizes for Trade Policies that destroyed Haitian Rice Farming', 1 April 2010, <http://www.democracynow.org/2010/4/1/clinton_rice>, accessed 17 August 2014.

D'Eramo, Marco. 'Populism for Oligarchs', *New Left Review*, 82, July/August 2013.

Dowd, Vincent. 'Singer Paul Robson's granddaughter recalls fight against racism', *BBC News*, 7 May 2014, <www.bbc.com/news/entertainment-arts-27291682>, accessed 14 August 2014.

Du Bois, W. E. B. 'The African Roots of War', *Atlantic Monthly*, Vol. 115, No. 5, May 1915.

Ekwe-Ekwe, Herbert. 'France must now leave Côte d'Ivoire', *Pambazuka News*, 527, 3 May 2011, <http://www.pambazuka.org/en/category/features/72912>, accessed 4 April 2014.

—— 'The concatenation of the African role in the war of 1914–1918 or World War I', *Pambazuka News*, 693, 11 September 2014, <http://pambazuka.org/en/category/features/92864>, accessed 11 September 2014.

Falola, Toyin and Tyler Fleming. 'African Civilizations: From the Pre-Colonial to the Modern Day'. In Robert Holton and William R. Nasson, eds, *World Civilizations and History of Human Development: Encyclopedia of Life Support Systems*. Eolss Publishers: Paris, 2010.

Fenton, Anthony. 'Haiti: Private Contractors Like Vultures Coming to Grab the Loot', *IPS*, 19 February 2010, <http://www.ipsnews.net/news.asp?idnews=50396>, accessed 27 February 2010.

Ford, Glen. 'Kidnapped girls become tools of US imperial policy in Africa', *Pambazuka News*, 679, 21 May 2014, <http://pambazuka.org/en/category/features/91842>, accessed 25 May 2014.

Frank, André Gunder. 'The Development of Underdevelopment'. In James D. Cockcroft, André Gunder Frank and Dale L. Johnson, eds, *Dependence and Underdevelopment: Latin America's Political Economy*. Garden City, NY: Anchor Books, 1972.

—— 'Economic Dependence, Class Structure and Development Policy'. In James D. Cockcroft, André Gunder Frank and Dale L. Johnson, eds, *Dependence and Underdevelopment: Latin America's Political Economy*. Garden City, NY: Anchor Books, 1972.

Fraser, John and Collins Mtika. 'West Cold-Shoulders Rebuilding Southern Africa', *IPS*, 29 August 2013, <http://www.ipsnews.net/2013/08/west-cold-shoulders-rebuilding-southern-africa/>, accessed 12 August 2014.

Fraser, Nancy. 'Feminism Co-opted: Feminism, Capitalism and the Cunning of History', *New Left Review*, 56, March/April 2009.

—— 'On Justice: Lessons from Plato, Rawls and Ishiguro', *New Left Review*, 74, March/April 2012.

Godoy, Julio. 'Africa: Global Warming behind Somali Drought', *IPS*, 26 August 2011, <http://www.ipsnews.net/2011/08/global-warming-behind-somali-drought>, accessed 30 April 2014.

Goffe, Leslie Gordon. 'The African-Americans who worked for apartheid', *New African*, 538, April 2014.

Goodman, Amy. 'Haiti, Forgive Us', 9 February 2010, <http://www.truthdig.com/report/item/haiti_forgive_us_20100209>, accessed 14 June 2013.

—— '"We Made a Devil's Bargain": Fmr President Clinton Apologises for Trade Policies that Destroyed Haitian Rice Farming'. Extract from interview with Clinton by *Haiti Liberté*'s Kim Ives, *Democracy Now!: The War and Peace Report*, 1 April 2010, <http://www.democracynow.org/2010/4/1/clinton_rice>, accessed 24 July 2014.

Goodwin, Clayton. 'Why Haiti is Poor', *New African*, 492, February 2010.

Gowans, Stephen. 'Why the West Loves Mandela and Hates Mugabe', *Global Research*, 9 December 2013, <http://www.globalresearch.ca/why-the-west-loves-mandela-and-hates-mugabe/5360995>, accessed 16 December 2013.

Graham, Yao. 'From Liberation into NEPAD', *African Agenda*, Vol. 5, Nos 2 & 3, 2002.

Hallinan, Conn. 'The New Scramble for Africa', *African Agenda*, Vol. 14, No. 3, 2011.

Hazeldine, Tom. 'The North Atlantic Counsel: Complicity of the International Crisis Group', *New Left Review*, 63, May/June 2010.

Hickel, Jason. 'Trading with the Enemy', *African Agenda*, Vol. 14, No. 3, 2011.

Hodgkin, T. 'A Note on the Language of African Nationalism'. In K. Kirkwood, ed., *African Affairs, No. 1*, 1st edn. London: Chatto and Windus, 1961.

Ibrahim, Kola. 'Boko Haram and the West's Intervention', *Pambazuka News*, 679, 21 May 2014, <http://pambazuka.org/en/category/features/91831>, accessed 25 May 2014.

Institute for Social Research, University of Michigan. 'Income Inequality now Greater in China than in US', 28 April 2014, <http://home.isr.umich.edu/releases/income-inequality-now-greater-china-us/>, accessed 21 August 2014.

IRIN. 'The downside of foreign land acquisitions', 19 January 2012, <http://www.irinnews.org/report/94680/west-africa-the-downside-of-foreign-land-acquisitions>, accessed 21 August 2014.

Jachnow, Joachim. 'What's Become of the German Greens?', *New Left Review*, 81, May/June 2013.

James, Andre C. 'The Butcher of Congo: King Leopold II of Belgium', *THE DIGITAL JOURNAL*, 4 April 2011, <http://digitaljournal.com/blog/11297>, accessed 20 August 2014.

Jammeh, Yahya.'We can rise faster than a rocket, if ...', *New African*, 539, May 2014.

John, Gus. 'Mandela: Goodness Personified, Terrorism Purified!', *gusjohn.com*, 8 December 2013, <http:www.gusjohn.com/2013/Mandela-goodness-personified-terrorism-purified>, accessed 16 December 2013.

Johnson, R. W. 'False Start in South Africa', *New Left Review*, 58, July/August 2009.

Kandil, Hazem. 'Revolt in Egypt', *New Left Review*, 68, March/April 2011.

Kebede, Messay. 'African Development and the Primacy of Mental Decolonisation', *Africa Development*, Vol. XXIX, No. 1, 2004.

Keenan, Jeremy. 'How terror came to the Sahel', *New African*, 560, April 2016.

King, Sharon Minor. 'WE HEAR YOU ALL ... But We Don't Understand What You Are Saying: Personal Reflections on the Joseph Project of Ghana, West Africa, Summer, 2007', <www.ghanaiandiaspora.com/wp/wp-content/uploads/2013/06/Sharon-Minor-King-Ph.D.pdf>, accessed 12 May 2012.

Krever, Tor. 'Dispensing Global Justice, Judging the ICC', *New Left Review*, 85, January/February 2014, <http://newleftreview.org/II/85/tor-krever-dispensing-global-justice>, accessed 12 August 2014.

Lee, Ching Kwan. 'The Spectre of Global China', *New Left Review*, 89, September/October 2014.

Lehmann, David. 'Political Incorporation versus Political Stability: The Case of the Chilean Agrarian Reform, 1965–70', *The Journal of Development Studies*, Vol. 7, No. 4, July 1971.

Lewis, Paul and Dan Lewis. 'White House denies "Cuban Twitter" ZunZuneo programme was covert', *The Guardian*, <http://www.theguardian.com/world/2014/apr/03/white-house-cuban-twitter-zunzuneo-covert>, accessed 9 August 2014.

Leys, Colin. 'Confronting the African Tragedy', *New Left Review*, Vol. 1, No. 204, March/April 1994.

Lopes, Carlos. 'How the World Bank's SAPs Impoverished Africa', *African Agenda*, Vol. 16, No. 3, 2013.

Lumumba, Patrice. 'Letter from Thysville Prison to Mrs Lumumba'. In Patrice Lumumba, ed., *The Truth about a Monstrous Crime of the Colonialists*. Moscow: Foreign Languages Publishing House, 1961.

Mafeje, Archie. 'The Ideology of Tribalism', *Journal of Modern African Studies*, Vol. 9, No. 2, 1971.

—— 'The fallacy of "dual economies" revisited: A case for East, Central and Southern Africa'. In P. Gutkind and P. Waterman, eds, *African Social Studies: A Reader.* London: Heinemann, 1977.

—— 'Africanity: A commentary by way of conclusion', *CODESRIA Bulletin*, 3 & 4, 2001.

Mandela, Nelson. 'Extract from *Statement from the Dock at the Opening of the Defence Case in the Rivonia Trial, Pretoria Supreme Court, South Africa, 20ᵗʰ April*, 1964', <http://www.goodreads.com/quotes/22390-during-my-lifetime-i-have-dedi cated-myself-to-this-struggle>, accessed 10 August 2014.

Merry, Robert W. 'Zbigniew Brzezinski interview with Robert W. Merry', *The National Interest*, 2012, <http://nationalinterest.org>, accessed 22 August 2012.

Milne, Seumas. 'Britain: Imperial nostalgia', *Le monde diplomatique*, English version, May 2005.

Mkandawire, Thandika. 'Globalisation, Structural Adjustment and "Choiceless Democracies"'. In Max Spoor, ed., *Globalisation, Poverty and Conflict: A Critical Development' Reader.* Dordrecht: Kluwer Academic Publishers, 2004.

Mohamed, Osman Abdi. 'Beyond the Dominant Terrorist Narrative', *The Thinker*, Vol. 64, Quarter 2, 2015.

Monbiot, George. 'Corporate carve-up', *Monbiot.com*, 10 June 2013, <http://www.monbiot.com/2013/06/10/corporate-carve-up>, accessed 12 May 2014.

—— 'Obama's Rogue State', *Monbiot.com*, 9 September 2013, <www.monbiot.com/2013/09/09/obamas-rogue-state/>, accessed 25 May 2014.

—— 'Loss Adjustment: When people say we should adapt to climate change, do they have any idea what that means?', *Monbiot.com*, 31 March 2014, <http://www.monbiot.com/2014/03/31/loss-adjustment/>, accessed 12 April 2014.

—— 'The Pricing of Everything', *Monibot.com*, 24 July 2014, <http://www.monbiot.com/2014/07/24/the-pricing-of-everything/>, accessed 21 August 2014.

Nehme, Majed et al. 'L'Héroique résistance populaire', *Afrique-Asie*, July/August 2012.

Nkrumah, Kwame. 'Address to the Conference of African Heads of State and Government', Addis Ababa, 24 May 1963, <http://panafricannews.blogspot.co.uk/2012/09/kwame-nkrumah-speech-at-founding.html>, accessed 21 August 2014.

Obama, Barack. 'Remarks of the President to Ghanaian Parliament', Accra, 11 July 2009, <http://www.whitehouse.gov/the-press-office/remarks-president-gha naian-parliament>, accessed 21 August 2014.

—— 'Remembering Nelson Mandela', Johannesburg, 10 December 2013, <http://www.nelsonmandela.org/news/entry/remembering-nelson-mandela-remarks-by president-barack-obama>, accessed 28 June 2014.

—— 'Remarks by the President at the United States Military Academy Commencement', 28 May 2014, <http://www.whitehouse.gov/the-press-office/2014/05/28/remarks-president-united-states military-academy-commencement-ceremony>, accessed 17 August 2014.

Obeng, Anthony V. 'Vassal States, Development Options and African Development'. In Jeggan C. Senghor and Nana K. Poku, eds, *Towards Africa's Renewal*. Aldershot: Ashgate Publishing Limited, 2007.

Ogun, Dele. *The Law, the Lawyers and the Lawless*. London: New European Publications, 2009.

Olokoshi, Adebayo. 'Africa from Lagos Plan of Action to NEPAD', *African Agenda*, Vol. 5, Nos 2 & 3, 2002.

Otas, Belinda. 'Why the AU is courting the Diaspora', *New African*, 519, July 2012.

Oxford Research Group. 'Press Release: Major New report Shows 11,420 Children Killed in Syrian Conflict', 24 November 2013, <http://www.oxfordresearchgroup. org.uk/publications/middle_east/press_release_new_report_stolen_futures_ hidden_death_toll_child_casualties>, accessed 14 August 2014.

Pearce, Fred. 'Land grabbers: Africa's hidden revolution', *The Observer*, 20 May 2012, <www.theguardian.com/world/2012/may/20/land-grab-ethiopi-saudi-agribusi ness>, accessed 10 May 2014.

Pheko, Motsoko. 'Which African renaissance are we talking about?', *Pambazuka News*, 664, <http://www.pambazuka.org/en/category/features/90447 2014-02-05>, accessed 5 February 2014.

Philip, Nourbese, Marlene. 'Letter to Haiti', *The New Legon Observer*, Vol. 4, No. 1, February 2010.

Pilger, John. 'South Africa Today: Apartheid by Another Name', 14 April 2014, <www. counterpunch.org/2014/14/south-africa-today-apartheid-by-another-name/>, accessed 14 April 2014.

—— 'Apartheid Did Not Die', *johnpilger.com*, 1998, <http://johnpilger.com/videos/ apartheid-did-not-die>, accessed 14 April 2014.

Polya, Gideon. '10th Anniversary of US Iraq Invasion: 2.7 Million Iraqi Deaths', *Countercurrents.org*, 20 March 2013, <http://www.countercurrents.org/polya200313. htm>, accessed 23 July 2014.

Porter, Bernard. 'Other People's Mail', *London Review of Books*, November 2009.

Rice, Xan. 'Sub-Saharan Africa: Where some purveyors of luxury goods are happy to tread', *Financial Times*, 2 June 2013, <http://www.ft.com/cms/s/0/57e0ef62-b70c-11e2-a249-00144feabdc0.html#axzz3AovSHA2B>, accessed 10 August 2014.

Robert, Anne-Cécile. 'Interventions militaries en Libye et en Côte d'Ivoire: Origines et vicissitudes du "droit d'ingérance"', *Le Monde Diplomatique*, 686, May 2011.

Rowden, Rick. 'The Myth of Africa's Rise: Why the rumours of Africa's explosive growth have been greatly exaggerated', *Democracy Lab*, 4 January 2013, <http://www.foreignpolicy.com/articles/2013/01/04/the_myth_of_africa_s_rise>, accessed 10 August 2014.

Rozoff, Rick. 'Africa: NATO seeks to recruit 50 new military partners', *Pambazuka News*, 519, 2003, <http://www.pambazuka.org/en/category/features/71392>, accessed 19 July 2014.

Sané, Pierre. 'Côte d'Ivoire: The Logic of the Absurd', *Pambazuka News*, 520, 3 October 2001, <http://pambazuka.org/en/category/features/71392>, accessed 14 April 2014.

Schneider, James. 'The Politics of Pity: Inside the White Saviour Industrial Complex', *New African*, 546, January 2015.

Sekyi, Kobina. 'The Future of the Subject Peoples', *The African Times and Orient Review*, October-December 1917.

Sherwell, Philip. 'Jamaica and Caribbean Demands for Reparations', *The Telegraph*, 11 March 2014, <http://www.telegraph.co.uk/news/worldnews/centralamericaandthecaribbean/10691024/Caribbean-states-demand-reparations-from-European-powers-for-slave-trade.html>, accessed 18 April 2014.

Smith, Ashley. 'How the NGOs are Profiting off a Grave Situation: Haiti and the Aid Racket', *Socialist Worker*, 14 January 2010, <http://socialistworker.org/2010/01/14/catastrophe-in-haiti>, accessed 26 April 2014.

Smith, Brian. 'Devastating floods sweep across Africa', *World Socialist Web Site*, 29 September 2007, <www.wsws.org/en/articles/2007/en/afri-s29.htlm>, accessed 4 April 2014.

Stockwell, John. 'The secret wars of the CIA', October 1987, <https://libcom.org/files/The%20secret%20wars%20of%20the%20CIA%20-%20John%20Stockwell.pdf>, accessed 21 August 2014.

Streeck, Wolfgang. 'Citizens as Customers: Considerations on the New Politics of Consumption', *New Left Review*, 76, July/August 2012.

Supio, Alain. 'Under Eastern Eyes', *New Left Review*, 73, January/February 2012.

Taiwo, Olufemi. 'Africa's Mendicant Rulers and their Intellectual Enablers', *Pambazuka News*, <http://pambazuka.org/en/category/comment/90438>, accessed 5 February 2014.

Tandon, Yash. 'Haiti: Microcosm of the crisis of development', *Pambazuka News*, 467, 28 January 2010, <http://www.pambazuka.org/en/category/features/61809>, accessed 15 February 2010.

Taylor, Ian. 'NEPAD: Towards the African Century or Another False Start?', *African Agenda*, Vol. 5, Nos 2 & 3, 2002.

Therborn, Göran. 'New Masses? Social Bases of Resistance'. *New Left Review*, 85 January/February 2014.

Transparency International. 'Corruption perception Index 2013', <http://www.trans parency.org/cpi2013/results>, accessed 10 November 2013.

Traoré, Aminata and Boubacar Boris Diop. 'African Impostures: Letters from a Proxy War', *New Left Review*, May/June 2014.

UPI. <www.upi.com/Top_News/World-News/2014/04/04/State-Department-nothing-classified-or-covert-about-Twitter-program/1701396616290/>, accessed 28 April 2014.

Wallace, Tina. 'NGO Dilemmas: Trojan Horses for Global Neoliberalism?', *Socialist Register*, 2003.

Wallerstein, Immanuel. 'The Range of Choice: Constraints on the Choice of Policies of Governments of Contemporary African Independent States'. In M. F. Lofchie, ed., *The State of the Nations: Constraints on Development in Independent Africa*. Berkeley, CA: University of California Press, 1971.

Wan, James. 'The Politics of Pity', *New African*, 546, January 2015.

Watkins, Susan. 'Annexations', *New Left Review*, 86, Mar/Apr 2014.

Weber, J. 'La region cacaoyère du Centre Sud Cameroun'. In Samir Amin, ed., *L'agriculture africaine et le capitalisme*. Paris: Anthropos, 1975.

Wittmann, Nora. 'The European Capital of Shame', *New African*, 530, July 2013.

Wolfe, Lonnie. 'World Population is top NSA Agenda: Club of Rome', *Executive Intelligence Review*, 10 March 1981, <http://home.iae.nl/users/lightnet/world/depopulation.htm>, accessed 10 June 2013.

Woods, Emira. 'Africa: burdened with too much oil', *African Agenda*, Vol. 9, No. 4, 2006.

Wroughton, Lesley. 'Oxfam urges World Bank to freeze land investments', *Reuters*, 4 October 2012, <http://www.reuters.com/article/2012/10/04/worldbank-oxfam-land-idUSL1E8L2LKF20121004>, accessed 20 August 2014.

Zivcic, Amanda. 'Haiti needs solidarity, not charity', interview of Marilyn Langlois, *Pambazuka News*, 11 March 2010, <http://www.pambazuka.org/en/category/features/62924>, accessed 11 March 2010.

Articles (author unnamed)

'400ppm: Climate Threshold Crossed, But No Solution in Sight!', *South Bulletin*, 35, 25 July 2013.
'Africa, le pauvre', <http://kwani.org/editorial/report_essay/37/Africa_le_pauvre. htm>, accessed 11 August 2014.
African Agenda. Vol. 5, Nos 2 & 3, 2002.
—— 'Cancun Climate Talks Saved But Climate Not Saved', Vol. 13, No. 6, 2010.
—— 'The tragic trajectory of Haiti', Vol. 13, Nos 1 & 2, 2010.
—— 'UN Climate Change Talks: Cancun Betrayal', Vol. 13, No. 6, 2010.
—— Vol. 14, No.1, 2011.
—— 'Climate Change Talks: Quibbling Whilst the Earth Burns', Vol. 14, No. 2, 2011.
—— 'Durban Climate Change Talks: People and Planet over Profit – Africa Demands Equity', Vol. 14, No. 4, 2011.
—— 'The downside of foreign land acquisitions', Vol. 15, No. 2, 2012.
—— 'Food prices on the rise', Vol. 15, No. 2, 2012.
Africawatch. February 2014.
Afrique-Asie. Editorial page. April 2011.
'Caribbean Repatory Justice Program: Ten Point Action Plan', <http://1804caribvoices. org/articles/2014/04/caribbean-reparatory-justice-program-ten-point-action-plan/>, accessed 20 August 2014.
'Centre for Scientific Research into Plan Medicine', <http://en.wikipedia.org/wiki/ Centre_for_Scientific_Research_into_Plant_Medicine>, accessed 21 August 2014.
'Civilizing Mission', <http://en.wikipedia.org/wiki/Civilizing_mission>, accessed 19 August 2014.
'Commission for Africa is Launched by PM Tony Blair: Panel Discusses Brandt and Sets Development Agenda', *Global Policy Forum*, <http://www.globalpolicy. org/component/content/article/211/44599.html>, accessed 20 August 2014.
Daily Graphic. Accra, 12 January 2011.
—— 'Uganda Angry at Cameron's Gay-Aid Threat', 2 November 2011.
—— 'Leave Us Alone', 3 November 2011.
—— 20 August 2013.
—— 21 August 2013.
—— 10 March 2014.
—— 24 March 2014.
—— 23 April 2014.
—— 24 July 2014.

'Diop: Birth of the Negro Myth', <https://abagond.wordpress.com/2011/07/16/ diop-birth-of-the-negro-myth/>, accessed 22 June 2014.

'Eco Currency: History of the Currency', <http://en.wikipedia.org/wiki/Eco_ (currency)#History_of_the_currency>, accessed 21 August 2014.

Ghanaian Times, The. 21 August 2013.

GNA. 23 July 2014.

'Haiti Demographics Profile 2014', <www.indexmundi.com/haiti/demographics_pro file.html>, accessed 15 May 2014.

'Haitian Diaspora', <https://en.wikipedia.org/wiki/Haitian_diaspora>, accessed 20 April 2014.

Joy Online. General News, 31 October 2013.

'Know Thyself', <http://en.wikipedia.org/wiki/Know_thyself>, accessed 21 August 2014.

Los Angeles Times, The. 18 August 1987.

'Marcus Garvey', <http://africanamericanquotes.org/marcus-garvey.html>, accessed 14 June 2014.

'Marcus Garvey: Conflict with Du Bois and others', <https://en.wikipedia.org/wiki/ Marcus_Garvey#Conflicts_with_Du_Bois_and_others>, accessed 18 August 2014.

'Marcus Garvey Quotes', <http://www.brainyquote.com/quotes/authors/m/marcus_ garvey.html>, accessed 13 May 2014.

'Marxists Internet Archive', <http://www.marxists.org/archive/lenin/works/1901/ witbd/>, accessed 10 August 2014.

New African, 'How Africa Developed Europe and USA', 444, October 2005.

—— 456, November 2006.

—— 503, February 2011.

'New Generation of African Leaders', <https://en.wikipedia.org/wiki/New_genera tion_of_African_leaders>, accessed 9 August 2014.

'Noam Chomsky', <http://en.wikipedia.org/wiki/Noam_Chomsky>, accessed 21 August 2014.

'Our Approach', <http://www.tonyblairoffice.org/africa/pages/our-approach>, accessed 20 August 2014.

'Poverty in Haiti', <https://en.wikipedia.org/wiki/Poverty_in_Haiti>, accessed 23 July 2014.

'Remarks by the President to the Ghanaian Parliament', <www.whitehouse.gov/the-press-office/remarks-president-ghanaian-parliament>, accessed 8 April 2014.

'Rural Poverty in Haiti', <www.ruralpoverty.org/country/home/tags/haiti>, accessed 23 July 2014.

'Stewart Synopsis', <http://www.stewartsynopsis.com/>, accessed 4 December 2013.

'Turkish finance minister vows to shore up economy', <www.ft.com/cms/s/o/57e0ef62-
  b70-11e2-a249-00144feabdco.html#axzz2zVWSBOAV>, accessed 15 May 2014.
United States Military Africa Command. <http://www.africom.mil/>, accessed 22
  October 2011.
US Strategy Toward Sub-Saharan Africa. Washington, DC: The White House, June
  2012.
Walk Free Foundation. *Global Slavery Index (2013)*.
'What countries attended the Berlin Conference?', <http://wiki.answers.com/Q/
  What_countries_attended_the_Berlin_Conference>, accessed 21 August 2014.
World Bank. *Accelerated Development in Sub-Saharan Africa: An Agenda for Action*.
  Washington, DC: World Bank, 1981.

Index

Africa in Development

Series Editor: Jeggan C. Senghor
Institute of Commonwealth Studies, University of London

While African development remains a preoccupation, policy craftsmen and a multiplicity of domestic and international actors have been engaged in the quest for solutions to the myriad problems associated with poverty and underdevelopment. Academic and scholarly responses have built on traditional and non-traditional analytical frameworks and promoted a multidimensional discourse on, for example, conflict management, peace and security systems, HIV/AIDS, democratic governance, and the implications of globalization.

This series is designed to encourage innovative thinking on a broad range of development issues. Thus its remit extends to all fields of intellectual inquiry with the aim of highlighting the advantages of a synergistic interdisciplinary perspective on the challenges of and opportunities for development in the continent. Of particular interest are studies with a heavy empirical content which also have a bearing on policy debates and those that question theoretical orthodoxies while being grounded on concrete developmental concerns.

The series welcomes proposals for collected papers as well as monographs from recent PhDs no less than from established scholars.

Book proposals should be sent to oxford@peterlang.com.
